ENOCH INSIGHTS

S.N.Strutt

Published by S.N.Strutt

ISBN 978-1-78222-580-5

Book design, layout and production management by Into Print
www.intoprint.net
+44 (0)1604 832149

CONTENTS

APPENDICES

CREDITS & ACKNOWLEDGEMENTS

COVER ART: © SUZANNA STRUTT

I would like to thank all my friends and associates as well as my personal family, who have encouraged me in the publishing of this book. They encouraged me to make this book available as a paper-back for easy reading, as many prefer having a paper-back copy to an electronic one. A special acknowledgement to Sherry Shiner for her background research into the history of the Book of Enoch, and why it was deliberately hidden for 1000 years. (See Appendix 1V and V)

INTRODUCTION TO THE BOOK OF ENOCH

The Book of Enoch is, in my opinion, one of the most interesting of the Apocryphal books that I have had the privilege of studying. Why? Because this book is, in few words, both *miraculous, supernatural & inspiring!* Contrary to what others have stated, I believe that this book *is* an accurate account given by God to Enoch, through His angel Uriel, as well as some short passages given to Noah, by perhaps the same angel. It is stated by Enoch himself, that he alone would see the visions that he saw (Enoch 19.3 "And I Enoch alone saw the VISION, the ends of all things; and no man shall see as I have seen.")

That is very similar to the Introduction to the book of Revelations 1.1: "The Revelation of Jesus Christ which God gave unto Him and signified it by His angel unto His servant John." The Book of Enoch, is probably the oldest book known to man, and was originally written about 5000 years ago, or between 700-950 years 'After CREATION', and well before the 'FLOOD' (1650 A.C.). I propose, that unfortunately in our modern times, many Christians are conditioned by "the traditions of the churches", only to believe the easy to believe topics, and that most people do not embrace the *truly miraculous*, which used to be much more accepted in the "less enlightened days" of man's wisdom.

I am reminded of the cryptic Bible verse (**1CO.2:14) '**But the natural man receives not the things of the Spirit of God: for they are foolishness unto him: neither can he know them, because they are spiritually discerned'.

I have heard writers dismiss most of the Book of Enoch as purely allegorical, with no real meaning to it. This is very often the modern way i.e. scepticism instead of simple faith. Another Bible verse comes to mind: "I fear lest by any means, even as Eve was corrupted by the Serpent, through his subtlety, so your minds should be corrupted from the simplicity that is in Christ" (Colossians 2.8). Those who write sceptically about the Book of Enoch *obviously have not taken the time, to really study what Enoch was saying.* It also takes faith in God to understand it.

Some facts about the Book of Enoch:

1) It was read by the Jewish people in the two centuries before Christ & by the early Christians, including those who were willing to be martyrs for Jesus.

2) The Book of Enoch was not included in the cannon of the Bible,

because the *council of Laodicea,* which was responsible for which books would be part of the original Canon in 365 AD, *decided to exclude any books deemed too radical or supernatural in content.*

3) Enoch himself is mentioned in the Bible in both the Old Testament in Genesis 5.18-24, & in the New Testament in Hebrews chapter 11.5

4) The Book of Enoch itself is mentioned in Jude verses14-16.

The big question is why was not much more said about Enoch in the Bible when he was instrumental in passing on most of God's Word and instructions from before the FLOOD, which was taken on the ark by Noah, for the sake of future generations. Why no mention of this big event in the Bible? It doesn't make any sense!

Enoch was an amazing person, who was totally dedicated to God Himself, and visited God's Throne, and received countless revelations directly from God and His angels, so why the lack of mentioning Enoch in the Bible, *when the early Christians were all believing in the Book of Enoch, and set it as one of their foundation stones?*

Obviously, someone back there in 300 AD *did not like the radical and supernatural ways of true Christianity, and the teachings of Creation,* and wanted to water down & compromise the message, probably in an attempt to become more accepted by the majority of the people of those Roman times, with their idol worshipping. *[5] (See **Appendix IV**: for **Background History of the Book of Enoch**)

As I mentioned in my first book *Out of the Bottomless Pit*, that Jesus himself had nothing good to say about the compromising Laodicean church in his day, except to state that it was a lukewarm church, and he would end-up spewing it out of his mouth. (Revelations 3.15-16)

5) The Book of Enoch has 108 Chapters, some of them being very short. It would seem at times in reading the book that certain portions of the book are sadly *missing.* As mentioned before, it becomes apparent in reading the Book of Enoch and other Apocryphal books, that most of the information given *is most definitely inspired by God.*

2PE.1:20 Knowing this first, that no prophecy of the scripture is of any private interpretation.

2PE.1:21 For the prophecy came not in old time by the will of man: but holy men of God spoke as they were moved by the Holy Ghost.

6) I am also convinced that certain books were *black-listed* in the past, because of their content. In the case of both the books of Enoch & II Ezdras, it was because it clearly showed the origins of evil, and how they were amplified by the fallen angels. Another factor: The books of both Enoch & II Ezdras, both prophesied about JESUS, centuries to millennia in advance of His 1ST and 2nd COMING.

Both of these Books, one around 5000 years ago and the other around 2500 years ago, were given in visions and dreams, and brought to firstly Enoch and then Ezra *by the same Arch-Angel* or otherwise known as one of the *angels of the Presence* of God, called Uriel, or as sometimes called in Jewish writings, Ariel

7) It is also important for Bible readers to understand that there used to be 15 more books in the current King James Bible until the late 19th century. Why were those 15 books also taken out from the Bible? Here is a list of all 15 of the Apocryphal books, which used to be included in the King James Bible until 1885:

1 Esdras; 2 Esdras; Tobit; Judith; Additions to Esther; Wisdom of Solomon; Ecclesiaticus; Baruch; Letter of Jeremiah; Prayer of Azariah; Susanna; Bel and the Dragon; Prayer of Manasseh; 1 Maccabees; 2 Maccabees

Other books of great importance: The fact is that the early Christians all referred to the "Book of Enoch" and the "SEPTUAGINT" version of the Old Testament, which was originally written in Greek. The Septuagint version of the Old Testament is more revealing, and has more details of the events, than even the King James version of the Bible.

Who would not want books such as both the 'Book of Enoch' & the 'Book of II Ezdras' available to the public?

I would venture to guess those who are not in favour of Christianity. These ancient texts prophesied *directly about Jesus,* proving that He was in fact the *Saviour* hundreds, and even thousands of years before he was actually born on earth.

There are 108 chapters in the Book of Enoch, with some of them very short. The content of this intriguing book, is jam-packed with very interesting visions of Heaven, Hell and Tartarus, angels good and bad, God's throne and descriptions of Jesus.

The Book of Enoch, as mentioned before, directly talks about Jesus, and gives a panorama of the sequence of Events from Creation until the New Heaven & New Earth, or around a span of 7000 years of World History.

8) It is claimed that the Book of Enoch was written or compiled around 200-300 BCE.

I would agree that it could have been re-compiled at that date, but not originally written at that date. Why? Because if you study the book of Enoch in detail, and at length, you will come to realize that many of the things described by Enoch could not have been 'created as an original writing' almost 4000 years after creation. There are simply too many exact details of people, places, creatures (which at least to our current knowledge), no longer existed in 200-300 BCE.

My take on the Book of Enoch is that it was written originally before the FLOOD, and was written on stone tablets, from around 700 AC to 987 AC or around 600 years before the flood at the latest, and taken by NOAH onto the ARK. The book was preserved until it was eventually re-written around 200 BCE. You will find that there were lots of Jewish books, which had both the written texts, such as the Torah, and also the oral versions of the Torah, passed down from father to son. I read recently that according to the Jewish tradition, it was necessary to have both the written texts, and the oral texts. Why? Because the written texts only gave a general idea such as the 10 commandments: "Thou shalt not make unto thee a graven image". The oral text would specify exactly what that meant, and how to personally apply the law. I would thus hold to the idea that the Book of Enoch was both in written form and probably also remembered orally by some, and the whole amount of information available at the time that yet remained in 200 BCE, was finally reassembled into the known Book of Enoch of today. I say that because some verses of the Book of Enoch seem to be missing.

There are many things in the Book of Enoch that simply could not have been known in 200 BCE, which you will have to study in depth for yourself, in order to also be convinced of this. It is a wonderful, as well as a much neglected book, in this modern world; as it *disproves many of man's modern ideas*, as it is indeed both *radical* & certainly points to the *supernatural.*

9) There are also some fantastic anomalies in the Book of Enoch to find answers for.

For example, according to Bible time-charts, Noah was supposedly born around 90 years after Enoch was taken up to heaven or translated. (Hebrews 11.5) So how could Noah have communicated with Enoch, as stated clearly in the Book of Enoch itself, in chapter 65?

I will attempt in this book to answer this question, and other interesting anomalies like it.

I have also, in thoroughly studying the books of JUBILEES, JASHER, II EZDRAS, found them absolutely fascinating, and wondered why were they NOT included in the Bible?

I intend to write about each of these books, given time. There are many connections between the above-mentioned books, with both similarities and differences. I would say they are all very fascinating, and interesting books, and an absolute must for serious readers of scriptures, and not ones to be neglected. As one Jewish Rabbi has stated, the Apocryphal books & Septuagint fill in the gaps or sometimes give greater details than even the Bible itself. After all, as the apostle John said at the end of the Bible, in the gospel of John, that if everything that had happened should be written in a book, even the world itself could not contain the volume of the books that would have to be written.

JOH.21:25 And there are also many other things which Jesus did, the which, if they should be written every one, I suppose that even the world itself could not contain the books that should be written. Amen.

So, in conclusion about the Bible itself, maybe it is just as well that it is not any larger in content.

I personally believe that the Bible is the most essential book to know, especially for the basics. However, for seasoned Christians, it is essential to broaden your vision & horizons in the knowledge of ancient texts, (both Jewish and non-Jewish) which parallel the Bible so well.

I will attempt to show how there has been a massive cover-up concerning the meaning of the Apocryphal books, and the dates given, often differ from one book to the other, about the timing of the same events. Why? Did those of the past try to hide certain information, and were certain books for the public, and others only for the 'Initiated'? This seems to be indicated by the Book of II Ezdras Chapter 14.44-48: "But keep the books...in order to give them to the wise among your people".

Disclaimer by the Author: In reading these ancient books, it is essential not to start reading them with a sceptical attitude: Meaning that if in your mind, every jot and tittle doesn't totally agree with the Bible, lock stock and barrel, then one simply rejects it all. Wrong move! Those who do that, are like unto a man who is shown a palatial garden full of flowers and interesting trees and creatures, but all he, the sceptic can do, is count the weeds, if there are any at all. His mind is already made up, as he simply does not want to listen, learn and simply enjoy the view.

PRO.18:13 He that answers a matter before he hears it, it is folly and shame unto him.

When I have both studied these books and written about them, I simply know that I don't know all the answers, and that only God knows the answers to all of these mysteries.

I have prayed that God would lead, guide and help me by His Holy Spirit to find verses in the Bible that do agree with verses in these ancient texts, & to also explain to the reader some interesting facts, and also expand some possibilities, along the journey of reading these books.

In my opinion, the Book of Enoch is amazingly accurate about most things of ancient history, but also talks about hidden things, which we may not fully understand in this life, as life was very different back in Enoch's time.

In direct contrast to the teachings of Evolution, one discovers that in reading the Apocryphal books of both Enoch and II Ezdras, that in the original creation of God, mankind was much stronger, taller, smarter and faster than we humans are today. (See **Appendix VII: GENE DISINTEGRATION**)

We are only now starting to learn a little of how it really was like back then, before the Great Flood.

Being optimistic and not sceptical is the foundation to learning anything worthwhile. The men who wrote the above-mentioned books were prophets of God, to whom God, even revealed names of nations, peoples, places even before they existed. Such is the nature of prophecy!

ECC.2:26 For God giveth to a man that is good in his sight wisdom, and knowledge, and joy.

JAM.1:5 If any of you lack wisdom, let him ask of God, that giveth to all men liberally, and upbraids not; and it shall be given him.

WHO WAS ENOCH?

Enoch was the son of Jared, and the 7th from Adam. He also was born in the 7th century after creation around 622 A.C. and according to the Bible & the Books of both Jasher and Jubilees, lived to be 365 years old. He was made king of kings, or emperor of the world, by 120 kings who lived in his time. (Around 700 years after creation.) He was translated in the year 987A.C. (years After Creation), and around 700 years before the FLOOD of 1650 A.C. He led mankind for 243 years, and while mankind followed Enoch's instructions, the earth was both at peace and stayed out of trouble, because the kings of the earth were afraid of Enoch and his god-like power. God kept at bay the influence of the fallen angels, who fell to earth during the life of Enoch's father Jared, as long as Enoch reigned on the earth. However, God decided to take Enoch up to heaven on a fiery flying horse, and he was told that as he had faithfully taught the sons of men on earth to honour God, now God would honour him by taking him to heaven earlier than was normal back then, to teach the Sons of God in Heaven, who were in fact the angels of God. Back then Methuselah, Enoch's son lived to be the oldest human who had ever lived, and died at the ripe old age of 969. Methuselah's son Lamech lived to be 777 years old, and died five years before the Great Flood. Methuselah died a few months before the Great Flood. God caused all the righteous to have died out before the Great Flood, with the exception of Enoch's great grandson Noah and his family.

Within two hundred years of Enoch's death, or circa 1170 years after Creation, the whole world strayed away from Enoch's teachings about God, and the kings of the earth would no longer listen to Methuselah, the son of Enoch who inherited his father's mantle and his title of king of kings, after Enoch's translation to heaven. Enoch was the only man who ever lived, who was instructed directly by the angels of God, and who had the power to address the fallen angels face to face, whom he rebuked for their rebellion against God. (Book of Enoch Chapter 15: Book of Jasher chapters 3-4: Jubilees chapter 4 verses 15-23: Sirach 49.14.)

THE FORMAT OF THIS BOOK

i) I have typed a chapter of the Book of Enoch, and included in each chapter my commentaries, which are just that: my opinions, speculations and theories, which are gleaned from much study of the subject matter. Most, if not all of which, could prove to be true, and are written with the express intention to motivate the reader to do a more thorough investigation for him or herself, to prove whether correct or not, as I am sure that some of the ideas, speculations and conjecture will be quite far out there, to some people.

ii) I have also put cross-references to the Bible, and other Apocryphal books where appropriate.

iii) **Details:**

The first '**comment'** in each chapter, will be noted as being '**Comment 1**' & then **C.2, C.3**, etc. The original Text from the Book of Enoch is in slightly larger text than either the 'comments' or 'Bible verses'. Three different types of writing are used. One for the original text, and another type of writing for my comments, and yet another for the Bible verses.

iv) The longest commentaries and conclusions are in the '**APPENDICES'** of this book of which there are around 25.

THE BOOK OF ENOCH

The original source of this particular copy of the Book of Enoch:

THE BOOK OF ENOCH - TRANSLATED BY R.H.CHARLES, D.LITT., D.D. - LONDON - SOCIETY FOR PROMOTING CHRISTIAN KNOWLEDGE -[1917]

CHAPTER 1

1 The words of the blessing of Enoch, wherewith he blessed the elect and righteous, who will be living in the 'day of tribulation', when all the wicked and godless are to be removed.

Comment:1: Who is Enoch addressing in the very first verse of chapter 1?

He is probably talking to those of us, who will be alive in the coming "GREAT TRIBULATION", as mentioned in Matthew 24.29-31 by Jesus himself & in the Book of Revelations 12.6,14.

MAT.24:29 Immediately after the *tribulation* of those days shall the sun be darkened, and the moon shall not give her light, and the stars shall fall from heaven, and the powers of the heavens shall be shaken.

REV.12:6 And the woman*[1] fled into the wilderness, where she hath a place prepared of God, that they should feed her there a thousand two hundred and threescore days. (*[1]Saved believers)

2 And he took up his parable and said, Enoch a righteous man, whose eyes were opened by God, saw the vision of the Holy One in the heavens, which the angels showed me, and from them I heard everything, and from them I understood as I saw, but not for this generation, but for a 'remote one' which is for to come.

C.2 "not for this generation, but for a 'remote one'". In other words, in the far future. In the Last Days, in which we *now* live. Enoch is addressing us, who live in the Last Days. Quite amazing, when one realizes that Enoch originally wrote this book around 5000 years ago!

3 Concerning the 'elect' I said, and took up my parable concerning them. The Holy Great One will come forth from His dwelling; and the eternal God will tread upon the earth, even on Mount Sinai and appear from His camp and appear in the strength of His might from the heaven of heavens.

C.3 The Book of Enoch is for the 'elect' to know about in particular.

The 'elect' are from all races, & are those who have received Jesus Christ, as their personal Saviour.

ACT.4:12 Neither is there salvation in any other (JESUS): for there is none other name under heaven given among men, whereby we must be saved.

C.4 Mount Sinai = same mountain that God gave the 10 Commandments to Moses on around 1500 BCE (Exodus 19.1-3)

4 And all shall be smitten with fear and the 'Watchers' shall quake; and great fear and trembling shall seize them unto the ends of the earth. And the high mountains shall be shaken and the high hills shall be made low and shall melt like wax before the flame.

C.5 'Watchers' = The fallen angels in this particular case. Watchers is a term used for both good and bad ANGELS.

DANIEL.4:17 "This matter is by the decree of the Watchers, and the demand by the word of the holy ones."

5 And the earth shall be wholly rent in sunder and all that is upon the earth shall perish and there shall be a judgement upon all; but with the righteous He will make peace and will protect the elect and mercy shall be upon them and they shall all belong to God and they shall be prospered and they shall all be blessed and He will help them all. Light shall appear unto them and he will make peace with them.

ISAIAH.24:1 Behold, the LORD makes the earth empty, and makes it waste, and turns it upside down, and scatters abroad the inhabitants thereof.

REVELATIONS.6:14 And the heaven departed as a scroll when it is rolled together; and every mountain and island were moved out of their places.

JOHN.8:12 Then spoke Jesus again unto them, saying, I am the light of the world: he that follows me shall not walk in darkness, but shall have the light of life.

6 And behold! He cometh with ten thousands of His holy ones to execute judgement upon all and to destroy all the ungodly and to convict all flesh of all the works of their ungodliness which they have ungodly committed, and of the hard things which ungodly sinners have spoken against Him.

JUDE.1:14 And Enoch also, the seventh from Adam, prophesied of these, saying, Behold, the Lord cometh with ten thousand times ten thousand of his saints.

C.6 This above verse, clearly shows how the disciples of Christ, had access to the Book of Enoch, 2000 years ago.

REV.14:1 And I looked, and, lo, a Lamb stood on the mount Sion, and with him an hundred forty and four thousand, having his Father's name written in their foreheads

CHAPTER 2

1 Observe ye everything that takes place in the heaven, how they do not change their orbits, and the luminaries which are in the heaven, how they all arise and set in order each in his season, and transgress not against their appointed order.

2 Behold ye the earth, and give heed to the things which take place upon it from the first to last, how steadfast they are, how none of the things upon earth change, but all the work of God appear to you. Behold the summer and the winter, how the whole earth is filled with water, and clouds and dew and rain lie upon it.

Comment: I have heard sceptical writers claim that the Book of Enoch is false, just because it mentions 'rain' before the Great Flood.

Just because the Bible states that it had 'not rained before the Great Flood' is probably talking about how that from the time of the Great Flood, it was clouds in the sky that caused rain to fall.

If we look scientifically at this seeming conundrum, we find that actually before the Great Flood, there was a canopy of water above the sky, which had the effect of making the earth like a green house with uniform temperature. This canopy of water was destroyed at the time of the Great Flood. I ask you what is the first thing that one notices on the inside surface of the glass of a greenhouse? Is it not drops of water caused by condensation? Even the Bible does state that a 'mist watered the ground'. So, mentioning the word rain in the Book of Enoch is no big deal in my books. Also remember that if this Book of Enoch, was reassembled in around 200-300 BCE, and if the writers did not fully understand the exact conditions before the Great Flood, they would have used a word they were familiar with such as 'rain'. No big issue here, in my opinion!

CHAPTER 3

1 Observe and see how in the winter all the trees seem as though they had withered and shed all their leaves, except 14 trees, which do not lose their foliage, but retain the old foliage from two to three years till the new comes.

CHAPTER 4

1 And again, observe ye the days of summer how the sun is above the earth over against it.

And ye seek shade and shelter by reason of the heat of the sun, and the earth also burns with growing heat you cannot tread on the earth, or on a rock by reason of its heat.

Commentary about the Book of Enoch chapters 2-4, & 5 verses 1-3.

These chapters are preparing the background for a very strong rebuke to the FALLEN ANGELS, mentioned in detail from chapter 6 onwards. Enoch explains how God's creation is always constant, consistent & on time and reliable, like the inner workings of a great clock, which obviously does have a maker, God Himself! In other words, nothing in our physical universe can happen without God's perfect timing for it to happen, including both the beginning and ending of the world as we now know it! These earlier chapters are outlines of what is to come in much later chapters, in the "Book of the Luminaries", which talk about the total absolute perfect precision of God's Creation in the Sun, the Moon, the stars and the universe down to the split-second.

ROM.1:20 For the invisible things of him from the creation of the world are clearly seen, being understood by the things that are made, even his eternal power and Godhead; so that they are without excuse.

CHAPTER 5

1 Observe ye how the trees cover themselves with green leaves and bear fruit; wherefore give ye heed and know with regard to all His works, and recognize how He that lives for ever hath made them so.

2 And all His works, go on thus from year to year for ever, and all the tasks which they accomplish for Him, and their tasks change not, but according as God hath ordained so is it done.

3 And behold how the sea and the rivers in like manner accomplish and change not their tasks from His commandments.

4 But Ye! Ye have not been steadfast, nor done the commandments of the Lord.

But ye have turned away and spoken proud and hard words with your impure mouths against His greatness. Oh, ye hard-hearted, ye shall find no peace.

Comment:1: Chapter 5 verse 4: '*But Ye!*' Who is Enoch addressing here? Enoch addresses the evil Watchers or the 'fallen angels'. Contrary to what is often taught, I believe that it is very possible that Satan and his fallen angels were around before God created the physical dimension, and the earth. I read a very interesting book, where Jesus was asked, why Satan had rebelled?

*In the book, Jesus mentioned that it came about, when God came to present Jesus, as His Beloved Son & Heir, to all those assembled in heaven, before the time of the creation of the physical universe.

Satan apparently did not like this, thinking that he himself, should be the most highly exalted, and then he rebelled against God, along with 1/3 of the angels in Heaven.' (***See APPENDIX IX**)

This, I think makes a lot of sense, why God would not forgive the "fallen angels" as you will see in later chapters. Also, why in chapter 5.4 the fallen angels shall find 'no peace'. There is no peace without the Prince of Peace, who is Jesus.

John.3:36 He that believeth on the Son, hath everlasting life: and he that believeth not the Son shall not see life; but the wrath of God abides on him.

5 Therefore shall ye execrate your days, and the years of your life shall perish, and the years of your destruction shall be multiplied in eternal execration and ye shall find no mercy.

C.2 Execration and no mercy? Execration means a curse is upon them.

No mercy, because they had *already rejected Jesus* before the creation of the world.

ACT.4:12 Neither is there salvation in any other: for there is none other name under heaven given among men, whereby we must be saved.

6 In those days ye shall make your names an eternal execration unto the righteous, and by you shall all who curse, curse, and all the sinners and godless shall imprecate by you and for you the godless there shall be a curse and all the (righteous) shall rejoice and there shall be forgiveness of sins and every mercy and peace and forbearance. There shall be salvation unto them, a goodly light, and for all of you sinners, there shall be no salvation, but on you all shall abide a curse.

C.3 Those who curse, do so by the help of fallen angels or demons. There is however forgiveness of sins by Salvation through the Saviour-Jesus.

ZEC.5:3 Then said he unto me, this is the curse that goes forth over the face of the whole earth: for every one that steals shall be cut off as on this side according to it; and every one that *swears* shall be cut off as on that side according to it.

JOH.1:9 That was the true Light, which lights every man that cometh into the world.

C.4 When Enoch uses the word '*sinners*' he is actually talking about the '*very wicked'* & especially the '*fallen angels*', and their sons the '*Giants*', who later, when they died, became '*the Demons*'.

7 But for the elect there shall be light and joy and peace, and they shall inherit the earth; and then there shall be bestowed upon the elect wisdom, and they shall live and never again sin, either through ungodliness or though pride, but they who are wise shall be humble.

MATTHEW 5:5 Blessed are the meek: for they shall inherit the earth.

8 And they shall not transgress, nor shall they sin all the days of their life, nor shall they die of the divine anger or wrath, but they shall complete the number of days of their life; and their lives shall be increased in peace, and the years of their joy shall be multiplied, in eternal gladness and peace all the days of their life.

DAN.12:3 And they that be wise shall shine as the brightness of the firmament; and they that turn many to righteousness as the stars for ever and ever.

JOH.14:27 Peace I leave with you, my peace I give unto you: not as the world giveth, give I unto you. Let not your heart be troubled, neither let it be afraid.

CHAPTER 6

1 And it came to pass when the children of men had multiplied, that in those days were born unto them beautiful and comely daughters.

Comment:1: In **Genesis chapter 6,** as well as **Jasher chapter 4,** & **Jubilees chapter 5**, it talks about the same topic of the fallen angels coming to earth and procreating with human women:

GEN.6:1 And it came to pass, when men began to multiply on the face of the earth, and daughters were born unto them,

GEN.6:2 That the sons of God saw the daughters of men that they were fair; and they took them wives of all which they chose.

GEN.6:3 And the LORD said, 'My spirit shall not always strive with man, for that he also is flesh: yet his days shall be an hundred and twenty years'.

GEN.6:4 There were giants in the earth in those days; and also after that, when the sons of God came in unto the daughters of men, and they bare children to them, the same became mighty men which were of old, men of renown.

Jasher 4.16,18. And all the sons of men departed from the ways of the Lord in those days, as they multiplied upon the face of the earth with sons and daughters, and they taught one another their evil practices, and they continued sinning against the Lord.**18** And their judges and rulers went to the daughters of men and took their wives by force from their husbands according to their choice and the sons of men (Sons of God?) in those days took from the cattle of the earth, the beasts of the field and the fowls of the air, and taught the mixture of animals of one species with another, in order to therewith provoke the Lord; and God saw the whole earth and it was corrupt, for all flesh had corrupted its ways upon earth, all men and all animals.

Jubilees 5.1-4 And it came to pass when the children of men began to multiply on the face of the earth and daughters were born unto them, that the angels of God saw them on at a certain year of this Jubilee, that they were beautiful to look upon; they took themselves wives of all whom they chose, and they bare unto them sons and they were giants. **2** And lawlessness increased on the earth and all flesh corrupted its way, alike men and cattle and beasts and birds and everything that walked on the earth- all of them corrupted their ways and their orders, and they began to devour each other, and lawlessness increased on the earth, and every imagination of the thoughts of all men was evil continually.**3** And God looked upon the earth, and behold it was corrupt, and all flesh had corrupted its orders, and all that were upon the face of the earth had wrought all manner of evil before His eyes.**4** And He said that He would destroy man and all flesh upon the face of the earth which He had created.

2 And the angels, the children of heaven, saw and lusted after them, and said to one another "Come, let us choose us wives from among the children of men and beget us children".

3 And Semjaza, who was their leader, said unto them, "I fear ye will not indeed agree to do this deed, and I alone shall have to pay the penalty of a great sin".

4 And they all answered him and said "Let us all swear an oath, and bind ourselves by mutual imprecations not to abandon this plan but to do this thing." Then swore they all together and bound themselves by mutual imprecations upon it.

C.2 Probably one of the reasons why Jesus said:

MAT.5:34 But I say unto you, swear not at all; neither by heaven; for it is God's throne:

MAT.5:35 Nor by the earth; for it is his footstool: neither by Jerusalem; for it is the city of the great King.

MAT.5:36 Neither shalt thou swear by thy head, because thou canst not make one hair white or black.

MAT.5:37 But let your communication be, Yea, yea; Nay, nay: for whatsoever is more than these *cometh of evil.*

5 And there were in all 200 who descended in the days of Jared on the summit of Mount Hermon, and they called it Mount Hermon, because they had sworn and bound themselves by mutual imprecations upon it.

C.3 The word 'Hermon', from 'Mount Hermon' actually means 'Forbidden' & 'Cursed'.

6 And these are the names of their leaders: Semjaza, their leader, Arakiba, Rameel, Kokabiel, Tamel, Ramiel, Danel, Ezeqeel, Baraqijal, Asael, Armaros, Batarel, Ananel, Zaqiel, Samsapeel, Satarel, Turel, Jomjael, Sariel. These are their chiefs of tens.

CHAPTER 7

1 And all the others together with them took unto themselves wives, and each chose for himself one, and they began to go in unto them and to defile themselves with them, and they taught them charms and enchantments, and the cutting of roots, and made them acquainted with plants.

Comment:1: The beginning of witchcraft

2 And they became pregnant, and they bare great giants, whose height was three thousand ells, who consumed all the acquisitions of men; and when men could no longer sustain them, the giants turned against them and devoured mankind.

C.2 Women on earth became pregnant with *giant* children, whose height was 3000 ells.

How high is 3000 ells? (Modern measurements 1 Ell=2.87 feet, which obviously can't be the same measurement as in ancient times, otherwise 3000 ells would equal around 9000 feet high!) Some say 3000 ells was in reality, back then, as high as 450 feet high! If there were giants so high as anywhere from 9 feet to 450 feet high, what did they eat? Well the fact is that they became cannibals! (*See the **Appendix**)

GEN.6:4 There were giants in the earth in those days; and also after that, when the sons of God came in unto the daughters of men, and they bare children to them, the same became mighty men which were of old, men of renown.

BARUCH 3.26-28 "There were the giants famous from the beginning, that were of so great a stature, and so expert in war. 27 Those did not the Lord choose, neither gave He the way of knowledge to them. 28 But they were destroyed, because they had no wisdom, and perished through their own foolishness."

3 And they began to sin against birds, and beasts and reptiles, and fish, and to devour one another's flesh, and drink the blood. Then the earth laid accusation against the lawless ones.

C.3 These Giants turned to cannibalism, and must have had incredible powers, such as we have never seen on earth in modern times, as they were literally the sons of angels and women. The amazing thing here is that, somehow they managed to corrupt the DNA of birds & beasts, as well as reptiles and fish to create hybrids or chimeras. Why did the fallen angels or Watchers create chimeras?

The problem they had, was that God had made all of his creation with a soul, which caused problems. If they could create a soulless chimera, which God simply had not created, then it was easier for evil spirits to enter in and control that hybrid. Thus, was the beginning of the minotaur, the centaur, reptilians & mermaids and many other chimeras. This apparently happened both before and after the Flood. These creatures and other monsters, giants and titans were made infamous by both Greek and Roman mythology and by most cultures on earth.

When the Giants, the sons of the 'fallen angels died', they became demons in the negative spirit world, who constantly lusted for power and violence, and were always looking for a human on the physical earth, or even better still, a hybrid to enter into, so as to temporarily return to the physical realm, in order to enjoy all the lusts, violence and power thereof.

If a demon possesses a human, it can be cast out, but if it enters a soul-less creature, such as a chimera, it is a much easier to remain in it. Most of these chimeras have not been detected by most people on earth at any given time in its history, both past and present. They tend to be hidden away somewhere, or very much keep to themselves. This comes under the topic of Crypto-zoology. (The study of 'hidden animals')

CHAPTER 8

1 And Azazel taught men to make swords and knives, and shields, and breastplates, and made known to them the metals of the earth and the art of working with them, and bracelets, and ornaments, and the use of antimony, and the beautifying of the eyelids, and all kinds of costly stones, and all colouring tinctures.

Comment:1: Men were taught to make war for the first time, and shown how to make effective weapons. Women were taught how to beautiful themselves, and to be experts at seducing both men and angels.

2 And there arose much godlessness, and they committed fornication, and they were led astray, and became corrupt in all their ways. Semjaza taught enchantments, and root-cuttings, Barquijal taught astrology, Kokabel the constellations, Ezeqeel the knowledge of the clouds, Araquiel the signs of the earth, Shamsiel the signs of the sun, and Sariel the course of the moon. And as men perished, they cried, and their cry went up to heaven.

C.2 *The angels that fell, didn't all fall at the same time, but were often seduced. It would seem that the 'fallen angels' acted more like very spoilt "17 year-olds", who tend to 'crash and burn' with their philosophy of 'whatever goes', and 'whatever is the excitement of the moment', without any consideration for the consequences of their 'foolhardy' and sometimes dangerous pranks and dares. Those into extreme sports and indeed the champions are often around 17 years old. It is, as if, at that age, teenagers often don't really care if they live or die, judging by their behaviour. (*Fact: 70% of fatalities in car accidents in the UK are 17 years old!) Of course not all 17-year-olds are dare-devils!*

It says about the "fallen angels" that they rebelled *before* they had even "risen as stars". In other words they were *very young and inexperienced.* Such a sad story that they ended up as *devils*, and their Giant progeny, upon their physical death, as *demons* roaming the earth to this day.

GEN.6:2 That the sons of God saw the daughters of men that they were fair; and they took them wives of all which they chose.

Result of the above: Fornication, and the whole earth became corrupt in all their ways- and eventually there was total anarchy.

1CO.11:10 For this cause ought the woman to have power on her head because of the angels.

C.3 This verse shows clearly that even in Paul's day, 2000 years ago, that he was concerned about the fallen angels and their lust for women, and thus he warned the women to keep their heads covered. Not that that would make much difference, as if the fallen angels are like Supermen, then they can probably see right through women's clothes!

CHAPTER 9

1 And then Michael, Uriel, Raphael and Gabriel looked down from heaven and saw much blood being shed upon the earth, and all lawlessness being wrought upon the earth; and they said to one another "The earth made without inhabitant cries the voice of their crying up to the gates of heaven."

2 And now to you, the holy ones of heaven, the souls of men make their suit, saying, "Bring our cause before the Most High." And they said to the Lord of Ages, "Lord of Lords, God of Gods, King of Kings, and God of Ages, the throne of Thy Glory stands unto all the generations of the ages, and thy name Holy and glorious and blessed unto all the ages!"

Revelations.19:16 And he hath on his vesture and on his thigh a name written, KING OF KINGS, AND LORD OF LORDS

3 Thou hast made all things, and power over all things hast Thou; and all things are naked and open in thy sight, and you see all, and nothing can hide itself from Thee. You see what Azazel hath done, who hath taught all unrighteousness on the earth and revealed the eternal secrets which were persevered in heaven, which men were striving to learn.

4 And Semjaza to whom Thou hast given authority to bear rule over his associates. And they have gone to the daughters of men upon the earth, and have slept with the women, and have defiled themselves, and revealed to them all kinds of sins. And the women have begotten giants, and the whole earth has thereby been filled with blood and unrighteousness.

5 And now, behold the souls of those who have died are crying and making their suit to the gates of heaven, and their lamentations have ascended; and cannot cease because of the lawless deeds which are wrought on the earth.

6 And you know all things before they come to pass, and you see these things and you do suffer them, and you do not say to us what we are to do to them in regard to these.

Comment:1: It is very interesting to see here, how that God was apparently waiting, until His top officers or arch-angels had realized how evil the earth had become, and came to report to Him about it. God doesn't usually do things suddenly and rashly, without involving the counsel of others.

LAM.3:33 For he doth not afflict willingly nor grieve the children of men.

2PE.3:9 The Lord is not slack concerning his promise, as some men count slackness; but is longsuffering to us-ward, not willing that any should perish, but that all should come to repentance.

C.2 In the above verse, it is almost as if God has been thinking and pondering His options concerning the horrors of violence going on down below on the earth, when His angels mentioning the very grave nature and condition of the fallen earth to God, it triggers a pre-planned response from God Himself. It is almost as if He was saying, "Ah, I have been waiting for you archangels to be concerned enough about the situation on earth, to challenge me to do something about it!" And of course, He did immediately react strongly!

CHAPTER 10

1 Then said the Most High, the Holy and Great One spoke, and sent Uriel to the son of Lamech, and said to him: "Go tell Noah and tell him in my name 'Hide thyself!' and reveal to him the end that is approaching, that the whole earth will be destroyed, and a deluge is about to come upon the whole earth, and I will destroy all that is upon it."

GEN.6:11 The earth also was corrupt before God, and the earth was filled with violence.

GEN.6:12 And God looked upon the earth, and, behold, it was corrupt; for all flesh had corrupted his way upon the earth.

GEN.6:13 And God said unto Noah, 'The end of all flesh is come before me; for the earth is filled with violence through them; and, behold, I will destroy them with the earth'.

JUBILEES 5.19 'All those who corrupted their ways and their thoughts before the FLOOD, no man's person was accepted save that of Noah alone'.

2 And now instruct him that he may escape and his seed may be preserved for all the generations of the world. And again the Lord said to Raphael: "Bind Azazel hand and foot, and cast him in the darkness, and make an opening in the desert, which in Dudael, and cast him therein, and place upon him rough and jagged rocks, and cover him with darkness, and let him abide there for ever, and cover his face that he may not see light."

JUD.1:6 And the angels which kept not their first estate, but left their own habitation, he hath reserved in everlasting chains under darkness unto the judgment of the great day.

Comments:1: Concerning Verses 1 & 2 "Go to Noah".

Observe that officially according to certain biblical time charts, Noah was not actually alive at the same time as Enoch, but was born some 90 years after the death of Enoch.

How is it then possible, that God told His Archangel Uriel, or Ariel to go to Noah... in the Book of Enoch chapter 10 verses 1-2.

This conundrum can actually be solved, by understanding that Enoch never actually died; but was translated to the heavenly plane. Let's consider what that could actually mean?

HEB.11:5 "By faith Enoch was translated that he should *not see death*; and was not found, because God had translated him: for before his translation he had this testimony, that he pleased God."

(**Enoch 12.1** Before these things, Enoch was hidden, and no man knew where he was hidden…)

C.2 INTERCESSOR

It is my conviction that Enoch was translated for a very important reason by God himself. Even as Jesus was to become our intercessor before God in the New testament, Enoch was also some type of intercessor between fallen angels, & God Himself.

According to the Book of Enoch and other Apocryphal books, Enoch was indeed very special.

I would venture to say that God deliberately chose Enoch to be a sort of *go-between the Heavenly spirit world and the physical dimension of earth*, including under the earth and Hell and Tartarus itself.

The world was kept pretty much in subjection for the 243 years that Enoch reigned on the earth. After God shortened his lifespan to only 365 years, within only a couple of centuries, the world had been totally corrupted, was violent, and totally perverse; mankind having been led astray by the fallen angels and their sons the giants, who subjugated mankind as much as they could.

Enoch never having physically died in pre-flood times, is matched in very similar details to Elijah being taken up to heaven in a whirlwind in the Old Testament.

2KI.2:1 And it came to pass, when the LORD would take up Elijah into heaven by a whirlwind, that Elijah went with Elisha from Gilgal.

C.3 Elijah who did not die physically was later prophesied to come back, and Jesus said that John the Baptist was Elijah. (Mark 9.11-13) With that in mind, it makes more sense that *Enoch could have indeed been a go-between the spiritual realm and the physical.* **(See the APPENDIX)**

Jasher 3.27-29 And at that time the sons of men were with Enoch …and the likeness of a great horse paced in the air…Enoch said, "On my account does this horse descent upon the earth. The time has come when I must go from you…"

Jubilees 4.23 And he (Enoch) was taken from amongst the children of men to the garden of Eden; for there he wrote down… the judgment of the world.

C.4 An amazing amount of information was revealed to Enoch by God and His angels during his lifetime.

(*Later* In chapter 14, of the Book of Enoch, we will see that Enoch approached God's throne, and he was asked to *re-visit the earth,* in order to chastise the Watchers for their iniquities, by God Himself.)

As mentioned before, Enoch apparently acted as some sort of pre-flood Intercessor, between God and men, and in this case, even fallen angels.

This is further evidenced in the Book of Enoch chapters 65, where Noah was desperate for answers and he looked for Enoch and found him at the "ends of the earth"

In Enoch Chapter 106 verse 8 Methuselah was also trying to find Enoch after he been translated, and also found him at the "ends of the earth"

In later chapters I will talk about the "ends of the earth" and where I think it could be? (See APPENDIX)

3 And on the day of the Great Judgment he shall be cast into the fire.

And heal the earth which the angels have corrupted, and proclaim the healing of the earth, that they may heal the plague. And that all the children of men may not perish through all the secret things that the Watchers have disclosed and have taught their sons.

4 And the whole earth has been corrupted through the works that were taught by Azazel, to him ascribe all sin.

C.5 The Final Fate of Satan & his band of fallen angels

REV.20:1 And I saw an angel come down from heaven, having the key of the bottomless pit and a great chain in his hand.

REV.20:2 And he laid hold on the dragon, that old serpent, which is the Devil, and Satan, and bound him a thousand years,

REV.20:3 And cast him into the bottomless pit, and shut him up, and set a seal upon him, that he should deceive the nations no more, till the thousand years should be fulfilled: and after that he must be loosed a little season.

REV.20:10 And the Devil that deceived them was cast into the lake of fire and brimstone, where the beast and the false prophet are, and shall be tormented day and night for ever and ever.

5 And to Gabriel said the Lord "Proceed against the bastards and the reprobates, and against the children of fornication, and destroy the children of fornication, the children of the Watchers from amongst men, and cause them to go forth. Send them one against the other that they may destroy each other in battle. For length of days they shall not have."

C.6 Here God is telling His angels to go forth and provoke the Giants to fight the one against each other, until they are all made an end of. So, the ancient mythological stories of the Greeks and Romans were real after all. It happened both before and after the Great Flood.

6 And no request that they make of thee shall be granted unto their fathers on their behalf. For they hope to live five hundred years.

7 And the Lord said unto Michael "Go bind Semjaza and his associates who have united themselves with women so as to have been defiled with them in all their uncleanness. And their sons have slain one another,

and they have seen the destruction of their beloved ones, bind them fast for seventy generations in the valleys of the earth till the day of their judgement and the consummation till the judgement that is for ever is consummated."*

C.7 'been defiled with them in all their uncleanness' Why was it considered unclean for angels to make love with the women on earth? What was the real issue? Are humans considered unclean, or imperfect? Who is this verse stating is unclean? The angels or the human women? Look at this verse from the last chapter:

Enoch 9.4 'And they have gone to the daughters of men upon the earth, and have slept with the women, and have *defiled themselves*, and *revealed to them all kinds of sins*. And the *women have begotten giants*, and the whole earth has thereby been *filled with blood and unrighteousness*.'

I actually feel sorry for the first women who lived on the earth before the flood, because according to some books such as the Bible: 'the angels lusted after the beautiful women and took wives of them as they chose'.

Jasher 4.18 'the angels' '*took the women by force from their husbands*'.

What was really going on back there? Why did the angels want to be with human women, when they could have been with the female angels in heaven, who are probably much more beautiful than human women as it is obvious, that if angels could make love to the human women, then female angels must also exist. Well it is in a word: REBELLION! Those fallen angels that followed Satan in His Rebellion turned to the ways of Pride and Arrogance, and turned away from Humility and love. The human woman were much easier for the fallen angels to dominate. The heavenly female angels and Virtues, would have probably tried to convince the fallen angels to repent, which they adamantly refused to do. Although the scriptures seem to indicate that the sexual union of 'fallen angels' and women was the main goal of the fallen angels, and to have their own sons, that is simply not the entire picture!

The fallen angels cohabited with the women for a season, but then they themselves became more and more depraved, leaving all standards of sexual morality, and became totally perverse, and started to want humans to worship to them as gods, and to make human sacrifices unto them. It has been ever so ever since that time! The fallen angels used and abused the women for a season, and then they descended into utter madness, perversion, and became hideous monsters just like Satan the Dragon and Serpent.

C.8 Bind them fast for **seventy generations*. How long was considered a generation in Enoch's time?

For people like Adam and Eve who lived to be over 900 years old, it would seem likely that a generation was from when mankind started having children, which was anywhere from 65 years old in the case of Enoch himself, to those much closer to the flood not having children until they were 160. I think a generation must have been around 100-120 years in those days. It is also stated that man's life would be reduced eventually to only 120 years by God himself.

So, if we assume that a generation was around 100 years for the sake of argument, then these first fallen angels such as Semjaza and his associates were to be locked up for a good 7000 years in the valleys of the earth. It goes on to say in this very 7th verse "till the day of their judgement and of their consummation, till the judgment that is forever is consummated".

According to the biblical timeline and other Jewish books, the earth is currently just around 6000 years old. When the Messiah returns, a 1000-year Golden Age will begin. So, the 6000 years, plus the 1000 years of the Golden Age, otherwise known as the MILLENNIUM makes around 7000 years of World's History. After which the GREAT WHITE THRONE JUDGEMENT will occur according to the Book of Revelations.

C.9 If we want to be more exact as to the length of a generation back then, well there is a roundabout way to calculate it. If we consider that those first 200 angels that fell, probably got locked up around the time of Noah according to the Book of Enoch chapter 9-10. Noah was born around 1050 AC. So God sending His angel to warn Noah to get ready for the Great Flood would have probably have happened around 1200 AC, and approximately the same time that the 200 first fallen angels were finally locked up. It is stated that they should be locked up for 70 generations. We know that the whole span of earth's history in biblical terms, that it is supposed to be around 7000 years in total. Why? It is symbolic for how God took 6 days to create His entire physical creation and that He rested on the 7th day. So 1000 years for every day of God's creation, gives us the biblical 7000 years of World History. If we round up the numbers and say for sake of argument that the first 200 angels got locked up circa 1000 A.C. So that would make a generation more accurately put at 85.5 years for a generation. Imagine just starting to have children at 85 years old! Amazing, and older than the age at which most people, die today in modern times!

REV.20:11 And I saw a great white throne, and him that sat on it, from whose face the earth and the heaven fled away; and there was found no place for them.

8 In those days they shall be led off to the abyss of fire, and to the torment and the prison in which they shall be confined for ever; and whosoever shall be condemned and destroyed will from henceforth be bound together with them to the end of all generations

JUD.1:6 And the angels which kept not their first estate, but left their own habitation, he hath reserved in everlasting chains under darkness unto the judgment of the great day.

REV.20:10 And the devil that deceived them was cast into the lake of fire and brimstone, where the beast and the false prophet are, and shall be tormented day and night for ever and ever.

9 And destroy all the spirits of the reprobate and the children of the Watchers, because they have wronged mankind. Destroy all wrong from the face of the earth, and let every evil work come to an end, and let the Plant of Righteousness appear.

C.10 WATCHERS: DAN.4:17 "This matter is by the decree of the watchers (The good ones in heaven), and the demand by the word of the holy ones: to the intent that the living may know that the most High rules in the kingdom of men, and giveth it to whomsoever he will, and sets up over it the basest of men."

10 And it shall prove a blessing. The works of righteousness and truth shall be planted in truth and joy forever more.

11 And then shall all the 'righteous escape' and shall live till they begat thousands of children and all the days of their youth and their old age shall they complete in peace.

C.11 And then shall all the 'righteous escape'. Is this possibly talking about the RAPTURE that occurs at the 2nd coming of Christ?

1TH.4:16 For the Lord himself shall descend from heaven with a shout, with the voice of the archangel, and with the trump of God: and the dead in Christ shall rise first:

1TH.4:17 Then we which are alive and remain shall be caught up together with them in the clouds, to meet the Lord in the air: and so shall we ever be with the Lord.

C.12 *Or* is this talking about *another Rescue of God's Millennial children,* of those who are still in their physical bodies & who get saved during the Millennium, and are finally tested at the end of the Millennium, when according to the Bible in Revelation 20, Satan is released from his prison of the Bottomless pit, for a very short season.

REV.20:7 And when the thousand years are expired, Satan shall be loosed out of his prison…

12 And then shall the whole earth be tilled in righteousness, and shall be planted with trees and full of blessing; and all desirable trees shall be planted on it, and they shall plant vines on it; and the vine which they plant thereon shall yield wine in abundance, and as for all the seed which is sown thereon each measure shall bare a thousand, and each measure of olives shall yield ten presses of oil.

C.13 VERSES 10-12 DESTROY ALL EVIL…and let the PLANT of RIGHTEOUSNESS & TRUTH APPEAR. **TIMEFRAME: THE MILLENNIUM**

C.14 This is obviously talking about JESUS.

ISAIAH.11:4 But with *righteousness* shall he judge the poor, and reprove with equity for the meek of the earth: and he shall smite the earth: with the rod of his mouth, and with the breath of his lips shall he slay the wicked.

ISAIAH.11:5 And righteousness shall be the girdle of his loins, and faithfulness the girdle of his reins.

REV.19:11 And I saw heaven opened, and behold a white horse; and he that sat upon him was called *Faithful and True*, and in righteousness he doth judge and make war.

REV.19:15 And out of his mouth goes a sharp sword, that with it he should smite the nations: and he shall rule them with a rod of iron: and he treads the winepress of the fierceness and wrath of Almighty God.

REV.21:8 But the fearful, and unbelieving, and the abominable, and murderers, and whoremongers, and sorcerers, and idolaters, and all liars, shall have their part in the lake which burns with fire and brimstone: which is the second death.

13 And cleanse thou the earth from all oppression, and from all unrighteousness, and from all sin, and from all godlessness, and all the uncleanness that is wrought upon the earth destroy from off the earth.

14 And all the children of men shall become righteous, and all nations shall offer adoration and shall praise Me, and all shall worship Me.

And the earth shall be cleansed from all defilement, and from all sin, and from all punishment, and from all torment, and I will never again send upon it from generation to generation forever.

C.15 No More WAR or Oppression.

ISA.11:9 They shall not hurt nor destroy in all my holy mountain: for the earth shall be full of the knowledge of the LORD, as the waters cover the sea.

REV.22:3 And there shall be no more curse: but the throne of God and of the Lamb shall be in it; and his servants shall serve him:

CHAPTER 11

1 And in those days, I will open the store chambers of blessing which are in heaven, so as to send them down upon the earth over the works and labour of the children of men. And truth and peace shall be associated together throughout all the days of the world and throughout all the generations of men.

Comment:1: 'I will open the *store chambers of blessing* which are in heaven'.

It would appear that God is holding back the very greatest blessings until last, after the Great Cosmic battle of the universe is won and Righteousness reigns supreme, and evil is vanquished permanently.

REV.22:3 And there shall be no more curse: but the throne of God and of the Lamb shall be in it; and his servants shall serve him:

ISA.9:6 For unto us a child is born, unto us a son is given: and the government shall be upon his shoulder: and his name shall be called Wonderful, Counsellor, The mighty God, The everlasting Father, *The Prince of Peace*.

ISA.9:7 Of the increase of his government and peace there shall be no end, upon the throne of David, and upon his kingdom, to order it, and to establish it with judgment and with justice from henceforth even for ever. The zeal of the LORD of hosts will perform this.

CHAPTER 12

1 Before these things Enoch was hidden, and no one of the children of men knew where he was hidden, and where he abode, and what had become of him; and his activities had to do with the Watchers and his days were with the holy ones.

Comment:1: This verse here, is *not* saying necessarily, that Enoch is being translated, at least perhaps not quite yet, but that he is hidden from men, while he devotes his time to spending it with the Holy watchers in heaven.

Book of Jasher: 'And it was in the year of Adam's death (930 A.C.), which was the two hundred and forty-third year of the reign of Enoch, in that time Enoch resolved to separate himself from the sons of men and to secret (hide) himself, as at the first, in order to serve the Lord.'

C.2 There is a verse in the Book of Enoch about Enoch's translation: (Enoch 39.3) "And in those days a whirlwind carried me off from the earth and set me down at the end of the heavens".)

2 And I, Enoch was blessing the Lord of majesty and the king of the ages, and lo! The Watchers called me-'Enoch scribe of righteousness, go declare unto the Watchers of the heaven who have left the high heaven, and holy eternal place, and have defiled themselves with women, and have done as the children of earth do, and have taken unto themselves wives', "Ye have wrought great destruction on the earth; and Ye shall have no peace for forgiveness of sin; and inasmuch as they delight themselves in their children, and the murder of their beloved ones shall they see, and over the destruction of their children shall they lament, and shall make supplication unto eternity, but mercy and peace shall ye not attain."

CHAPTER 13

1 And Enoch went and said, "Azazel, thou shalt have no peace, a severe sentence has gone forth against thee to put thee in bonds and thou shalt have no toleration nor request granted to thee because of the unrighteousness which thou has taught, and because of all the works of godlessness and unrighteousness and sin which thou hast shown to men."

Comment:1: No forgiveness, because they had already rejected Jesus, God's only begotten Son, before the creation of the earth, whilst still in heaven, or in Pre-Adamic times.

2 Then I went and spoke to them all together, and they were all afraid, and fear and trembling seized them; and they besought me to draw up a petition for them that they might find forgiveness and to read their petition in the presence of the Lord of heaven.

3 For from henceforth they could not speak with Him, nor lift up their eyes to heaven for shame of their sins for which they had been condemned.

C.2 Here it is evident that the fallen angels had lost some of their former powers and abilities: *'they could not speak with Him, nor lift up their eyes to heaven for shame of their sins for which they had been condemned.'* *

C.3 The most dangerous thing that any of us on earth can do is to repeatedly resist God's Holy Spirit.

PRO.29:1 He, that being often reproved hardens his neck, shall suddenly be destroyed, and that *without remedy.*

4 Then I wrote out their petition, and the prayer in regard to their spirits and their deeds individually and in regard to their requests that they should have forgiveness and length of days. And I went off and sat down at the waters of Dan, in the land of Dan, to the south of the west of Hermon. I read their petition and fell asleep.

C.4 Land of Dan, near Mt Hermon. Later in time the location of the lost, 13th tribe of Israel.

5 And behold a dream came to me, and visions fell down upon me, and I saw visions of chastisement, and a voice come bidding (me) to tell it to the sons of heaven, and reprimand them.

6 And when I awoke, I came unto them, and they were all sitting gathered together, weeping in Abelsjail, which is between Lebanon and Seneser, with their faces covered.

7 And I recounted before them all the visions which I had seen in sleep, and I began to speak the words of righteousness, and to reprimand the heavenly Watchers.

C.5 Enoch was given unusual powers from God, to reprimand the fallen angels right to their faces! No one in history has repeated that!

CHAPTER 14

1 The book of the words of righteousness, and of the reprimand of the eternal Watchers in accordance with the command of the Holy Great One in that vision.

I saw in my sleep what I will now say with a tongue of flesh and with the breath of my mouth: which the Great One has given to men to converse therewith and understand with the heart.

Comment:1: 'tongue of flesh' Here Enoch is making the point that he is still in a human body and not a spirit, or heavenly body. At least not quite yet.

2 As He has created and given to man the power of understanding the word of wisdom, so hath He created me also and given the power of reprimanding the Watchers, the children of heaven.

3 I wrote out your petition, and in my vision it appeared thus, that your petition will not be granted unto you throughout all the days of eternity, and that judgement has been finally passed upon you: yea your (petition) will not be granted unto you; and from henceforth you shall not ascend into heaven unto all eternity and in bonds of the earth, the decree has gone forth to bind you for all the days of the world.

JOB.1:6 Now there was a day when the sons of God came to present themselves before the LORD, and Satan came also among them.

C.2 In the Book of Job, it is made clear that both Satan and other Sons of God, or angels could appear before the throne of God. However, these *first 200 angels* that fell were to be bound for all the days of the earth (7000 years), and they would no longer be allowed to ascend into heaven.

4 And that previously you shall have seen the destruction of your beloved sons and ye shall have no pleasure in them, but they shall fall before you by the sword. And your petition on their behalf shall not be granted, nor yet on your own; even though you weep and pray and speak all the words contained in the writing which I have written.

C.3 These first two hundred fallen angels are to witness their own sons the giants fighting one another until they make a complete end of each other at least in the physical world of the flesh. When their sons died they became the origin of the Demon spirits.

5 And the vision was shown to me thus: Behold, in the vision clouds invited me and a mist summoned me and the course of the stars and lightnings sped and hastened me, and the winds in the vision caused me to fly and lifted me upward, and bore me into heaven.

C.4 An unusually descriptive & beautiful verse of being borne up to heaven.

6 And I went in till I drew nigh to a wall which is built of crystals and surrounded by tongues of fire and it began to affright me. And I went into the tongues of fire and drew nigh to a large house which was built of crystals; and the walls of the house were like tessellated floor (made) of crystals, and its groundwork was of crystal.

C.5 'tessellated floor'=mosaic

C.6 *"Crystals and Tongues of Fire"*

EZE.1:22 "And the likeness of the firmament upon the heads of the living creature was as the colour of the *terrible crystal*, stretched forth over their heads above."

ACT.2:3 "And there appeared unto them *cloven tongues like as of fire*, and it sat upon each of them."

7 Its ceiling was like the path of the stars, and the lightnings, and between them were the fiery cherubim, and their heaven was (clear) as water. A flaming fire surrounded the walls, and its portals blazed with fire.

8 And I entered into that house, and it was hot as fire and cold as ice. There were no delights of life therein. Fear covered me, and trembling got hold upon me. And as I quaked and trembled, I fell upon my face, and I beheld a vision, and lo! there was a second house, greater than the former, and the entire portal stood open before me, and it was built of flames of fire.

C.6 How could a house be "hot as fire and cold like ice. No delights of life?" That is a mystery, as it certainly does not sound like an inviting place.

C.7 A second greater house...a *PORTAL* stood open..

Enoch mentions portals frequently, some apparently spiritual and others apparently physical gateways or *doors to other places*...

REV.4:1 After this I looked, and, behold, *a door was opened in heaven*: and the first voice which I heard was as it were of a trumpet talking with me; which said, 'Come up hither, and I will shew thee things which must be hereafter.'

9 And in every respect, it so excelled in splendour and magnificence and extent that I cannot describe to you its splendour and its extent: And its floor was of fire, and above it were lightnings and the path of the stars, and its ceiling also was flaming fire.

C.8 REV.4:5 "And out of the throne proceeded *lightnings and thunder* and voices..."

10 And I looked and saw therein a lofty *throne*. Its appearance was as crystal, and the *wheels* thereof as the shining sun, and there was the vision of *cherubim*: And from underneath the throne came streams of flaming

fire, so that I could not look thereon; and the Great Glory sat thereon, and His raiment shone more brightly than the sun and was whiter than any snow.

EZE.1:13 "As for the likeness of the living creatures, their appearance was like *burning coals of fire,* and like the appearance of lamps: it went up and down among the living creatures; and the fire was bright, and out of the fire went forth lightning."

DAN.7:9 "I beheld till the thrones were cast down, and the Ancient of days did sit, whose garment was white as snow, and the hair of his head like the pure wool: *his throne was like the fiery flame, and his wheels as burning fire."*

REV.1:14 "His head and his hairs were white like wool, as white as snow; and his *eyes were as a flame of fire."*

REV.1:15 "And his *feet like unto fine brass, as if they burned in a furnace*; and his *voice as the sound of many waters."*

REV.4:6 "And before the throne there was a *sea of glass* like unto *crystal*: and in the midst of the **throne**, and round about the throne, were *four beasts full of eyes before and behind."*

11 None of the angels could enter and could behold His face by reason of the magnificence and glory, and no flesh could behold him. The flaming fire was round about Him, and a great fire stood before Him, and none around could draw nigh Him.

Ten thousand times ten thousand (stood) before him, yet he needed no counsellor.

C.9 Here are some excellent Bible verses which concur:

DAN.7:10 "A fiery stream issued and came forth from before him".

REV.1:16 "…and out of his mouth went a *sharp two-edged sword*: and his *countenance was as the sun shines in his strength."*

REV.7:9 After this I beheld, and, lo, a great multitude, which no man could number, of all nations, and kindreds, and people, and tongues, stood before the throne, and before the Lamb, clothed with white robes, and palms in their hands;

REV.7:15 "Therefore are they before the throne of God, and serve him day and night in his temple: and he that sits on the throne shall dwell among them."

12 And the most holy ones who were nigh to Him did not leave by night nor depart from Him. And until then, I had been prostrated on my face, trembling and the Lord called me with His own mouth, and said to me, "Come hither Enoch and hear my word".

13 And one of the holy ones came to me and waked me, and he made

me rise up and approach the door and I bowed my face downwards.

DAN.7:15 "I Daniel was grieved in my spirit in the midst of my body, and the visions of my head troubled me."

REV.1:17 "And when I saw him, I fell at his feet as dead. And he laid his right hand upon me, saying unto me, 'Fear not; I am the first and the last'".

CHAPTER 15

1 And He answered me and said to me, and I heard His voice, "Fear not, Enoch thou righteous man and scribe of righteousness. Approach hither and hear my voice, and go, say to the Watchers of Heaven, who have sent thee to intercede for them." "You should intercede for men, and not men for you."

Comment:1: The Watcher Angels were a specific class of angels, who were designed by God to read the thoughts and intents of the minds & hearts of humans. Their job was to communicate & intercede directly with God on the behalf of humans.

When the 200 Fallen 'Watcher Angels' rebelled, they then used their unique talents against mankind, and it was easy for them to deceive people, because they knew the intentions of people's hearts.

2 Wherefore have ye left the high, holy and eternal heaven, and lain with women, and defiled yourselves with the daughters of men and taken to yourselves wives and done like the children of earth, and begotten giants (as your) sons?

GEN.6:2 That the sons of God saw the daughters of men that they were fair; and they took them wives of all which they chose.

GEN.6:4 There were giants in the earth in those days; and also after that, when the sons of God came in unto the daughters of men, and they bare children to them, the same became mighty men which were of old, men of renown.

Jubilees 5.1 …And it came to pass when the children of men began to multiply on the face of the earth and daughters were born unto them, that the angels of God, saw them on a certain year, that they were beautiful to look upon; and they took themselves wives of all whom they chose, and bare unto them sons, and they were giants.

3 And though ye were holy, spiritual living the eternal life, you have defiled yourselves, with the blood of women, and begotten children with the blood of flesh, and as the children of men, have lusted after flesh, and as those also do who die and perish.

4 Therefore have I given them wives also that they might impregnate them and begat children by them, that thus nothing might be wanting to them on earth.

Comment:1: 'nothing might be wanting'. This would tend to suggest, that in the spirit world, contrary to what is often taught in churches, there is sex, and there is procreation and that's how God gets more souls in the heavenly realms. The point being that the fallen angels were able to have sex with the women on earth. However, it was not just because the women were beautiful, but because the fallen angels needed a way to dominate the physical plane, and try to corrupt the seed of mankind, so that the promised Messiah would not be able to show up.

5 But you were formerly spiritual, living the eternal life, and immortal for all generations of the world. And therefore, I have not appointed wives for you. For as for the spiritual ones of the heaven, in heaven is their dwelling.

Jubilees 7.21 For owing to these three things came the flood upon the earth, namely owing to the fornication wherein the Watchers against the laws of their ordinances went a whoring after the daughters of men, and took themselves wives of all which they chose; and made the beginning of uncleanness.

2PE.2:4 For if God spared not the angels that sinned, but cast them down to hell, and delivered them into chains of darkness, to be reserved unto judgment.

6 And now, giants, who were produced from the spirits, and flesh, shall be called evil spirits upon the earth, and on the earth shall be their dwelling. Evil spirits have proceeded from their bodies, because they are born from men, and from the Holy Watchers is their beginning and primal origin. They shall be evil spirits on earth, and evil spirits shall they be called.

C.2 The fallen angels didn't actually co-habit with the women for very long, before they started more perverse actions, and doing things with animals, in order to create soulless chimeras, which were much easier to directly possess and control, by the dead spirits of the slain giants, who then became the start of the demons. The fallen angels mighty sons, the giants, were getting slain in battle with other demi-gods. By creating chimeras, the fallen angels made a way for their sons, the demons, to come back to the physical plain of the earth, by possessing the chimeras.

Jubilees 7.22 "And they begat sons the Naphidim, and they were all unalike, and they *devoured one another*; and the giants slew the Naphil, and the Naphil slew the Eljo, and the Eljo mankind, and one man another".

C.3 How tall were these different classes of giants and titans? There are skeletons that have been found that I know of, that are up to 45 feet high. I have also heard of one of 75 feet high. Scary just to think about what it was like for humans back then before the flood. It also might explain why so many underground cities have been found. What were those ancient people hiding from. Was it from man-eating giants as well as monsters?

2PE.2:12 But these, as natural brute beasts, made to be taken and destroyed, speak evil of the things that they understand not; and shall utterly perish in their own corruption;

7 As for the spirits of heaven, in heaven shall be their dwelling, but

as for the spirits of the earth which were born upon the earth, on the earth shall be their dwelling. And the spirits of the giants afflict, oppress, destroy, attack, do battle, and work destruction on the earth, and cause trouble. They take no food, but nevertheless hunger and thirst, and cause offences.

Jubilees 10.5… "For these are malignant, and created to destroy."

8 And these spirits shall rise up against the children of men and against women, because they have proceeded from them

Jubilees 10.2 "And the sons of Noah came to Noah and told him concerning the demons which were leading astray and blinding and slaying his sons' sons"

CHAPTER 16

1 From the days of the slaughter and destruction and death of the giants, from the souls of whose flesh the spirits, having gone forth, shall destroy without incurring judgement; thus they shall destroy until the day of the consummation, the great judgment in which the age shall be consummated, over the Watchers and the godless yea, shall be wholly consummated.

Comment:1: Here '**The Consummation'** *means the* WRATH of GOD.
The demons which are the spirits of the giants, some of which, shall roam free until the WRATH of God, and they are finally locked up for good in the 'Bottomless Pit', along with Satan. Notice that it clearly states that the demons shall not incur judgement until the Wrath of God, and also the Final Great White Throne Judgement. This explains why the demons spoke the following to Jesus in His days on earth:

MAT.8:29 And, behold, they cried out, saying, 'What have we to do with thee, Jesus, thou Son of God?' 'Art thou come hither to *torment us before the time*?'

DAN.9:27 ...he shall make it desolate, even until the **consummation,* and that determined shall be poured upon the desolate.

REV.15:7 And one of the four beasts gave unto the seven angels seven golden vials full of the *Wrath of God*, who lives for ever and ever.

2 And now as to the Watchers who have sent thee to intercede for them, who have been afore-time in heaven, (say to them): You have been in heaven, but all the mysteries had not yet been revealed to you, and you knew worthless ones, and these in the hardness of your hearts, you have made known to the women, and through these mysteries women and men work much evil on earth. Say to them therefore, "Ye have no peace."

C.2 What did God mean, in the above verse, by saying that the fallen angels knew only "worthless mysteries", and not the important ones?
The following are examples of different mysteries mentioned in the Bible:

2TH.2:7 For the *mystery* of iniquity doth already work.

REV.17:5 And upon her forehead was a name written, MYSTERY, BABYLON THE GREAT, THE MOTHER OF HARLOTS AND ABOMINATIONS OF THE EARTH.

REV.10:7 But in the days of the voice of the seventh angel, when he shall begin to sound, the *mystery* of God should be finished, as he hath declared to his servants the prophets.

1CO.15:51 Behold, I shew you a *mystery*; We shall not all sleep, but we shall all be changed..

EPH.3:4 Whereby, when ye read, ye may understand my knowledge in the *mystery* of Christ..

EPH.6:19 And for me, that utterance may be given unto me, that I may open my mouth boldly, to make known the *mystery* of the gospel,

EPH.5:32 This is a great *mystery*: but I speak concerning *Christ and the church.*

C.3 In conclusion: about 'all the mysteries had not yet been revealed to you, and you knew worthless ones'. God is stating matter of fact, that the fallen angels had jumped the gun, as they had no idea about all the above-mentioned mysteries, and especially about the mystery of Christ and the Bride. All the evil of Satan and his fallen angels could not stop the mysteries of God from being fulfilled, including Jesus coming as the Messiah and Redeemer of all mankind.

C.4 The last verse ends up saying, "Ye shall have no peace."

THERE IS NO PEACE WITHOUT THE PRINCE OF PEACE - JESUS

The *greatest mystery* has been that God, in the form of His Son Jesus, is the Saviour of all of mankind. The tragedy for the fallen angels is, that they had already rejected Jesus sometime before the creation of the earth, in Pre-Adamic times. They did not really realize the great importance of who Jesus was, as Jesus is humble and loving, as well as all powerful. Satan and His band of roving fallen angels, don't have the beautiful qualities that Jesus, the Son of God, has. They rejected Jesus because of their pride.

HEB.1:2 Hath in these last days spoken unto us by his Son, whom he hath appointed heir of all things, by whom also he made the worlds.

HEB.1:4 Being *made so much better than the angels*, as he hath by inheritance obtained a more excellent name than they.

HEB.1:5 For unto which of the angels said he at any time, '*Thou art my Son, this day have I begotten thee?*' And again, 'I will be to him a Father, and he shall be to me a Son?'

CHAPTER 17 Earth and Hell (Sheol)

1 And they took and brought me to a place in which those who were there were like flaming fire, and when they wished, they appeared as men.

Comment:1: This shows that the angels, can most definitely, change their form.

HEB.1:7 And of the angels he says, 'Who makes his angels spirits, and his ministers a *flame of fire.'*

2 And they brought me to a place of darkness, and to a mountain the point of whose summit reached to heaven.

3 And I saw the places of the luminaries and the treasuries of the stars and of the thunder and in the uttermost depths, where were a fiery bow and arrows and their quiver, and a fiery sword and all the lightnings.

REV.6:2 And I saw, and behold a white horse: and he that sat on him had a *bow*; and a crown was given unto him: and he went forth conquering, and to conquer.

ZEC.9:14 And the LORD shall be seen over them, and his *arrow* shall go forth as the *lightning*

REV.11:5 And if any man will hurt them, *fire* proceeds out of their mouth, and devours their enemies: and if any man will hurt them, he must in this manner be killed.

REV.19:21 And the remnant were slain with the *sword* of him that sat upon the horse, which *sword* proceeded out of his mouth

REV.4:5 And out of the throne proceeded *lightnings* and *thunders* and voices

2TH.1:8 In *flaming fire* taking vengeance on them that know not God, and that obey not the gospel of our Lord Jesus Christ.

JUBILEES 1.28 "And all the *luminaries* be renewed for healing and for peace and for blessing"

C.2 There are many interesting verses in the Bible about the topics of verse 3. Luminaries and the treasure of the stars are dealt with in a later chapter of the Book of Enoch. Luminaries are sometimes referred to as the angels and sometimes to as the stars of the heavens.

4 And they took me to the living waters and to the fire of the west, which receives every setting of the sun. And I came to a river of fire in which the fire flows like water and discharges itself into the great sea towards the west.

C.3 This verse is very mysterious as 'living waters' is normally a reference to the waters coming out of God's throne. The 'river of fire' normally has the connotation of something to do with the Lake of Fire. Why does it discharge itself into the great sea towards the west? Is this location that Enoch is visiting a physical location inside the earth or is it a spiritual location such as Tartarus?

REV.7:17 For the Lamb which is in the midst of the throne shall feed them and shall lead them unto *living fountains of waters:* and God shall wipe away all tears from their eyes.

REV.20:14 And death and hell were cast into the *lake of fire*. This is the second death.

REV.20:15 And whosoever was not found written in the book of life was cast into the *lake of fire*.

5 I saw the great rivers and came to the great river and to the great darkness, and went to the place where no flesh walks.

C.4 *'A place where no flesh walks'* & *'to the great darkness'*. It would appear that Enoch is being shown the spiritual side of the 'inner earth', or better said the 'negative spirit world'.

6 I saw mountains of the darkness of winter and the place whence all the waters of the deep flow. I saw the mouths of <u>all</u> the rivers of the earth and the mouth of the deep.

C.5 'mouths' of <u>all the rivers</u> of the earth and the <u>mouth of the deep.</u> Sounds like all the rivers are connected to the mouth of the deep. What is the mouth of the deep?

A mouth is normally a small and narrow part of a given body. This verse seems to tell us, that there is a narrow entrance, or there are entrances and connections between the rivers of the earth and the <u>deep,</u> or the <u>inner earth</u>. Some state that our planet is actually hollow, and has <u>narrow entrances</u> to the inner earth situated at the poles. It is also reported that the inner world fresh water rivers, come out of the North and South poles (so-called).

According to all the famous explorers, they never found the poles, but found themselves descending inside the earth's apertures to discover new lands full of tall trees, and what was thought to be extinct dinosaurs. (Admiral Bird -1947)

Here are a few very interesting verses from II Ezdras, written originally by Ezra, in around 500 BCE:

II Ezdras Chapter 4.7 (angel Uriel speaking) "And he said to me, "If I had asked you, 'How many dwellings are *in the heart of the sea*, or how many streams are at the *source of the deep*, or how many streams are above the firmament, or which are the *exits of hell*, or which are the *entrances of paradise*?'""

II Ezdras 4.41 "In Hades, the chambers of the souls are *like the womb*."

II Ezdras 7.3 "There is a *sea set in a wide expanse* so that it is broad and vast, but it has an *entrance* set in *a narrow place*, so that it is like a river."

CHAPTER 18

1 I saw the treasuries of all the winds. I saw how He had furnished with them the whole creation and the firm foundations of the earth; and I saw the corner-stone of the earth. I saw the four winds which bear the earth and the firmament of the heaven.

Comment:1: What exactly are the foundations of the earth and the corner-stone?

JOB.38:4 Where were you when I laid the foundations of the earth? Declare, if thou hast understanding?

JOB.38:6 Whereupon are the foundations thereof fastened? Or who laid the corner stone thereof;

PRO.8:29 "When he appointed the *foundations of the earth*"

Only God knows the answer to that question, but it sure is intriguing. It is very interesting that Enoch actually got to see both the Foundations and the Corner Stone of the earth.

2 And I saw how the winds stretch out the vaults of heaven and have their station between heaven and earth. These are the pillars of the heaven. I saw the winds of heaven which turn and bring the circumference of the sun and all the stars to their setting.

3 I saw the winds on the earth carrying the clouds. I saw the paths of the angels. I saw at the end of the earth the firmament of the heaven above; and I proceeded and saw a place which burns day and night, where there are seven mountains of magnificent stones, three towards the east, and three towards the south.

C.2 This is simply amazing, and something that none of us in modern times have actually seen. Mountains made of magnificent stones.

4 And as for those towards the east, one was of coloured stone, and one of pearl, and one of jacinth, and those towards the south of red stone; but the middle one reached to heaven like the throne of God of alabaster, and the summit of the throne was of sapphire.

REV.4:2 And immediately I was in the spirit: and, behold, a throne was set in heaven, and one sat on the throne.

REV.4:3 And he that sat was to look upon like a jasper and a sardine stone: and there was a rainbow round about the throne, in sight like unto an emerald.

5 And I saw a flaming fire and beyond these mountains is a region the end of the earth. There the heavens were completed, and I saw a deep

abyss with columns of heavenly fire, and among them I saw columns of fire fall which were beyond measure alike towards the height and towards the depth.

6 And beyond that abyss, I saw a place which had no firmament of the heaven above and no firmly founded earth beneath it. There was no water upon it, and no birds, but it was a waste and horrible place. I saw there seven stars like great burning mountains, and to me, when I inquired regarding them,

C.3 '*Seven stars'*? Seven Mountains? I don't know if it has any relevance, but could these particular 'fallen angels' represent the '**7 Empires of mankind'** that became dominant after the Great Flood? The 1st being Egypt, then 2nd Assyria, 3rd Babylon, 4th Media-Persia, 5th Greece, 6th Rome and the 7th being the final World-Wide government of the Anti-Christ. (See APPENDIX for class on 'Satan, King of Empires'.) Let's imagine, that before the Great Flood, Satan and the fallen angels were causing havoc on the earth, but after the Flood, Satan decided that he wanted to rule mankind, and therefore inspired his top fallen angels to get mankind organized into making governments instead of the awful anarchy that persisted before the Great Flood. As we all know as each world Empire fell it happened in a very destructive manner almost as though one huge spiritual negative power was battling with another for control.

REV.17:9 And here is the mind which hath wisdom. The *seven heads* are *seven mountains*, on which the woman sitteth.

REV.17:10 And there are *seven kings*: five are fallen, and one is, and the other is not yet come; and when he cometh, he must continue a short space.

REV.17:11 And the *beast* that was, and is not, even he is the *eighth*, and is of the seven, and goes into perdition.

Apart from these 7 Empires of man, there was the very first Empire after the Great Flood of Nimrod and the Tower of Babel. Nimrod is said to have been a Demi-god who had many powers, and was in total rebellion against God. Some writers have speculated that the spirit of Nimrod shall return to possess the leader of the last kingdom of man on earth, the Anti-Christ.

C.4 I think it very likely that God had a very good talk with Satan at the time after the Great Flood, when all of Satan's plans had come to nought and had in fact been all but washed away.

God seems to have some sort of councils in heaven to which Satan is some-times present:

JOB.1:6 Now there was a day when the sons of God came to present themselves before the LORD, and Satan came also among them.

JOB.1:7 And the LORD said unto Satan, from where did you come? Then Satan answered the LORD, and said, 'From going to and fro in the earth, and from walking up and down *in* it'.

God must have told Satan that He would no longer tolerate total anarchy upon the earth and that there needed to be some semblance of order and control, and that He would no longer allow chaos to reign. So Satan started to become the 'prince of the air' and 'Satan, King of Empires', by possessing the very worst of the leaders of the empires of mankind, as he will also do with the Final Empire of the Anti-Christ, which will be the very worst of all. Satan is trying to get out from under the restrains and shackles that God placed upon him at the time of the Great Flood- i.e. 'No more total ANARCHY!' However, the Bible states that in the last days of the Anti-Christ's world empire, there shall be a time of 'TRIBULATION' such as was never seen before in history, and according to the Apocryphal book of ***II Ezdras***, eventually the 'spirit of unrest' shall return, and things will once again descend into the TOTAL ANARCHY that existed before the Great Flood of Noah. This won't happen until God himself removes the restrains put on Satan, and only then, will the happenings of the ***Book of Revelation chapter 9*** will start to occur.

REV.9:2 And he opened the bottomless pit; and there arose a smoke out of the pit, as the smoke of a great furnace; and the sun and the air were darkened by reason of the smoke of the pit.

REV.9:5 And to them it was given that they should not kill them, but that they should be tormented five months: and their torment was as the torment of a scorpion, when he strikes a man.

REV.9:6 And in those days shall men seek death, and shall not find it; and shall desire to die, and death shall flee from them.

REV.9:11 And they had a king over them, which is the angel of the bottomless pit, whose name in the Hebrew tongue is Abaddon, but in the Greek tongue hath his name Apollyon.

7 The angel said "this place is the *end of heaven and earth. This has become a prison of the stars and the host of heaven*; and the stars which roll over the fire are they which have transgressed the commandment of the Lord in the beginning of their rising, because they did not come forth at their appointed times."

C.5 This sounds like the worst place of all inside the earth: **TARTARUS**

2PE.2:4 For if God spared not the angels that sinned, but cast them down to hell, and delivered them into chains of darkness, to be reserved unto judgment.

8 And He was wroth with them and bound them till the time when their guilt should be consummated (even) for ten thousand years.

C.6 Most of us would be unhappy to spend some days in jail; but imagine having to be locked up for 10,000 years!

JUD.1:6 And the angels which kept not their first estate, but left their own habitation, he hath reserved in everlasting chains under darkness unto the judgment of the great day.

CHAPTER 19

1 And Uriel said to me, "Here shall stand the angels who have connected themselves with women, and their spirits assuming many different forms are defiling mankind and shall lead them astray into sacrificing to demons as gods, (here shall they stand) till the day of the great judgment in which they shall be judged till they are made an end of."

Comment:1: Here it clearly shows that angels are able to be *shape-shifters*. All through history sacrificing to Demons as gods has been very common place, though it *still exists in modern times*, it is mostly camouflaged.

2 And the women also of the angels who went astray shall become sirens, and I, Enoch alone saw the vision, the ends of all things, and no man shall see as I have seen.

C.2 Enoch states that he alone saw this vision, and that no man shall see as he has seen. This statement in a very real sense, proves that it was Enoch himself, seventh from Adam that *originally wrote this book*.

CHAPTER 20

1 And these are the names of the holy angels who watch: Uriel, one of the holy angels, who is over the world and over Tartarus: Raphael, one of the holy angels, who is over the spirits of men: Raguel, one of the holy angels, who takes vengeance on the world of the luminaries: Michael, one of the holy angels, to wit, he that is set over the best part of mankind and over chaos:

DAN.12:1 And at that time shall Michael stand up, the great prince which stands for the children of thy people: and there shall be a time of trouble, such as never was since there was a nation even to that same time: and at that time thy people shall be delivered, every one that shall be found written in the book.

Comment:1: Uriel is the angel who takes Enoch to visit the different places both in the physical and spiritual realms. He is also the same angel who visited EZRA in the Book of II Ezdras.

II Ezdras: Chapter 4 verse.1 "Then the angel that had been sent to me, whose name was Uriel answered..."

2 **Saraquael**, one of the holy angels, who is set over the spirits who sin in the spirit: Gabriel, one of the holy angels, who is over paradise and the serpents and the Cherubim: Remiel, one of the holy angels, whom God set over those who rise.

LUK.1:19 And the angel answering said unto him, I am *Gabriel*, that stands in the presence of God; and am sent to speak unto thee, and to shew thee these glad tidings.

C.2 Remiel, one of the holy angels, whom God 'set over those who rise'. In other words, Remiel has something to do with those who 'rise from the dead'.

CHAPTER 21

1 And I proceeded to where things were chaotic; and I saw there something horrible. I saw neither a heaven above nor a firmly founded earth, but a place chaotic and horrible.

Comment:1: This chapter sounds like the time-frame after the 'Great White Throne Judgement' at the end of the Millennium, when God finally casts all the fallen angels into the Lake of Fire.

REV.20:15 And whosoever was not found written in the book of life was cast into the lake of fire.

2 And there I saw seven stars of the heaven bound together in it, like great mountains and burning with fire; then I said, "For what sin are they bound, and on what account have they been cast in hither?"

3 Then said Uriel, one of the holy angels, who was with me, and was chief over them, and said, "Enoch, why dost thou ask, and why art thou eager for the truth? These are the number of the stars of heaven, which have transgressed the commandments of the Lord, and are bound here till ten thousand years, the time entailed by their sins are consummated,"

C.2 Here it specifically mentions that the angels are bound for 10,000 years. Could it be that some of the angels have been bound since the beginning of time, or around 6000 years ago, and that they have another 4000 years of imprisonment? In another verse in this Book of Enoch, it states that some of the fallen angels would be locked up for 70 generations. Perhaps a generation back then, before the Flood, was around 100 years.

4 And from thence I went to another place, which was still more horrible than the former, and I saw a horrible thing. A great fire which burnt and blazed, and the place was cleft as far as the abyss, being full of great descending columns of fire, neither its extent or magnitude could I see, nor could I conjecture.

5 Then I said, "How fearful is the place and how terrible to look upon!"

6 Then Uriel answered me, one of the holy angels who was with me, and said unto me, "Enoch, why hast thou such fear and affright?"

7 And I answered, "Because of this fearful place, and because of the spectacle of the pain."

8 And he said unto me, "This place is the prison of the angels, and here they will be imprisoned for ever."

REV.20:1 And I saw an angel come down from heaven, having the key of the bottomless pit and a great chain in his hand.

REV.20:2 And he laid hold on the dragon, that old serpent, which is the Devil, and Satan, and bound him a thousand years,

REV.20:3 And cast him into the bottomless pit, and shut him up, and set a seal upon him, that he should deceive the nations no more, till the thousand years should be fulfilled: and after that he must be loosed a little season.

CHAPTER 22

1 And thence I went to another place, and he showed me in the west another great and high mountain of hard rock; and there was in it ***four hollow places***, deep and wide and very smooth. How smooth are the hollow places and deep and dark to look at.

2 Then Raphael answered, one of the holy angels who was with me, and said unto me, "These ***hollow places*** have been created for this very purpose, that the ***spirits of the souls of the dead should assemble therein***, yea that ***all the souls of the children of men should assemble here."***

Comment:1: These hollow places must be very large indeed if they can contain all the souls of men who have ever lived.

C.2 'HOLLOW PLACES' Most people today believe that the earth is solid, as taught since about 1950, in the science community, without giving any proof. It makes much more sense, however that the earth is actually hollow. Why ? Most things in nature are hollow, in order to contain other things within themselves.

The earth is stated to contain HELL, PARADISE, TARTARUS, and many other lands. So isn't it logical, to deduce that the earth must be hollow, in order to contain these other places. (Please see **APPENDIX XIV & XV for HOLLOW EARTH & INNER EARTH)**

C.3 I know that most of us have probably thought, that these above-mentioned places, are spiritual in nature, rather than physical. However, what if they are in fact both; part spiritual and part physical, and thus they do need some space. Thus, a hollow earth would be more suitable to contain all these places.

C.4 If one thinks about it seriously, we ourselves are partly physical, and partly spiritual. It has been stated, that there are many dimensions, some going up and some down. The higher dimensions are more spiritual, and the lower ones more physical.

3 "And these places have been made to receive them till the day of their judgement, and till their period appointed, till the great judgement (comes) upon them."

REV.20:13 And the sea gave up the dead which were in it; and death and hell delivered up the dead which were in them: and they were judged every man according to their works.

4 I saw the spirits of the children of men who were dead, and their voice went forth to heaven and made suit. Then I asked Raphael, the angel

who was with me, and I said unto him, "This spirit, whose is it whose voice goes forth and makes suit (implores)?"

5 And he answered me saying, "This is the spirit which went forth from Abel, whom his brother Cain slew, and he makes his suit against him till his seed is destroyed from the face of the earth and ***his seed is annihilated*** from amongst the seed of men."

C.5 *'his seed is annihilated'*. This would appear to be talking about 'Satan's Seed'.

1JN.3:12 Not as Cain, who <u>*was*</u> of that <u>*wicked one*</u> (Satan), and slew his brother. And wherefore slew he him? Because his own works were evil, and his brother's righteous.

JASHER 1.22 And Abel answered Cain saying, 'Surely God who has made us in the earth, he will avenge my cause, and He will require my blood from thee should thou slay me.'

ANTIQUITIES OF THE JEWS-JOSEPHUS 2.2 [Concerning Cain] *'He augmented his household substance with much wealth, by raping and violence;* he *excited his acquaintance to procure pleasures and spoils by robbery*, and *became a great leader of men into wicked courses.* He also introduced a change in that way of simplicity wherein men lived before; and was the author of *measures and weights*.' Was Cain the very first of the evil and corrupt murdering Merchants?

6 Then I asked regarding it, and regarding all the hollow places, "Why (was) one separated from the other?"

7 And he answered me and said unto me, "These three have been made, that the spirits of the dead might be separated. And such a division has been made for the spirits of the righteous, in which (are) there as the bright springs of water. And such as has been made for sinners when they die and are buried in the earth and judgement has not been executed on them in their lifetime."

C.6 FOUR distinct places for the different types of the dead. 1) A Hollow Place to implore God for revenge by the righteous, and where there is also **PARADISE** inside the earth 2) **LIMBO? -** Another hollow place for the undecided. 3) **HELL** - A hollow place for the unrepentant sinners, 4) **LAKE of FIRE** - A hollow place for the very wicked.

8 Here their spirits shall be set apart in this great pain, till the great day of judgement and punishment and torment of those who curse for ever, and retribution for their spirits. There He shall bind them forever.

C.7 This last verse seems to be talking about the verse worst spirits, who like Satan, will end up being cast into the LAKE of FIRE.

As mentioned before cursing was originally started by the fallen angels, and those who curse and swear, do it by the power of bad spirits or demons, whether people know it consciously or not!

9 And such a division has been made for the spirits of those who make their suit, who make disclosures concerning their destruction, when they were slain in the days of the sinners.

C.8 A special 'hollow place' for all of the souls that have been slain who implore God for vengeance.

REV.6:9 And when he had opened the fifth seal, I saw under the altar the souls of them that were slain for the word of God, and for the testimony which they held:

REV.6:10 And they cried with a loud voice, saying, 'How long, O Lord, holy and true, dost thou not judge and avenge our blood on them that dwell on the earth?'

10 And such as has been made for the spirits of men who were not righteous but sinners, who were complete in transgression, and that of the transgression, they shall be companions, but their spirits shall not be slain in the day of judgement nor shall they be raised from thence.

C.9 This sounds like a very great multitude of un-saved peoples, who will not live during the coming Millennium, but will be awakened after it, at the great Final Judgement of the Great White Throne Judgement. They were not judged at the coming Wrath of God, because they had already died in ages gone past.

REV.20:5 But the rest of the dead lived not again until the thousand years were finished. This is the first resurrection.

11 Then I blessed the Lord of glory and said, "Blessed be my Lord, the Lord of Righteousness, who rules for ever."

(SEE **APPENDIX XIV & XV** for **HOLLOW EARTH** for detailed study)

CHAPTER 23

1 From thence I went to another place to the west of the ends of the earth, and I saw a burning fire, which ran without resting, and paused not from its course day or night but (ran) regularly. And I asked saying, "What is this which rests not?"

2 Then Raguel one of the holy angels who was with me, answered me and said unto me, "This course of fire, which thou has seen is the fire in the west which persecutes all the luminaries of heaven!"

Comment: The fallen angels are really going to get it in the end, along with the wicked incorrigibles. - **The Lake of Fire**

ISA.33:14 The sinners in Zion are afraid; fearfulness hath surprised the hypocrites. Who among us shall dwell with the devouring fire? Who among us shall dwell with everlasting burnings?

ISA.66:24 And they shall go forth, and look upon the carcases of the men that have transgressed against me: for their worm shall not die, neither shall their fire be quenched; and they shall be an abhorring unto all flesh.

CHAPTER 24

1 And from thence, I went to another place of the earth, and he showed me a mountain range of fire, which burnt day and night. And I went beyond it and *saw seven magnificent mountains*, all differing from the other, and the stones thereof were magnificent and beautiful. Magnificent as a whole of glorious appearance and fair exterior. Three towards the east, one founded upon the other, and deep rough ravines, no one of which joined with any other.

II EZDRAS 2.19 And the same number of springs, flowing with milk and honey, and *seven high mountains* on which roses and lilies grow; by these I will fill your children with joy.

2 And the seventh mountain was in the midst of these, and it excelled them in height resembling the seat of a throne; and fragrant trees encircled the throne. And amongst them was a tree such as I had never yet smelt, neither was any amongst them nor were others like it. It has a fragrance beyond all fragrance, and its leaves and blooms and wood wither not forever. Its fruit is beautiful, and its fruit resembles the dates of a palm.

REV.21:2 And I John saw the holy city, new Jerusalem, coming down from God out of heaven, prepared as a bride adorned for her husband.

REV.21:3 And I heard a great voice out of heaven saying, 'Behold, the *tabernacle of God* is with men, and he will dwell with them, and they shall be his people, and God himself shall be with them, and be their God'.

Comment: This tabernacle of God, is a mountain 250 times higher than Mount Everest.

REV.21:16 And the city lies foursquare, and the length is as large as the breadth: and he measured the city with the reed, ***twelve thousand furlongs***. The length and the breadth and the height of it are equal.

C.2 ***Twelve thousand furlongs*** = 1500 miles long, wide and high. Some mountain!

3 Then I said, "How Beautiful is this tree, and fragrant, and its leaves are fair, and its blooms very delightful in appearance."

REV.22:1 And he shewed me a pure river of water of life, clear as crystal, proceeding out of the throne of God and of the Lamb.

REV.22:2 In the midst of the street of it, and on either side of the river, was there the ***tree of life***, which bare ***twelve manner of fruits***, and yielded her fruit every month: and the ***leaves of the tree were for the healing of the nations.***

4 Then answered Michael, one of the holy and honoured angels who
was with me, and was their leader.

CHAPTER 25

1 And he said unto me, "Enoch, why dost thou ask me regarding the fragrance of the tree, and why dost thou wish to learn the truth?"

2 Then I answered him saying, "I wish to know about everything, but especially about this tree."

3 And he answered saying, "This high mountain which thou hast seen, whose summit is *like* the *throne of God*, is His throne, where the Holy Great One, the Lord of Glory, the Eternal King, will sit when He shall come down to visit the earth with goodness. Note the future tense 'will' God's Throne inside the earth? God's throne is mobile?"

REV.21:10 And he carried me away in the spirit to a *great and high mountain*, and shewed me that *great city, the holy Jerusalem*, descending out of heaven from God,

REV.21:11 Having the glory of God: and her *light was like unto a stone most precious*, even like a jasper stone, clear as crystal;

REV.22:3 And there shall be no more curse: but the throne of God and of the Lamb shall be in it; and his servants shall serve him:

4 And as for this fragrant tree, no mortal is permitted to touch it till the great judgement, when He shall take vengeance on all and bring everything to its consummation for ever. It shall then be given to the righteous and holy.

5 Its fruit shall be for food to the elect. It shall be transplanted to the holy place, to the temple of the Lord, the Eternal King.

Comment:1: Why was the 'tree of life' *transplanted*, and from exactly where? The tree of life was originally in the Garden of Eden, and has been taken by God into the heavenly *New Jerusalem*.

GEN.3:22 And the LORD God said, 'Behold, the man is become as one of us, to know good and evil: and now, lest he put forth his hand, and take also of the *tree of life*, and eat, and *live for ever...*'

REV.22:2 In the midst of the street of it, and on either side of the river, was there the *tree of life*, which bare twelve manner of fruits, and yielded her fruit every month: and the leaves of the tree were for the healing of the nations.

6 Then shall they rejoice with joy and be glad, and into the holy place shall they enter. Its fragrance shall be in their bones; and they shall live a long life on the earth, such as their fathers lived. In their days shall no sorrow or plague of torment or calamity touch them.

GEN.5:5 And all the days that Adam lived were *nine hundred and thirty years*: and he died.

C.2 In the Golden Age soon to come, known as the Millennium, with Jesus as King of Kings and Lord of Lords, people will live to almost 1000 years old, after God has totally restored the Pre-Flood atmospheric conditions that existed on earth before the flood.

C.3 *Ageing,* is apparently caused by dangerous radiation, from both the sun and from the cosmos. Apparently prior to the GREAT FLOOD, there used to be a protective layer of water surrounding the earth, about 100 miles up in the atmosphere, which kept out ultra violet and cosmic radiation.

7 Then blessed I the God of Glory, the Eternal King, who hath prepared such things for the righteous, and hath created them and promised to give them.

ISA.2:2 And it shall come to pass in the last days, that the mountain of the LORD's house shall be established in the top of the mountains, and shall be exalted above the hills; and all nations shall flow unto it.

ISA.2:3 And many people shall go and say, 'Come ye, and let us go up to the mountain of the LORD, to the house of the God of Jacob; and he will teach us of his ways, and we will walk in his paths: for out of Zion shall go forth the law, and the word of the LORD from Jerusalem.'

ISA.2:4 And he shall judge among the nations, and shall rebuke many people: and they shall beat their swords into ploughs, and their spears into pruninghooks: nation shall not lift up sword against nation, neither shall they learn war any more.

CHAPTER 26

1 And I went from hence to the *middle of the earth*, and I saw a blessed place in which there were trees with branches abiding and *blooming of a dismembered tree*; and there I saw a holy mountain, underneath the mountain to the east there was a stream and it flowed to the south.

2 And I saw towards the east another mountain higher than this, and between them a deep and narrow ravine. In it also ran a stream underneath the mountain.

3 And to the west thereof there was another mountain, lower than the former and of small elevation, and a ravine deep and dry between them; and another dry ravine was at the extremities of the three mountains; and all the ravines were deep and narrow, (being formed) of hard rock, and trees were not planted upon them.

4 And I marvelled at the rocks, and I marvelled at the ravine, yea, I marvelled very much.

CHAPTER 27

1 Then said I, "For what object is this blessed land, which is entirely filled with trees, and this accursed valley between?"

2 Then Uriel, one of the holy angels who was with me answered and said, "This accursed valley is for those who are accursed for ever. Here shall all the accursed be gathered together who utter with their lips against the Lord unseemly words and of His Glory speak hard things. Here shall they be gathered together, and here shall be their place of judgement."

3 In the last days there shall be upon them the spectacle of righteous judgement in the presence of the righteous for ever. Here shall the merciful bless the Lord of Glory, the Eternal King. In the days of judgement over the former, they shall bless Him for the mercy in accordance with which He has assigned them (their lot).

4 Then I blessed the Lord of Glory and set forth His glory and lauded Him gloriously.

CHAPTER 28

1 And thence I went towards the east, into the midst of the mountain range of the desert, and I saw a wilderness and it was solitary, full of trees and plants and *water gushed forth from above;* rushing like a copious water-course (which flowed) towards the north-west it caused clouds and dew to ascend on every side.

Comment: This sounds like a very high waterfall, practically coming out of the cloud level, it is so high.

CHAPTER 29

1 And thence I went to another place in the desert, and approached to the east of this mountain range, and there I saw aromatic trees exhaling the fragrance of frankincense and myrrh, and the trees also were similar to the almond tree.

CHAPTER 30

1 And beyond these, I went afar to the east, and I saw another place, a valley full of water, and therein there was a tree, the colour of fragrant trees such as the mastic. And on the sides of those valleys, I saw fragrant cinnamon. And beyond these I proceeded to the east.

CHAPTER 31

1 And I saw other mountains, and amongst them were groves of trees, and there flowed forth from them nectar, which is named Sarara and Galbanum.

2 And beyond these mountains, I saw another mountain to the *east of the ends of the earth*, whereon were aloe trees, and all the trees were full of Stacte, being like almond trees.

Comment:1: the 'ends of the earth' must be an exact location, in order for the above-mentioned mountain to be described as being East of the 'ends of the earth'.

C.2 If we think of the earth as being but a globe in shape, then it would appear that the 'ends of the earth' could be any point on the globe. However, the truth of the matter is that the earth is not quite global, but flattened somewhat at the poles. Some have described the earth as being more like a donut in shape. To give exact measurements. The holes at the poles are supposed to be around 1200 miles in diameter, where the most Northern land of the North Pole gradually descends inside the earth and comes out upside down relative to us on the inner surface of the planet.

C.3 With all that in mind, the 'ends of the earth' possibly being the entrances to Inner Earth or the Gateways or portals to the dimensional Inner World. Experts claim that there are 12 dimensional gates around the world. All set at 30 degrees Latitude, and most of which are in the sea just to the right of a large land mass. Two of the gates or Portals are the North and South Poles.

C.4 In conclusion, although *there are many gates or portals*, it would seem logical that the *'ends of the earth' is an exact location*, it is much more likely to be *at the polar entrances to the inner worlds*, than at any other points on the earth.

3 And when one burnt it, it smelt sweeter than any fragrant odour.

CHAPTER 32

1 And after these fragrant odours, as I looked towards the north over the mountains, I saw seven mountains full of choice nard, and fragrant trees and cinnamon and pepper.

2 And thence I went over the summits of these mountains, far towards the east of the earth, and passed above the Erythraean* sea, and went far from it and passed over the angel Zotiel

Comment:1: The *Erythraean sea in modern times is said to be around the Indian Ocean, close to Saudi Arabia. However, let's think for a moment: if everyone died in Noah's Flood, except for 8 persons, how do we know what the various lands and seas were called before the Flood? Also, it is likely as others have also said, that after the Flood, men would have started naming the new lands, seas, mountain ranges which were now all completely different than before the Flood, according to names they had heard before. As in the case of the Erythraean sea could have actually been an entirely different location in Enoch's time, and was probably a location *inside the earth* in his time. The Great Flood totally changed the mountain ranges and the seas.

C.2 Before the Great Flood there was a lot more land area on the earth in general, and sea levels were much lower. The high mountains of today such as the Himalayas were forced up because of the terrible convulsion of the Flood, where enormous cracks in the earth's crust appeared and formed the 'plates' all around the planet, which are today known as the tectonic plates. Point being, is that the earth and its lands and seas were totally different after the Flood than before it, and all the lands would have appeared unrecognisable to Noah and his sons right after the Great Flood.

3 And I came to the Garden of Righteousness and saw beyond those trees many large trees growing there and of goodly fragrance, large, very beautiful and glorious, and the tree of wisdom, whereof they eat and know great wisdom.

C.3 This Garden of Righteousness is taking about the 'Garden of Eden'.

4 That tree is in height like the fir, and its leaves are like (those of) the Carob tree; and its fruit is like clusters of the vine, very beautiful, and the fragrance of the tree penetrates afar.

C.4 According to this verse, it would seem that the forbidden fruit which Eve gave to Adam from the Tree of the Knowledge of Good and Evil, was not the traditionally known apple, but a fruit like a grape, but probably larger and very delicious, and very beautiful to behold!

5 Then I said, "How beautiful is the tree, and how attractive is its look!"

C.5 The Tree of the Knowledge of Good and Evil. This explains why Eve was tempted to eat of this tree, as it was indeed both very attractive, and its mesmerizing aroma, could also be detected from far away.

6 Then Rafael, the Holy angel, who was with me, answered me and said, "This is the tree of wisdom, of which thy father (Adam) old (in years) and thy aged mother (Eve), who were before thee, have eaten, and they learnt wisdom, and their eyes were opened, and they knew that they were naked and they were driven out of the garden."

C.6 Notice here that the Tree of the Knowledge of Good and Evil is exactly that. There is Good knowledge which gives wisdom, and other knowledge which is evil.

GEN.2:17 But of the tree of the *knowledge of good and evil*, thou shalt not eat of it: for in the day that thou eat thereof thou shalt surely die.

GEN.3:11 And he said, '*Who told thee that thou was naked*? Hast thou eaten of the tree, whereof I commanded thee that thou shouldest not eat?'

GEN.3:24 So he (God) *drove out the man*; and he placed at the east of the *garden of Eden Cherubims*, and a *flaming sword* which turned every way, to keep the way of the tree of life.

CHAPTER 33

1 And from thence, I went to the 'ends of the earth', and saw there great beasts, and each differed from the other, and I saw birds also differing in appearance and beauty and voice, the one differing from the other.

Comment: Enoch saw many different types of very large beasts at the *'ends of the earth'*.

C.2 According to both the famous and highly decorated Admiral Byrd of the USA, who flew inside the earth on several occasions (1927, 1947, 1956). He mentioned the exact things that we have read in the past few chapters, including this last verse. 1) Circular Polar entrances at both the North and South Poles 2) High mountains 3) Lots of forests 4) Deep Ravines 5) Rivers & Waterfalls 6) Huge creatures such as the Mammoths and other monsters roaming around far below his aircraft.

2 And to the east of those beasts, I saw the ***ends of the earth***, whereon the heaven rest and the *portals of heaven open*.

C.3 '***Ends of the earth where the portals are open'***. It would seem to suggest, that at the ends of the earth there are some kind of portals, which by definition would suggest that sometimes they could be open and at other times they could also be closed. These portals, sound similar to the Bermuda Triangles, known on earth in modern times. Areas on the earth where ships, planes, submarines, and even satellites, high up in the atmosphere, have vanished into thin air, under very special circumstances, and exact locations on the planet. Some scientists have stated that the disappearances of both people, ships and aircraft, happens in areas where there are 'portals' to other dimensions or some kind of overlap in both time and space.

The above-mentioned portal, is most probably talking about either the Northern of Southern Circular Polar Entrances into Inner earth. These entrances at the ends of the earth are not small and are stated to be around 1200 miles in diameter when open. They would seem to be dimensional gates that sometimes allow people and ships or planes to enter. On other occasions, people travelling near the same area wouldn't even notice the entrances as they are 'closed' or 'cloaked' Why was Admiral Byrd allowed inside the earth? He himself stated that 'He was permitted by those who live inside the earth.' There are many more details which you can read in my first book: *Out of the Bottomless Pit*.

3 And I saw how the stars of heaven come forth, and I counted the portals, out of which they proceed, and wrote down all their outlets, of each individual star by itself, according to their number and their names, their courses and their positions, and their times and their months, as Uriel the holy angel who was with me showed me.

C.4 This verse is very revealing, as again Enoch is apparently seeing the inner workings of the dimension immediately behind our physical dimension. We here in the physical realm only see the sun in the sky and the stars slowly passing through the heavens. Enoch could see much more than that and could see the forces that control our universe. I suppose it would be like comparing someone looking at an old pocket watch. We in the physical realm only notice the ornate watch and see the hands of the watch telling the time. However, with Enoch it was as if God opened up the very watch and showed Enoch the inner workings of the watch itself with all of its spinning wheels big and small. That would explain why often Enoch's descriptions are hard for us to fathom or to visualize.

4 He showed all things to me and wrote them down for me & also their names he wrote for me, and their laws and their companies.

CHAPTER 34

1 And from thence, I went towards the *north* to the *ends of the earth*, and there I saw a great and *glorious device*, at the ends of the whole earth.

Comment:1: 'great and *glorious device*', at the 'ends of the whole earth'. This is a strange expression to use and we normally think of a device as something mechanical. It would be good to see what the original word was used by Enoch in Hebrew, as it is possible that the translators used this word *device* because they couldn't think of more appropriate word to use.

I am convinced that this 'great and glorious device' at the 'ends of the earth' is probably talking about the great Northern Aperture which descends into the INNER EARTH. (Where the North Pole is supposed to be, but isn't) Here are some very interesting verses from the book of Job:

The following verses from the Book of Job, are a perfect description of the Northern Opening into the 'Hollow Earth'.

JOB.26:7 "*He stretches out the north over the 'empty place', and hangs the earth upon nothing"*

C.2 This sounds like the big hole at the North Pole of the earth, is being described.

JOB.38:8 "*Or who shut up the sea with doors, when it breaks forth*, as if it had issued *out of the womb?"*

C.3 Apertures/doors at the North and South Poles (so-called), with the seas going through these apertures, and thus the appearance 'as if the seas' had issued '*out of the womb?'* As mentioned before, these doors are also 'dimensional gates', which are sometimes open and sometimes closed.

JOB.38:30 The waters are hid as with a stone, and the *face of the deep is frozen.*

C.4 Talking again about the so-called North and South poles of the earth
According to those who have travelled inside the earth through the northern opening, there is a great & high barrier of Ice inside the round aperture, which blocks progress of further travelling, at least by ship, and thus the description: '*The waters are hid as with a stone, and the face of the deep is frozen.'*

JOB.38:13 That it might take hold of the *ends of the earth*, that the *wicked might be shaken out of it?*

JOB.38:17 Have the gates of death been opened unto thee? Or hast thou seen the doors of the shadow of death?

C.5 Apparently, there are a lot, of both wicked people, giants and monsters, living on the inside inner earth surface, who will be judged when God arises to judge the earth. The inner earth, which was originally an incredibly beautiful place, and in pristine condition at the time of the Garden of Eden, has unfortunately, in more modern times become a hornets nest of all kinds of unsavoury critters, both physical and spiritual, and none of them recognise Jesus as the Saviour, but rather they worship the 'god of the underworld' Satan, often called the 'Ascendant Master' by oriental religions.

REV.11:18 And the nations were angry, and thy wrath is come, and the *time of the dead*, that *they should be judged*, and that thou shouldest give reward unto thy servants the prophets, and to the saints, and them that fear thy name, small and great; and shouldest *destroy them which destroy the earth.*

C.6 It is clear to see that there is a *link between higher and lower dimensions*, such as *HADES (Hell), TARTARUS (lake of fire)*, which could be classified as *lower dimensions*, and the refuge of *PARADISE* (higher dimension), noted as being inside the earth, by Jesus, and called *"The Bosom of Abraham"*, and also the physical *INNER EARTH*, where apparently *there are physical beings of all types* living, including humans, giants, dragons, dinosaurs and a whole lot more!

God obviously took Enoch on an amazing tour of the INNER EARTH and even as far as the NORTHERN PORTAL, from which he then returned to the OUTER SURFACE of the earth?

When Enoch is describing the following "portals of heaven, the question to be asked is, was he describing the Heavenly Portals from the vantage point of the INNER EARTH or the OUTER EARTH? Did Enoch himself live on the inside of the earth, as well as all other inhabitants of earth prior to the Great Flood. Did mankind start living on the outer surface of the earth after the Great Flood of Noah?"

I will explain more about these points in detail, later. (**See the Appendix**)

2 And here I saw three portals of heaven open in the heaven; through each of them proceed north winds. When they blow there is cold, hail, frost, snow, dew, and rain.

3 And out of one portal they blow for good, but when they blow through the other two portals, it is with violence and affliction on the earth, and they blow with violence.

C.7 This is also quite an odd description that through one portal the winds blow for good, and through the other two portals for *"violence and affliction"*. This verse would seem to indicate that these particular portals are much more than just physical portals as they cause *"violence and affliction"* upon the earth. This reminds me of the spiritual forces which afflict our world today: **The 4 Horsemen of the Apocalypse in Revelations chapter 6.**

REV.6:8 And I looked, and behold a pale horse: and his name that sat on him was *Death*, and *Hell* followed with him. And *power was given unto them over the fourth part of the earth, to kill with sword, and with hunger, and with death, and with the beasts of the earth.*

CHAPTER 35

1 And form thence, I went towards the west to the ends of the earth, and saw three portals of the heaven open such as I had seen in the east, the same number of portals, and the same number of outlets.

Comment: Why is there only one verse in this chapter? It seems very odd to have only one verse representing a whole chapter! Has something been deliberately omitted from chapters such as this one?

CHAPTER 36

1 And from thence, I went towards the south to the ends of the earth, and saw there three open portals of the heaven, and thence there come dew, rain, and wind.

2 And from thence I went to the east to the ends of the heaven, and saw here the three eastern portals of heaven open and small portals above them.

3 Through each of these small portals pass the stars of heaven, and run their course to the west on the path which is shown to them.

4 And as often as I saw, I blessed always the Lord of Glory, and I continued to bless the Lord of Glory, who has wrought great and glorious wonders, to show the greatness of His work to the angels and to spirits, and to men, that they might praise His work, and all His creation; that they might see the work of His might and praise the great works of His hands and bless Him for ever.

Comments:**1**: In chapters 34-36 we read about 12 PORTALS and also "three eastern portals of heaven open and small portals above them"?

The traditional way has been to interpret these 12 portals as nothing more than the 12 SIGNS of the ZODIAC, through which we see the different Star Constellations according to what time of the year it is at any given time. I am not so sure about that traditional interpretation. To me it looks like the 12 portals are talking about the forces behind this physical world and which control the physical universe. Man looks up at the sky and in his head tries to figure out how the universe is put together, without God and without other dimensions.

Unfortunately science is not able to explain the many wonders of the cosmos without acknowledging that there has to be a great Creator behind this amazing universe. If one studies the Bible and other important books like this Book of Enoch, it is so clear, that there is both a wonderful Creator who can do anything, and that He is not limited by physical laws of Physics, as man so often is.

We have to look "outside the box" in order to find answers for very strange writings such as the 12 Portals and the small portals above through which pass the stars.

Let's look at a couple of Bible verses:

REV.7:1 And after these things I saw four angels standing on the four corners of the earth, *holding the four winds of the earth,* that the wind should not blow on the earth, nor on the sea, nor on any tree.

DAN.7:2 Daniel spake and said, I saw in my *vision* by night, and, behold, the four winds of the heaven strove upon the *great sea.*

C.2 In the first verse, it is talking about the physical earth, and in the second verse it is talking about spiritual forces.

I believe that before the Great Flood, there was a canopy of water surrounding the earth, about 100 miles above the earth, where the forces of gravity and centrifugal forces balanced each other out.

I also believe as you know that the earth is hollow, with two large openings at the north and south poles. *These openings are somewhat camouflaged in a mysterious way*, like strange dark forces are at work, to conceal these apertures from mankind.

This is not difficult to explain, when you have already read how that God has confined countless fallen angels, Devils and Demons to the heart of the earth. Although there is probably an inner world (physical), there are also lower dimensions inside the earth, as I mentioned before. So it is logical to deduce that those who rule spiritually the Netherworld such as Satan and his band of fallen angels, that generally they don't like mankind to either go into the inner world, or even be aware of its existence. That would certainly disprove the 'Big Lie of Evolution'. According to modern science, the earth is solid!

So far in the Book of Enoch we have seen that God showed Enoch our outer world, and the inner earth and also heaven. He was being shown how things work like the intricate wheels inside a large watch.

It is very difficult for me to write about these things, when most of the basic building blocks of knowledge, are simply not known to most people, as most don't study enough of the *truth*. That is very sad, as God has many wonders for us all to study, if we read the right books, that are trying to tell us the truth and not fill us with deliberate disinformation.

You can read many details about the HOLLOW EARTH on my website: www.outofthebottomlesspit.co.uk I have also written a lot about this topic in my book *Out of the Bottomless Pit.*

C.3 Another possibility, is that there are 12 known Bermuda Triangles on the outside surface of the planet known to science, at least to those willing to listen. In my book *Out Of The Bottomless Pit*, I talked in detail about the Bermuda Triangles.

The Parables

CHAPTER 37

1 The second vision, which he saw, the vision of wisdom, which Enoch, the son of Jared, the son of Mahalalel, the son of Cainan, the son of Enos, the son of Seth, the son of Adam, saw.

2 And this is the beginning of the words of wisdom which I lifted up my voice to speak and say to those which dwell upon the earth.: Hear, ye men of old time, and see, ye that come after, the words of the Holy One, which I will speak before the Lord of Spirits.

3 It were better to declare (them only) to the men of old time, but even from those that come after we will not withhold the beginning of wisdom.

4 Till the present day such wisdom has never been given by the Lord of Spirits, as I have received according to my insight, according to the good pleasure of the Lord of Spirits, by whom the lot of eternal life have been given unto me.

5 Now three parables were imparted to me and I lifted up my voice and recounted them to those that dwell upon the earth.

CHAPTER 38

1 The first parable.

When the congregation of the righteous shall appear, and sinners shall be judged for their sins, and be driven from the face of the earth:

2 And when the Righteous One shall appear before the eyes of the righteous, whose elect works hang upon the Lord of spirits. Light shall appear unto the righteous and elect who dwell on the earth. Where then will be the dwelling of the sinners, and where the resting place of those who have denied the Lord of Spirits? It has been good for them, if they had not been born.

ISA.42:6 I the LORD have called thee in righteousness, and will hold thine hand, and will keep thee, and give thee for a covenant of the people, for a light of the Gentiles;

MAT.26:24 The Son of man goes *as it is written of him*: but woe unto that man by whom the *Son of man* is betrayed! It had been good for that man if he had *not been born.*

3 When the secrets of the righteous shall be revealed and the sinners judged, and the godless driven from the presence of the righteous and elect.

PSA.37:35 I have seen the wicked in great power, and spreading himself like a green bay tree.

PSA.37:36 Yet he passed away, and, lo, he was not: yea, I sought him, but he could not be found.

4 From that time those that possess the earth shall no longer be powerful and exalted, and they shall not be able to behold the face of the holy, for the Lord of Spirits has caused His light to appear on the face of the holy, righteous, and elect.

ISA.60:1 Arise, shine; for thy light is come, and the glory of the LORD is risen upon thee.

ISA.60:2 For, behold, the darkness shall cover the earth, and gross darkness the people: but the LORD shall arise upon thee, and his glory shall be seen upon thee.

5 Then shall the kings and the mighty perish and be given into the hands of the righteous and holy. And thenceforward none shall seek for themselves mercy from the Lord of Spirits. For their life is at an end.

ISA.28:15 Because ye have said, 'We have made a *covenant with death*, and with hell are we at agreement; when the overflowing scourge shall pass through, it shall not come unto us: for we have made lies our refuge, and under falsehood have we hid ourselves':

REV.6:15 And the *kings of the earth, and the great men, and the rich men*, and the chief captains, and the mighty men, and every bondman, and every free man, hid themselves in the dens and in the rocks of the mountains;

REV.6:16 And said to the mountains and rocks, Fall on us, and hide us from the face of him that sits on the throne, and from the *wrath of the Lamb*:

REV.6:17 For the great day of his wrath is come; and who shall be able to stand?

CHAPTER 39

1 And it shall come to pass in those days, that elect and holy children will descend from the high heaven, and their *seed will become one with the children of men.*

Comment:1: 'elect and holy children' will 'descend from the high heaven', and 'their *seed will become one with the children of men'.* Here is yet another fascinating verse, that is difficult to understand the full scope of, what is being said. We started off this Book of Enoch, in chapter 6 with rebellious 'fallen angels' lusting after the women on earth, and mating with them and producing children, which became both giants and cannibals, *because at that particular time, it was not God's will.*

C.2 What if, at some point in the far future however, things will be very different, and it will no longer be considered evil, for those in heaven to mingle with the children of men. Humanity will no longer be considered unclean. So much so, that the 'children of heaven' will 'become one' with the 'children of men' could also be interpreted as meaning those in heaven marrying those on earth, and having children with them. When would that happen?

C.3 Remember that humans were considered unclean for the angels of God to mingle with. After the Great White Throne Judgement, there simply *won't be any uncleanness anymore in any form whatsoever!*

C.4 This sounds like the time of the 'New Heaven and the New Earth'. and right after the Great White Throne Judgement. Only after the Great White Throne Judgement will *all evil have finally been totally expunged from the earth* and from *the spirit world*. So that finally, those in heaven can now get on well with those on the earth and we finally can 'see eye to eye'.

2 And in those days, Enoch received books of zeal and wrath, and books of disquiet and expulsion. And mercy shall not be accorded to them says the Lord of Spirits.

C.5 Books of zeal and wrath and of disquiet. Where are all of these books? Is it not just possible that the Book of Enoch is a compilation of different books that Enoch wrote in his lifetime, of which we only have part?

3 And in those days, a *whirlwind* carried me off from the earth, and *set me down at the end of the heavens.*

C.6 A very dramatic description: A '*whirlwind' carried Enoch to the Ends of the 'heavens'.*

He was taken up to the heavenly plane. Let's examine other similar scriptures in the Bible:

JOB.38:1 Then the LORD answered Job out of the whirlwind.

PSA.19:6 His going forth is from the '*end of the heaven'*, and his circuit unto the ends of it: and there is nothing hid from the heat thereof.

4 And there I saw another vision, the dwelling places of the holy and the resting places of the righteous.

REV.4:1 After this I looked, and, behold, a door was opened in heaven: and the first voice which I heard was as it were of a trumpet talking with me; which said, 'Come up hither, and I will shew thee things which must be hereafter.'

5 Here mine eyes saw their dwellings with His righteous angels, and their resting places with the holy. They petitioned, interceded and prayed for the children of men, and righteousness flowed before them as water, and mercy like dew upon the earth. Thus, it is among them for ever.

REV.21:10 And he carried me away in the spirit to a great and high mountain, and shewed me that great city, the holy Jerusalem, descending out of heaven from God,

6 And in that place mine eyes saw the Elect One of righteousness and of faith.

and I saw his dwelling place under the wings of the Lord of spirits, and righteousness shall prevail in his days, and the righteous shall be without number before Him for ever and ever.

ISA.42:1 Behold my servant, whom I uphold; mine elect, in whom my soul delights; I have put my spirit upon him: he shall bring forth judgment to the Gentiles

PSA.96:10 Say among the heathen that the LORD reigns: the world also shall be established that it shall not be moved: he shall judge the people righteously.

PSA.96:11 Let the heavens rejoice, and let the earth be glad; let the sea roar, and the fullness thereof.

PSA.96:12 Let the field be joyful, and all that is therein: then shall all the trees of the wood rejoice

PSA.96:13 Before the LORD: for he cometh, for he cometh to judge the earth: he shall judge the world with righteousness, and the people with his truth.

7 And all the righteous and elect before Him shall be strong as *fiery lights*, and their mouth shall be full of blessing, and their lips extol the name of the Lord of spirits, and righteousness before Him shall never fail, and uprightness shall never fail before Him.

DAN.12:3 And they that be wise shall shine as the brightness of the firmament; and they that turn many to righteousness as the stars for ever and ever.

8 There I wished to dwell, and my spirit longed for that dwelling-place; and there heretofore hath been my portion, for so has it been established concerning me before the Lord of spirits.

REV.7:9 After this I beheld, and, lo, a great multitude, which no man could number, of all nations, and kindreds, and people, and tongues, stood before the throne, and before the Lamb, clothed with white robes, and palms in their hands;

REV.7:10 And cried with a loud voice, saying, Salvation to our God which sits upon the throne, and unto the Lamb.

9 In those days, I praised and extolled the name of the Lord of spirits with blessings and praises, because He hath destined me for blessing and glory according to the good pleasure of the Lord of spirits.

PSA.145:1 I will extol thee, my God, O king; and I will bless thy name for ever and ever.

PSA.145:2 Every day will I bless thee; and I will praise thy name for ever and ever.

10 For a long time my eyes regarded that place, and I blessed Him, and praised Him, saying "Blessed is He, and may He be blessed from the beginning and for evermore."

PSA.145:3 Great is the LORD, and greatly to be praised; and his greatness is unsearchable.

PSA.145:4 One generation shall praise thy works to another, and shall declare thy mighty acts.

11 And before Him there is no ceasing. He knows before the world was created, what is for ever, and what will be from generation unto generation.

PSA.145:5 I will speak of the glorious honour of thy majesty, and of thy wondrous works.

PSA.145:6 And men shall speak of the might of thy terrible acts: and I will declare thy greatness.

12 Those who sleep not bless thee. They stand before thy Glory, and bless praise and extol, saying, "Holy, Holy, Holy is the Lord of spirits. He fills the earth with spirits."

PSA.145:7 They shall abundantly utter the memory of thy great goodness, and shall sing of thy righteousness.

ISA.6:3 And one cried unto another, and said, *Holy, holy, holy*, is the LORD of hosts: the whole earth is full of his glory.

REV.4:8 And the four beasts had each of them six wings about him; and they were full of eyes within: and they rest not day and night, saying, *Holy, holy, holy*, LORD God Almighty, which was, and is, and is to come.

13 And here my eyes saw all those who sleep not. They stand before Him and bless and say, "Blessed be Thou, and blessed be the Name of the Lord for ever and ever. And my face was changed, for I could no longer behold."

CHAPTER 40

1 And after that I saw thousands of thousands and ten thousand times ten thousand. I saw a multitude beyond number and reckoning, who stood before the Lord of Spirits.

REV.7:9 After this I beheld, and, lo, *a great multitude, which no man could number*, of all nations, and kindreds, and people, and tongues, stood before the throne, and before the Lamb, clothed with white robes, and palms in their hands;

REV.7:10 And cried with a loud voice, saying, Salvation to our God which sits upon the throne, and unto the Lamb.

2 And on the four sides of the Lord of Spirits, I saw *four presences*, different from those that sleep not, and I learnt their names. For the angels that went with me made known to me their names, and showed me all the hidden things.

Comment: 'I saw *four presences*, different from those that sleep not'. Here Enoch is referring to the 4 Beasts 'who sleep not'.

LUK.1:19 And the angel answering said unto him, I am Gabriel, that stand *in the presence of God;* and am sent to speak unto thee, and to shew thee these glad tiding

Jubilees 2.1 And the *angel of the presence* spake to Moses according to the Word of the Lord, saying: Write the complete history of the creation, how in six days the Lord God finished all His works and all that He created...

3 And I heard voices of those four presences as they uttered praises before the Lord of Glory.

4 The first voice blessed the Lord of Spirits of ever and ever.

5 And the second voice I heard blessing the elect One, and the elect ones, who hang upon the Lord of spirits.

6 And the third voice, I heard pray and intercede for those who dwell on the earth and supplicate in the name of the Lord of spirits.

7 And I heard the fourth voice, fending off the *great Satans*, forbidding them to come before the Lord of Spirits to accuse them who dwell on the earth.

Comment: Why is the word Satans or Satan in the plural used? You might say, I thought that there was only one Satan? Here it is referring to other 'fallen angels' like Satan.

REV.12:9 And the *great dragon* was cast out, that old serpent, called the Devil, and *Satan*, which deceives the whole world: he was cast out into the earth, and his angels were cast out with him.

REV.12:10 And I heard a loud voice saying in heaven, 'Now is come salvation, and strength, and the kingdom of our God, and the power of his Christ: for the *accuser of our brethren is cast down*, which accused them before our God day and night.'

8 After that I asked the angel of peace who went with me, who showed me everything that is hidden; "Who are these four presences, which I have seen and whose words I have heard and written?"

9 And he said to me, "This is Michael, the merciful and long-suffering; and second, who is set over all the diseases and all the wounds of the children of men is Raphael; and the third, who is set over the powers, is Gabriel; and the fourth who is set over the repentance unto hope of those who inherit eternal life is called Phanuel. These are the four angels of the Lord of spirits and the four voices I heard in those days."

Book of Tobias Chapter 12.15 "I am *Raphael,* *one of the seven* *holy angels*, which present the prayers of the saints, and which go in and out before the glory of the Holy One."

CHAPTER 41

After that I saw all the secrets of the heavens, and how the kingdom is divided, and how the actions of men are weighed in the balance.

REV.14:13 And I heard a voice from heaven saying unto me, 'Write, Blessed are the dead which die in the Lord from henceforth: Yea, says the Spirit, that they may rest from their labours; and their works do follow them.'

Comment: 'kingdom is divided' This is probably talking about the choice between good and evil. 'Weighed in the balance' God weighs all men in the balance to see if their deeds in their life were good or evil.

GAL.6:7 Be not deceived; God is not mocked: for whatsoever a man soweth, that shall he also reap.

2 And there I saw the mansions of the elect and the mansions of the holy, and mine eyes saw there all the sinners being driven from thence which deny the name of Lord of Spirits, and being dragged off, and they could not abide because the punishment which proceeds them from the Lord of Spirits.

JOH.14:2 In my Father's house are many *mansions:* if it were not so, I would have told you. I go to prepare a place for you.

REV.21:2 And I John saw the holy city, new Jerusalem, coming down from God out of heaven, prepared as a bride adorned for her husband.

REV.21:3 And I heard a great voice out of heaven saying, Behold, the tabernacle of God is with men, and he will dwell with them, and they shall be his people, and God himself shall be with them, and be their God.

REV.21:24 And the nations of them which are saved shall walk in the light of it: and the kings of the earth do bring their glory and honour into it.

3 And there mine eyes saw the secrets of the lightning, and of the thunder, and the secrets of the winds, how they are divided to blow over the earth, and the secrets of the clouds and dew, and there I saw from whence they proceed in that place from whence they saturate the dusty earth.

4 And there I saw closed chambers, out of which the winds are divided, the chambers of the hail and winds, the chamber of the mist, and of the clouds, and the cloud thereof hovers over the earth from the beginning of the world.

5 And I saw the chambers of the sun and moon, whence they proceed and when they come again, and their glorious return, and how one is

superior to the other, and their stately orbit, and how they do not leave their orbit, and they add nothing to their orbit, and they take nothing from it, and they keep faith with each other, in accordance with the oath by which they are bound together.

Comment:1: Here Enoch clearly states that both the *sun and the moon are in orbit*. What are they both orbiting, if not the earth? Here is another description of the sun in its orbit:

PSA.19:6 His going forth is from the end of the heaven, and his circuit unto the ends of it: and there is nothing hid from the heat thereof.

C.2 Could it just be that science has it all wrong concerning the Helio-centric view, and perhaps the old-fashioned view of the Geo-centric solar system, is actually the right one?

6 And first the sun goes forth and traverses his path according to the commandments of the Lord of Spirits, and mighty is His name for ever and ever.

7 And after that I saw the hidden and the visible path of the moon, and she accomplishes the course of her path in that place by day and by night. The one holding a position opposite to the other before the Lord of Spirits, and they give thanks, and praise and rest not. For unto them is their thanksgiving rest

C.3 CHAMBERS, HIDDEN AND VISIBLE

How could the sun come out of a *chamber*, or the moon for that matter? Isn't it true that even today the scientists are only guessing about how the whole universe works, because they simply don't know much about how it all works. The scientists have stated that they know there are other dimensions behind this one. I would agree with that much, and I think that in that context, we find the meaning of **CHAMBERS & HIDDEN** = *Dimensions behind the physical realm* which keep everything under perfect control.

That is why the whole universe is a mystery to both scientists and all of us, because *you only see a very small part of what is really going on* and the inner workings behind the face of our universe, most of which is invisible.

8 For the [1]sun changes oft for a blessing or a curse, and the course of the path of the moon is light to the righteous, and darkness to the sinners in the name of the Lord, who made a separation between the light and the darkness, and divided the spirits of men, and strengthened the spirits of the righteous, in the name of His righteousness.

C.4 [1]'Sun changes oft for a blessing or a curse' How can the sun be both a blessing and a curse? This depends upon the cycles of the sun which change every 11 years. A one end of the sun's cycle it is colder and at the other end it is hotter. Under the certain alignment of different weather conditions it actually gets far too hot in certain places on the planet, which could be counted as a curse.

C.5 'And the course of the path of the moon is light to the righteous, and darkness to the sinners' The righteous consider the moon to be a blessing. As the moon reflects the light of the sun, in a similar way God's true 'church of believers reflect' His light to the world.
Those who are into the occult see the moon in an evil light, and consider it as an evil omen and certain phases of the moon are used for black magic.

9 For no angel hinders and no power is able to hinder; for He appoints a judge for them all and He judges them all before Him.

C.6 No angel or power *is able to hinder* the actual creation itself, such as the sun, the moon and their orbits. I have heard of some crazy scientists, talking about blowing up the moon, for whatever nefarious & crazy reasons. Well even if they tried, they would be prevented by God Himself and His angels. The truth be said, 'Everything in the greater creation of the universe is under God's perfect control, down to the split second-timing of the orbits of all the astral and planetary bodies.' Of course, it is indeed true that man is totally destroying his own planet earth with pollution in the seas and on the earth and even the skies. One of these days God will finally judge man and fix all the damage done to His creation.

REV.11:18 And the nations were angry, and thy wrath is come, and the time of the dead, that they should be judged, and that thou shouldest give reward unto thy servants the prophets, and to the saints, and them that fear thy name, small and great; and shouldest *destroy them which destroy the earth*.

CHAPTER 42

1 Wisdom found no place where she might dwell, then a dwelling place was assigned her in the heavens.

Comment:1: According to **Proverbs chapter 8** (the whole chapter), which is talking about the *Holy Spirit Or Wisdom calls herself the companion of God.*

PRO.8:22 The LORD *possessed me* in the beginning of his way, before his works of old.

PRO.8:23 I was set up from everlasting, from the beginning, or ever the earth was.

C.2 I will expand upon this idea, as for many it will be shocking to find out that the *Holy Spirit is actually female.* It makes perfect sense, when one thinks about it.

God the Father, the Holy Spirit Mother, Jesus the Son of God, and all those who genuinely love Jesus as the Bride of Christ.

It all makes sense and a perfect balance. It would sound strange with God, Jesus and the Holy Spirit all being very strongly Masculine. Where would be the Feminine representative of the Godhead?

Genesis clearly states that *God created us all in His image*. (Male and Female)

It is interesting to note that God was speaking to someone, when HE created the earth, and was about to create man. It sounds like God was talking to the Holy Spirit, His wife.

It then goes on to say that He created us Male and Female:

GEN.1:26 And God said, '*Let us* make man in our image, after our likeness: and let them have dominion over the fish of the sea, and over the fowl of the air, and over the cattle, and over all the earth, and over every creeping thing that creeps upon the earth.'

GEN.1:27 So God created man in his own image, in the image of God created he him; *male and female* created he them

2 Wisdom went forth to make her dwelling among the children of men, and found no dwelling place. Wisdom returned to her place, and to her seat among the angels.

3 And unrighteousness went forth from her chambers; whom she sought not she found, and dwelt with them, as rain in a desert and dew on a thirsty land.

C.3 Sadly, Wisdom couldn't find many wise and receptive people to dwell with on earth, and was generally replaced by unrighteousness, so she returned to take her place in heaven, among the angels. *The Holy Spirit of God*, only goes where she is wanted, and does not force herself on anyone.

THE HOLY SPIRIT, QUEEN OF HEAVEN

C.4 I always did think of God as our heavenly father and his Spirit of Love as our Heavenly Mother-making Her His Spirit Queen of Love! It meets a human need of visualising the loving Motherhood of God in His Motherly Holy Spirit.

This makes the trinity more comprehensible, the Third Person of His Spirit more understandable, complete as Father, Mother and Son! This is vividly picturing His abstract Spirit of Love in a more concrete way by personifying Her as She should be--a Motherly conception of His Holy Spirit of Love! His Spirit-Queen of Love! The God-Mother! Queen of Heaven!

What do we think of when we see hearts and flowers and a beautiful woman? Love! So why not picture God's Love, His Spirit, Third Person of the Trinity, as a real Person? Which She is! His Holy Queen of Love! God the Mother! God the Holy Spirit!

These scriptures in the old testament using "she" and "her" referring to His spirit of Wisdom in Prov.3:13-18; 4:5-9; 7:4; 8:1-36 and 9:1-12 have always been noted by Bible authorities as being some of the descriptions of the Holy Spirit in the Old Testament.

Of course, because of its Jewish writers and the peculiarities of Hebrew and Jewish male chauvinist bent, the Bible often uses "he" and "him" or "it" when it means to also include either or both sexes.

I like to think of the holy spirit as the god-mother, always gently loving, wooing, comforting, winning, soothing and healing like a Mother-characteristics usually associated more with the feminine than the masculine.

God chose it and inspired Solomon to write of Her as such!

PROVERBS 8:2-3: "She stands in the top of high places by the way in the places of the paths. She cries at the gates, at the entry of the city, at the coming in at the doors."

PROVERBS 8:22-31 : "The Lord possessed me in the beginning of His way, before His works of old. I was set up from everlasting, from the beginning, or ever the earth was. When there were no depths, I was brought forth; when there were no fountains abounding with water."

"Before the mountains were settled, before the hills was I brought forth! While as yet He had not made the Earth, nor the fields, nor the highest part of the dust of the world"

"When he prepared the heavens, I was there! When He set a compass upon the face of the depth. When He established the clouds above: when He strengthened the fountains of the deep. When He gave to the sea His decree, that the waters should not pass His commandment: When He appointed the foundations of the Earth."

"Then I was by him, as one brought up with him! And I was daily His delight, rejoicing always before Him. Rejoicing in the habitable part of His Earth; and my delights were with the sons of men!"

C.5 Witnessing

Christ himself is also spoken of as "the beginning of the creation of God" (Rev. 3:14), and as having been present at the Creation (John 1:1-3). So, the person speaking here in Proverbs 8 was neither God the Father nor the Son, but God the Mother, His Holy Spirit! *Then this "She" of proverbs 8, had to be the Holy Spirit!* This then completes the original cozy little divine Holy Family of the Trinity: Father, Mother and Son! The true Trinity! * (See **APPENDIX XVI** for more on the Feminine Holy Spirit.)

CHAPTER 43

1 And I saw other lightnings and the stars of the heaven, and I saw how He called them by their names, and they hearkened unto Him.

Comment:1: How can the stars of heaven, being un-alive hearken unto God? It is very interesting to note that often the *"stars of heaven"* are referring to angels, as shown clearly in the following verse:

REV.12:4 And his tail drew the third part of the *stars of heaven*, and did cast them to the earth: and the dragon stood before the woman which was ready to be delivered, for to devour her child as soon as it was born.

2 And I saw how they are weighed in a righteous balance, according to their proportions of light. I saw the width of the spaces and the day of their appearing, and how their revolution produces lightning, and I saw their revolution according to the number of the angels, and how they keep faith with each other.

C.2 It would appear that there are angels in charge of and responsible for the care of the physical the moon & the stars, to keep everything in their correct orbits. It is indeed marvellous to look at the heavens and the stars in wonder at how everything is kept in perfect order and synchronization. Obviously, someone is taking care of it all-God and His angels. When one looks at the beautiful stars at night it feels like being close to the power of God Himself. One can feel the peace of God which passes all understanding, possibly because of the presence of His angels who guard or watch over each of these heavenly bodies.

3 And I asked the angel who went with me who showed me what was hidden, "What are these?"

4 And he said to me, "The Lord of Spirits hath showed thee their parabolic meaning. These are the names of the holy who dwell on the earth and believe in the name of the Lord of Spirits for ever and ever."

C.3 The *Saints* are also said to *shine as the "stars of heaven":*

DAN.12:3 And *they that be wise shall shine as the brightness of the firmament*; and they that turn many to righteousness *as the stars* for ever and ever.

CHAPTER 44

1 Also another phenomenon I saw in regard to the lightnings; how some of the stars arise and become lightnings, and cannot part with their new form.

Comment:1: This is a very interesting verse, as it is says that there is a connection between *stars changing or morphing into lightnings.* There are many verses which talk about lightening's coming out of the throne of God and more. *Lightnings* would suggest the powers and incredible speed of changeability, and flight speed ability of angels. Angels are known to be able to *change form* at will. (Enoch 17.1)

REV.4:5 And out of the throne proceeded *lightnings and thunder and voices:* and there were seven lamps of fire burning before the throne, which are the seven Spirits of God.

LUK.10:18 And he said unto them, I beheld Satan as lightning fall from heaven.

CHAPTER 45

1 And this is the Second Parable concerning those who deny the name of the dwelling of the holy ones and the Lord of Spirits.

2 And into the heaven they shall not ascend, and on the earth they shall not come; such shall be the lot of sinners who have denied the name of the Lord of Spirits, who are thus preserved for the day of suffering and tribulation.

3 On that day, Mine Elect One, shall sit on a throne of glory, and shall try their works and their places of rest are innumerable, and their souls shall grow strong within them when they see Mine elect ones, and those who have called upon My glorious name.

Comment:1: Notice how that God is talking about another being other than Himself, as sitting on a throne of glory, *"Mine Elect One"* this is similar to the following verse:

DAN.7:13 I saw in the night visions, and, behold, one like the *Son of man* came with the clouds of heaven, and came to the *Ancient of days,* and they brought him near before him.

DAN.7:14 And there was given him dominion, and glory, and a kingdom, that all people, nations, and languages, should serve him: his dominion is an everlasting dominion, which shall not pass away, and his kingdom that which shall not be destroyed.

Jesus in the New Testament was often called the *Son of man*:

MAT.10:23 But when they persecute you in this city, flee ye into another: for verily I say unto you, Ye shall not have gone over the cities of Israel, till the *Son of man* be come. (His 2nd Coming.)

4 Then will I cause *Mine Elect One* to dwell among them, and I will transform the heaven and make it an eternal blessing and light.

5 And I will transform the earth and make it a blessing; and I will cause *Mine elect ones* to dwell upon it; but the sinners and evil-doers shall not set foot thereon.

MAT.24:31 And he shall send his angels with a great sound of a trumpet, and they shall gather together *His elect* from the four winds, from one end of heaven to the other.

6 For I have provided and satisfied with peace My righteous ones, and have caused them to dwell before Me; but for sinners there is judgement impending with Me, so that I shall destroy them from the face of the earth.

ISA.11:4 But with righteousness shall he judge the poor, and reprove with equity for the meek of the earth: and he shall *smite the earth*: with the *rod of his mouth*, and with the breath of his lips shall he *slay the wicked.*

DAN.7:27 And the kingdom and dominion, and the greatness of the kingdom under the whole heaven, shall be *given to the people of the saints of the Most High*, whose kingdom is an everlasting kingdom, and *all dominions shall serve and obey him.*

REV.19:21 And *the remnant were slain with the sword of him* that sat upon the horse, which *sword proceeded out of his mouth*: and all the fowls were filled with their flesh.

CHAPTER 46

1 And there I saw One who had a head of days, and his head was white like wool. With Him was another being whose countenance had the appearance of a man, His face was full of graciousness, like one of the holy angels.

DAN.7:9 I beheld till the thrones were cast down, and the Ancient of days did sit, whose garment was white as snow, and the *hair of his head like the pure wool*: his throne was like the fiery flame, and his wheels as burning fire.

DAN.7:13 I saw in the night visions, and, behold, one like the *Son of man* came with the *clouds of heaven*, and came to the *Ancient of days*, and they brought him near before him.

2 CO.8:9 For ye know the *grace of our Lord Jesus Christ*, that, though he was rich, yet for your sakes he became poor, that ye through his poverty might be rich.

2 And I asked the angel who went with me and showed me all the hidden things, concerning that Son of Man, who he was, and whence he was, and why he went with the Head of Days? He answered me and said unto me:

3 This is the Son of Man, who hath righteousness, with whom dwelleth righteousness, and who reveals all the treasures of that which is hidden, because the Lord of Spirits hath chosen him, and whose lot hath the pre-eminence before the Lord of spirits in uprightness for ever.

PRO.2:4 If thou seek her (WISDOM) as silver, and search for her as for *hidden treasures;*

PRO.2:5 Then shalt thou understand the fear of the LORD, and find the knowledge of God.

4 And this Son of Man whom thou hast seen shall raise up the kings and the mighty from their seats, and the strong from their throne. He shall loosen the reins of the strong, and break the teeth of the sinners.

PSA.3:7 Arise, O LORD; save me, O my God: for thou hast smitten all mine enemies upon the cheek bone; thou hast *broken the teeth* of the ungodly.

5 He shall put down the kings from their thrones and kingdoms, because they do not extol and praise Him, nor humbly acknowledge whence the kingdom was bestowed upon them.

REV.6:15 And *the kings* of the earth, and the *great men*, and the *rich men*, and the chief captains, and the mighty men, and every bondman, and every free man, hid themselves in the dens and in the rocks of the mountains;

REV.6:16 And said to the mountains and rocks, 'Fall on us, and hide us from the face of him that sits on the throne, and from the *wrath of the Lamb'*:

REV.6:17 For *the great day of his wrath is come; and who shall be able to stand?*

6 He shall put down the countenance of the strong and shall fill them with shame. Darkness shall be their dwelling, and worms shall be their bed, and they shall have no hope of rising from their beds, because they do not extol the name of the Lord of Spirits.

ISA.65:13 Therefore thus says the Lord GOD, Behold, my servants shall eat, but ye shall be hungry: behold, my servants shall drink, but ye shall be thirsty: behold, my servants shall rejoice, but ye shall be *ashamed:*

MAR.9:44 Where their *worm dies not*, and the fire is not quenched.

PSA.107:10 Such as sit in *darkness* and in the *shadow of death*, being bound in affliction and iron;

PSA.107:11 Because they *rebelled against the words of God*, and contemned the counsel of the most High:

7 And these are they who judge the stars of heaven, and raise their hands against the Most High, and tread upon the earth and dwell upon it. All their deeds shall manifest unrighteousness, and their power rests upon their riches, and their faith is in the gods which they have made with their hands, and they deny the name of the Lord of Spirits.

Comment:1: The above verse 7 is describing the coming Anti-Christ and his empire or the 7th and last World Empire of Mankind. The coming one world government will have 10 leaders who 'have horns' or are demon possessed, and shall rule the earth together with Satan through the Anti-Christ.

REV.17:12 And the ten horns which you saw are ten kings, which have received no kingdom as yet; but receive power as kings one hour with the beast.

REV.17:13 These have one mind, and shall give their power and strength unto the beast.

REV.17:14 These shall make war with the Lamb, and the Lamb shall overcome them: for he is Lord of lords, and King of kings: and they that are with him are called, and chosen, and faithful.

DAN.7:25 And he shall *speak great words* against the Most High, and shall wear out the saints of the most High, and think to change times and laws: and they shall be given into his hand until a time and times and the dividing of time.

REV.13:6 And he opened his mouth in blasphemy against God, to *blaspheme his name*, and his tabernacle, and *them that dwell in heaven.*

8 They persecute the houses of His congregations, and the faithful who hang upon the name of the Lord of Spirits.

REV.12:17 And the dragon was wroth with the woman, and went to make war with the remnant of her seed, which keep the commandments of God, and have the testimony of Jesus Christ.

MAT.5:10 Blessed are they which are *persecuted* for righteousness' sake: for theirs is the kingdom of heaven.

MAT.5:11 Blessed are ye, when men shall revile you, and *persecute you*, and shall say all manner of evil against you falsely, for my sake.

MAT.5:12 Rejoice, and be exceeding glad: for great is your reward in heaven: for so *persecuted* they the *prophets* which were before you.

CHAPTER 47

1 And in those days, shall have ascended the prayer of the righteous, and the blood of the righteous from the earth before the Lord of Spirits.

REV.6:10 And they cried with a loud voice, saying, 'How long, O Lord, holy and true, dost thou not *judge and avenge our blood on them that dwell on the earth?'*

2 In those days the holy ones who dwell above in the heavens shall unite with one voice and supplicate and pray and praise, and give thanks and bless the name of the Lord of Spirits, on behalf of the blood of the righteous which has been shed, and that the prayer of the righteous may not be in vain before the Lord of Spirits. That judgement may be done unto them, and that they may not have to suffer for ever.

REV.6:11 And white robes were given unto every one of them; and it was said unto them, that they should rest yet for a little season, until their *fellow servants also and their brethren, that should be killed as they were,* should be fulfilled.

3 In those days I saw the Head of Days when He seated himself upon the throne of His glory, and the books of the living were opened before Him: and all His host which is in heaven above and His counsellors stood before Him.

DAN.7:10 A fiery stream issued and came forth from before him: millions ministered unto him, and ten thousand times ten thousand stood before him: the judgment was set, and *the books were opened.*

REV.3:5 He that overcomes, the same shall be clothed in white raiment; and I will not blot out his name out of the *book of life*, but I will confess his name before my Father, and before his angels.

4 And the hearts of the Holy were filled with joy, because the number of the righteous had been offered, and the prayer of the righteous had been heard, and the blood of the righteous had been required before the Lord of Spirits.

PSA.9:12 When he makes inquisition for *blood*, he remembers them: he forgets not the cry of the humble.

REV.8:3 And another angel came and stood at the altar, having a golden censer; and there was given unto him much incense, that he should offer it with the *prayers of all saints* upon the golden altar which was before the throne.

CHAPTER 48

1 And in that place, I saw the fountain of righteousness which was inexhaustible; and around it were many fountains of wisdom; and all the thirsty drank of them, and were filled with wisdom, and their dwellings were with the righteous and holy and elect.

REV.22:1 And he shewed me a *pure river of water of life*, clear as crystal, *proceeding out of the throne of God and of the Lamb*

2 And at that hour that Son of Man was named in the presence of the Lord of Spirits, and his name before the Head of Days.

DAN.7:13 I saw in the night visions, and, behold, one like the *Son of man* came with the clouds of heaven, and came to the Ancient of days, and they brought him near before him.

ACT.2:22 Ye men of Israel, hear these words; *Jesus of Nazareth*, a man *approved of God* among you by *miracles* and *wonders* and *signs*, which *God did by him* in the midst of you, as ye yourselves also know.

3 Yea, before the sun and the signs were created, and before the stars of the heaven were made, His name was named before the Lord of Spirits.

JN.1:1 In the beginning was *the Word*, and the *Word was with God*, and the *Word was God*.

JN.1:2 The same was *in the beginning with God*.

JN.1:3 *All things were made by him; and without him was not anything made that was made.*

4 He shall be a staff to the righteous whereon to stay themselves and not fall, and he shall be a light of the Gentiles, and the hope of those who are troubled of heart.

ZEC.11:10 And I took *my staff*, even *Beauty*, and *cut it asunder*, that I might break my covenant which I had made with all the people.

ISA.53:5 But he was *wounded for our transgressions*, he was *bruised for our iniquities*: the *chastisement of our peace was upon him; and with his stripes we are healed*.

LUK.2:32 A *light to lighten the Gentiles*, and the *glory of thy people Israel*.

JOH.14:1 Let not your *heart be troubled*: ye *believe in God, believe also in me*.

5 All who dwell on earth shall fall down and worship before Him, and will praise and bless and celebrate with song the Lord of Spirits: and for

this reason that he been chosen and hidden before Him, before the creation of the world and for evermore.

JOH.1:1 In the beginning was *the Word*, and the *Word was with God*, and the *Word was God.*

REV.5:9 And they sung a new song, saying, 'Thou art worthy to take the book, and to open the seals thereof: for thou was slain, and hast redeemed us to God by thy blood out of every kindred, and tongue, and people, and nation'.

6 And the wisdom of the Lord of Spirits hath revealed him to the holy and righteous; for he that preserved the lot of the righteous, because they have hated and despised this world of unrighteousness, and have hated all its works and ways in the name of the Lord of Spirits; for in His name they are saved, and according to his good pleasure hath it been in regard to their life.

PHI.2:10 That at the <u>*name of Jesus*</u> every knee should bow, of things in heaven, and things in earth, and things under the earth;

PHI.2:11 And that every tongue should confess that <u>*Jesus Christ is Lord*</u>, to the glory of God the Father.

ISA.33:6 And *wisdom* and knowledge shall be the stability of thy times, and strength of *salvation:* the fear of the LORD is his treasure.

1JN.5:13 These things have I written unto you that believe on the *name* of the *Son of God;* that ye may know that *ye have eternal life (salvation)*, and that ye may *believe on the name of the Son of God.*

REV.12:11 And they overcame him by the blood of the Lamb, and by the word of their testimony; and they *loved not their lives unto the death.*

7 In those days downcast in countenance shall the kings of the earth have become, and the strong who possess the land because of the works of their hands. For on the day of their anguish and affliction shall not be able to save themselves.

ISA.2:17 And the *loftiness* of man shall be *bowed down,* and the *haughtiness* of men shall be *made low*: and the *LORD alone* shall be *exalted* in that day.

DAN.7:26 But the *judgment shall sit*, and they shall take away his dominion, to consume and to destroy it unto the end. (Talking about the fall of the ANTICHRIST and end of the Kings of the earth)

REV.17:12 And the ten horns which thou saw are *ten kings*, which have received no kingdom as yet; but receive *power as kings one hour with the beast*. (Coming ANTI-CHRIST and the 7th world empire of man and Satan)

REV.17:14 These shall make war with the Lamb, and the Lamb shall overcome them: for he is *Lord of lords*, and *King of kings*: and they that are with him are *called, and chosen, and faithful.*

8 And I will give them over into the hands of Mine elect. As straw in the fire so shall they burn before the face of the holy; as lead in the water shall they sink before the face of the righteous, and no trace of them shall any more be found.

DAN.7:22 Until the Ancient of days came, and judgment was given to the saints of the Most High; and the *time came that the saints possessed the kingdom.*

DAN.7:27 And the kingdom and dominion, and the greatness of the kingdom under the whole heaven, shall be given to the *people of the saints of the Most High*, whose kingdom is an everlasting kingdom, and *all dominions shall serve and obey him.*

9 And on the day of their affliction there shall be rest on the earth, and before them they shall fall and not rise again; and there shall be no one to take them with his hands and raise them. For they have denied the Lord of Spirits and His Anointed. The name of the Lord of Spirits be blessed.

EXO.33:14 And he said, 'My presence shall go with thee, and I will give thee *rest'*.

ISA.9:6 For unto us a child is born, unto us a *Son is given*: and the *government shall be upon his shoulder*: and his name shall be called *Wonderful, Counsellor, The mighty God, The everlasting Father, The Prince of Peace.*

CHAPTER 49

1 For wisdom is poured out like water, and glory fails not before Him for evermore. For he is mighty in all the secrets of righteousness, and unrighteousness shall disappear as a shadow, and have no continuance; because the Elect One stands before the Lord of Spirits, and his glory is for ever and ever, and his might unto all generations.

Comment: As mentioned before, the 'Elect One' *is* Jesus

2 And in him dwells the spirit of wisdom, and the spirit which gives insight, and the spirits of understanding and of might, and the spirit of those who have fallen asleep in righteousness.

DAN.12:2 And many of them that *sleep* in the dust of the earth shall awake, some to everlasting life, and some to shame and everlasting contempt.

DAN.12:3 And they that be *wise* shall shine as the brightness of the firmament; and they that turn many to *righteousness* as the stars for ever and ever.

3 And he shall judge the secret things, and none shall be able to utter a lying word before him; for He is the Elect One before the Lord of Spirits according to His good pleasure.

PSA.63:11 But the king shall rejoice in God; every one that swears by him shall glory: but the mouth of them that *speak lies* shall be stopped.

CHAPTER 50

1 And in those days a change shall take place of the holy and elect, and the light of days shall abide upon them, and glory and honour shall turn to the holy.

1CO.15:51 Behold, I shew you a mystery; We shall not all sleep, but we shall all be *changed,*

1CO.15:52 In a moment, in the *twinkling of an eye,* at the *last trump*: for the trumpet shall sound, and the dead shall be raised incorruptible, and we shall be *changed.*

Comment:1: Time-frame: At the 2nd Coming of Christ. (To see an extensive Time-frame of the future, please see the **Appendix** of this book)

2 On the day of the affliction on which evil shall have been treasured up against the sinners, and the righteous shall be victorious in the name of the Lord of Spirits.

He will cause the others to witness this, that they may repent, and forego the works of their hands.

3 They shall have no honour through the name of the Lord of Spirits, yet through His name shall they be saved, and the Lord of Spirits will have compassion on them, for His compassion is great. And He is righteous also in His judgement, and in the presence of His glory unrighteousness also shall not maintain itself. At His judgement the unrepentant shall perish before Him.

C.2 In these two last verses, Enoch is talking about those who know their Master's will, but didn't do it.

'*Yet through His name shall they be saved'* Even some of those who are *saved,* but don't tell anyone else about Salvation. Many will be saved, and get into heaven by the Grace of Salvation, by Jesus Christ, but they *won't have any reward,* because they *didn't witness about Jesus to others*, when they knew that they should have. Salvation is totally by Grace, but our rewards in heaven, depend on our faithfulness to witness about Jesus and salvation to others, during our lifetime.

TIT.3:5 Not by works of righteousness which we have done, but *according to his mercy he saved us*, by the washing of regeneration, and renewing of the Holy Ghost;

1CO.3:15 If any man's work shall be burned, he shall suffer loss: but he himself shall be saved; yet so as by fire.

REV.14:13 And I heard a voice from heaven saying unto me, Write, 'Blessed are the dead which die in the Lord from henceforth: Yea, saith the Spirit, that they may rest from their labours; and their works do follow them.'

LUK.9:26 For whosoever shall be ashamed of me and of my words, of him shall the Son of man be ashamed, when he shall come in his own glory, and in his Father's, and of the holy angels.

C.3 'ashamed of me and of my words' Jesus commandment to all of his disciples and believers is simply:

Mark 16.15 "And he said unto them, 'Go ye into all the world, and preach the gospel to every creature.'"

DAN.12:2 And many of them that sleep in the dust of the earth shall awake, some to everlasting life, and some to shame and everlasting contempt.

C.4 'unrighteousness also shall not maintain itself.' 'At His judgement the unrepentant shall perish before Him'.

4 And from henceforth I will have no mercy on them, says the Lord of Spirits.

CHAPTER 51

1 And in those days, shall the earth also give back that which has been entrusted to it, and Sheol also shall give back that which it has received, and hell shall give back that which it owes, for in those days the Elect One shall arise.

Comment:1: The time sequence mentioned here is right after the MILLENNIUM and THE GREAT WHITE THRONE JUDGEMENT (Related: REV.20:11 REV.20:12)

REV.20:13 And the sea gave up the dead which were in it; and *death* and *hell* delivered up the dead which were in them: and they were judged every man according to their works.

REV.20:14 And *death* and *hell* were cast into the *lake of fire*. This is the *second death.*

2 And He shall choose the righteous and holy from among them; for the day had drawn nigh that they should be saved.

REV.12:10 And I heard a loud voice saying in heaven, 'Now is come *salvation,* and strength, and the kingdom of our God, and the *power of his Christ*: for the accuser of our brethren is cast down, which accused them before our God day and night.'

3 And the elect One shall in those days sit on My throne, and his mouth shall pour forth all the secrets of wisdom and counsel, for the Lord of Spirits hath given them to him and hath glorified him.

ISA.2:3 And many people shall go and say, 'Come ye, and let us go up to the *mountain of the LORD,* to the house of the God of Jacob; and *He will teach us of his ways*, and we will walk in his paths: for out of Zion shall go forth the law, and the word of the LORD from Jerusalem.'

4 And in those days shall the mountains leap like rams, and the hills also shall skip like lambs satisfied with milk, and the faces of all the angels in heaven shall be lighted up with joy.

ISA.11:6 The wolf also shall dwell with the lamb, and the leopard shall lie down with the kid; and the calf and the young lion and the fatling together; and a little child shall lead them.

C.2 TIMEFRAME: THE MILLENNIUM

5 And the earth shall rejoice, and the righteous shall dwell upon it, and the elect shall walk thereon.

ISA.29:19 *The meek* also shall increase their *joy in the LORD*, and the poor among men shall *rejoice* in the *Holy One* of Israel.

MAT.5:5 Blessed are the *meek*: for they shall *inherit the earth.*

CHAPTER 52

1 And after those days in that place where I had seen all the visions of that which is hidden; for I had been carried off in a whirlwind and they had borne me towards the west.

2 There mine eyes saw all the secret things of the heaven that shall be, a mountain of iron, and a mountain of copper, and a mountain of soft metal, and a mountain of lead.

3 And I asked the angel who went with me, saying, "What things are these which I have seen in secret?"

4 And he said unto me, "All these things which thou hast seen shall serve the dominion of His Anointed that he may be potent and mighty on the earth."

5 And that angel of peace answered and, saying unto me, "Wait a little, and these shall be revealed unto thee all the secret things which surround the Lord of Spirits."

6 And these mountains which thine eyes hast seen: the mountain of iron, and the mountain of copper, and the mountain of silver, and the mountain of gold, and the mountain of soft metal, and the mountain of lead.

All these shall be in the presence of the Elect One, as wax before the fire, and like water which streams down from above upon those mountains, and they shall become powerless before his feet.

DAN.2:44 And in the *days of these kings* shall the *God of heaven* set up a *kingdom,* which shall *never be destroyed:* and the kingdom shall not be left to other people, but it shall *break in pieces and consume all these kingdoms,* and it shall stand for ever.

DAN.2:45 Forasmuch as thou saw that the *stone was cut out of the mountain* without hands, and that it *broke in pieces the iron, the brass, the clay, the silver, and the gold*; the *great God hath made known to the king what shall come to pass hereafter*: and the dream is certain, and the interpretation thereof sure.

7 And it shall come to pass in those days that none shall be saved, either by gold or by silver, and none shall be able to escape.

ISA.2:20 In that day a man shall cast his idols of *silver,* and his idols of *gold,* which they made each one for himself to worship, to the moles and to the bats;

8 And there shall be no iron for was, nor shall one clothe oneself with a breastplate. Bronze shall be of no service, and tin shall be of no service and shall not be esteemed, and lead shall not be desired.

MIC.4:3 And he shall judge among many people, and rebuke strong nations afar off; and they shall *beat their swords into ploughs*, and their *spears into pruninghooks*: *nation shall not lift up a sword against nation, neither shall they learn war any more.*

ISA.11:9 They shall *not hurt nor destroy* in all my holy mountain: for the earth shall be full of the knowledge of the LORD, as the waters cover the sea.

9 All these things shall be denied and destroyed from the surface of the earth, when the elect One shall appear before the face of the Lord of Spirits.

CHAPTER 53

1 There mine eyes saw a deep valley with open mouths, and all who dwell on the earth and sea and islands shall bring to him gifts and presents and tokens of homage, but that deep valley shall not become full.

Comment:1: This is indeed a mysterious verse. A deep valley with open mouths. What does it actually mean? Abysses in the Valley perhaps or is it a great vault for storage of all the gifts and presents and tokens of homage to the KING OF KINGS

2 And their hands shall commit lawless deeds, and sinners devour all whom they lawlessly oppress; yet the sinners shall be destroyed before the face of the Lord of Spirits, and they shall be banished from off the face of His earth; and they shall perish for ever and ever.

3 For I saw all the angels of punishment abiding there, and preparing all the instruments of Satan.

4 And I asked the angel of peace who went with me, "For whom are they preparing these instruments?"

5 And he said unto me: "They prepare these for the kings and the mighty of this earth, that they may thereby be destroyed."

6 And after this the Righteous and Elect One shall cause the house of his congregation to appear; henceforth these shall be no more hindered in the name of the Lord of Spirits.

7 And these mountains shall not stand as the earth before His righteousness; but the hills shall be as a fountain of water, and the righteous shall have rest from the oppression of sinners.

C.2 These *"mountains"* is referring to the *"kings of the earth"*, or its *true evil rulers.*

The *hills*, sometimes refers to God's people who shall be as a fountain of water to refresh the peoples of the earth.

PSA.65:12 They drop upon the pastures of the wilderness: and the *little hills rejoice* on every side.

PSA.65:13 The pastures are clothed with flocks; the *valleys* also are covered over with corn; they *shout for joy, they also sing.*

CHAPTER 54

1 And I looked and turned to another part of the earth, and saw there a deep valley with burning fire; and they brought the kings and the mighty and began to cast them into this deep valley.

REV.18:23: For thy merchants were the great men of the earth; for by thy sorceries were all nations deceived.

2 And there mine eyes saw how they made these chains of immeasurable weight; and I asked the angel of peace who went with me, saying, "For whom are these chains being prepared?"

3 And he said unto me, "These are being prepared for the hosts of Azazel, so that they may take them and cast them into the abyss of complete condemnation and they shall cover their jaws with rough stones as the Lord of spirits commanded."

REV.20:1 And I saw an angel come down from heaven, having the key of the bottomless pit and a great chain in his hand.

REV.20:2 And he laid hold on the *dragon, that old serpent, which is the Devil, and Satan, and bound him* a thousand years,

REV.20:3 And *cast him into the bottomless pit, and shut him up,* and set a seal upon him, that he should *deceive the nations no more*, till the thousand years should be fulfilled: and after that he must be loosed a little season.

Comment:1: Some of the most evil-beings that have ever lived in the spirit world are Lucifer and His band of fallen angels. In the physical realm, the fallen angels have always had their henchmen in the form of demonic powers and entities who literally get into or possess the very *rich and elite* who are classified in the Bible as the Merchants and Kings of the Earth.

To qualify for the LAKE of FIRE, *one has to be one of the worst types imaginable.*

Hell is normally enough for most wicked humans as a punishment, like a prison sentence. Most however, will eventually be released and forgiven by God. Only the worst and totally incorrigible beings who *refuse to acknowledge their sins,* and diabolical crimes against humanity, and also refuse to come to be forgiven by Jesus, King of Kings and Lord of Lords, will end up in the *Lake of Fire.*

REV.20:15 And whosoever was not found written in the book of life was cast into the lake of fire.

C.2 That last Bible verse, is referring to the *GREAT WHITE THRONE JUDGEMENT of GOD*, which happens 1000 years after the Millennium.

During the Millennium, everyone on earth would have had the opportunity to know that Christ is real, and is the KING of KINGS.

"Though Mercy be shown the wicked, yet will he not learn righteousness."

ISA.26:10 'Let grace be shown to the wicked, yet he will not learn righteousness; In the land of uprightness he will deal unjustly, and will not behold the majesty of the LORD.'

C.3 In spite of that, at the end of the Millennium, after Satan is released from the bottomless pit for a short season, hordes of people, without number, follow him again:

REV.20:7 And when the thousand years are expired, Satan shall be loosed out of his prison,

REV.20:8 And shall go out to deceive the nations which are in the four quarters of the earth, Gog, and Magog, to gather them together to battle: the number of whom is as the sand of the sea.

REV.20:9 And they went up on the breadth of the earth, and compassed the camp of the saints about, and the beloved city: and *fire came down from God out of heaven, and devoured them.*

4 And Michael, Gabriel, Raphael and Phanuel shall take hold of them on that great day, and cast them into the burning furnace, that the Lord of Spirits may take vengeance on them for their unrighteousness in becoming subject unto Satan, and leading astray those who dwell on the earth.

REV.20:10 And the Devil that deceived them was cast into the lake of fire and brimstone, where the beast and the false prophet are, and shall be tormented day and night for ever and ever.

C.4 Between *Rev 20.3* mentioned above and *Rev 20.10*, there is a 1000-year interval in time. The first verse, just before the start of *The Millennium,* and the other at the end of it.

5 And in those days shall punishment come from the Lord of Spirits, and he will open all the chambers of waters which are above the heavens, and of the fountains which are beneath the earth. And all the waters shall be joined with the waters. That which is above the heavens is the masculine, and the water which is beneath the earth is the feminine.

C.5 I think that it is talking about the *Great Flood of Noah,* and that it would effect the *physical* peoples of the *Outer Earth and the Inner Earth.*

Waters above "masculine", and waters below "feminine", as the INNER EARTH is compared to the "WOMB of the Earth" in the Book of 2nd Ezdras 4.41 "In Hades the chambers of the souls are like the womb."

6 And they shall destroy all who dwell on the earth and those who dwell under the "ends of the heaven"; and when they have recognised their

unrighteousness which they have wrought on the earth, then by these shall they perish.

C.6 It is very interesting, that this verse does **not** say 'destroy all who dwell on the earth only', but '**also** those', who **dwell under** the "**ends of heaven**" *Who and where exactly is that talking about?* (**See Enoch chapter 18**)

CHAPTER 55

1 And after that the Head of Days repented and said, "In vain have I destroyed all who dwell on the earth." And He swore by His great name, "From henceforth I will not do so to all who dwell on the earth, and I will set a sign in the heaven; and this shall be a pledge of good faith between Me and them for ever, so long as heaven is above the earth. This is in accordance with My command."

GEN.9:12 And God said, "This is the *token of the covenant* which I make between me and you and every living creature that is with you, for perpetual generations:"

GEN.9:13 "I do set my (Rain)bow in the cloud, and it shall be for a *token of a covenant* between me and the earth."

Comment:1: You are probably wondering how is this possible, that Enoch is talking about the Great Flood and God's reactions to it happening, long before it actually happened? A very good question. According to some sources, the Book of Enoch is divided into 4 parts, with one or more of those parts, assembled together by Noah. As you know Noah lived both before and after the Flood, so the writings about the Flood in the Book of Enoch, could have been a small insert into the Book of Enoch by Noah himself, sort of 'after- the-fact'? Or perhaps, Enoch was just seeing the future in both vision and prophecy time and time again, including the amazing details of the coming Great Flood, and describing it exactly as it was to happen, around 500 years before it was to actually be fulfilled?

2 When I have desired to take hold of them by the hand of the angels on the day of tribulation and pain because of this, I will cause My chastisement and My wrath to abide on them, says God, the Lord of Spirits.

REV.16:1 And I heard a great voice out of the temple saying to the seven angels, 'Go your ways, and pour out the vials of the *wrath of God* upon the earth.'

3 Ye mighty kings who dwell on the earth, ye shall have to behold Mine Elect One, how he sits on the throne of glory and judges Azazel, and all his associates, and all this host in the name of the Lord of Spirits.

REV.19:15 And out of his mouth goes a *sharp sword*, that with it he should *smite the nations*: and he shall *rule them with a rod of iron*: and he treads the *winepress* of the fierceness and *wrath of Almighty God.*

REV.14:20 And the *winepress* was trodden without the city, and *blood came out of the winepress, even unto the horse bridles, by the space of a thousand and six hundred furlongs.*

REV.19:16 And he hath on his vesture and on his thigh a name written, *KING OF KINGS, AND LORD OF LORDS.*

CHAPTER 56

1 And I saw there the hosts of the angels of punishment going, and they held scourges and chains of iron and bronze, and I asked the angel of peace who went with me, saying, "To whom are these who hold the scourges going?"

2 And he said unto me: "To their elect and beloved ones, that they may be cast into the chasm of the abyss of the valley; and then that valley shall be filled with 'their elect and beloved', and the days of their lives shall be at an end, and the days of their leading astray shall not thenceforward be reckoned."

Comment:1: The destruction of the former giants, (disembodied spirits, known as the demons), does *not happen until the "GREAT WHITE THRONE JUDGEMENT",* mentioned in Revelations 20.11.

REV.20:11 "And I saw a *great white throne,* and him that sat on it, from whose face the earth and the heaven fled away; and there was found no place for them."

C.2 What a punishment! The fallen angels of Satan will be forced to gather together all of their loved ones and offspring, such as the giants, and many other strange entities, chimeras etc., and have to cast them into the chasm of the abyss of the valley.

The fallen angels will witness the total destruction of all their descendants, and will also be instrumental in causing it to come to pass.

This reminds me of the verse, "Whatsoever a man (angel) soweth, shall he also reap!"

3 And in those days the angels shall return, (fallen angels), and hurl themselves upon the Parthians and Medes. They shall stir up the kings, so that a spirit of unrest shall come upon them, and they shall rouse them from their thrones, that they may break forth as lions from their lairs, and hungry wolves among their flocks.

C.3 Was Enoch talking about the 4th *World empire** of the *Parthians (Persians) and Medes.* Or was he actually talking about a *new vicious emerging power* which follows *Satan*, after he has *been released from the Bottomless Pit at the end of the Millennium?*

According to Ezekiel 38 and 39, *Persia* or modern-day *Iran*, will work together *with GOG (The Anti-Christ) and MAGOG (The Russians)*

Perhaps at the end of the Millennium, these *same forces unite* to come up against Israel and the *"Camp of the Saints"*, as it stated above that *the fallen angels shall return (when released from the Bottomless Pit, together with Satan), and hurl themselves upon the Parthians and Medes.*

(In other words, they take over those peoples, and bring them to War against the Elect in Jerusalem, Israel, or Jesus' Millennial capital city.)

4 And they shall go up and tread underfoot the land of His elect ones, and the land of His elect ones shall be before them as a threshing floor and a highway.

REV.20:7 And when the thousand years are expired, *Satan shall be loosed out of his prison,*

REV.20:8 And shall go out *to deceive the nations* which are in the *four quarters of the earth, Gog, and Magog,* to gather them together to battle: the number of whom is as the sand of the sea.

5 But the "city of my righteousness" shall be hindrance to their horses, and they shall begin to fight among themselves, and their right hand shall be strong against themselves, and a man shall not know his brother, nor a son his father or his mother, till there be no end of number of corpses through their slaughter, and punishment be not in vain.

C.4 Is the "*city of my righteousness*" mentioned here by Enoch the exact same as the "*camp of the saints*" in Jerusalem at the end of the Millennium?

REV.20:9 And they went up on the breadth of the earth, and compassed the *'camp of the saints* about, and the beloved city': and *fire came down from God out of heaven, and devoured them.*

6 In those days Sheol shall open its jaws, and they shall be swallowed up therein, and their destruction shall be at an end.

Sheol shall devour the sinners in the presence of the elect.

C.5 This verse really gives the time sequence away (End of the Millennium), as mentioned in Revelations chapter 20:

REV.20:11 And I saw a *great white throne,* and him that sat on it, from whose face the earth and the heaven fled away; and there was found no place for them.

REV.20:12 And I saw the *dead, small and great,* stand before God; and the *books were opened:* and another book was opened, which is the book of life: and the *dead were judged* out of those things which were written in the books, according to their works.

REV.20:13 And the *sea gave up the dead* which were in it; and death and hell delivered up the dead which were in them: and they were judged every man according to their works.

REV.20:14 And *death and hell* were cast into the *lake of fire.* This is the second death.

REV.20:15 And whosoever was not found written in the book of life was cast into the lake of fire.

CHAPTER 57

1 And it came to pass after this that I saw another host of wagons, and men riding thereon, and coming on the winds of the east, and from the west to the south.

Comments:1: The mystery is the word *wagons,* and why the use of this word? Also, how could the wagons come '*on winds of the east'* as well as '*from the west to the south'?* These wagons don't sound like any normal wagons at all. Also notice the word 'ANOTHER'. Whatever these type of wagons are, Enoch has noticed them before somewhere.

2 And the noise of their wagons was heard, and when this turmoil took place, the holy ones from heaven remarked it, and the "pillars of the earth" were moved from the one end of the heaven to the other, in one day.

And they shall all fall down and worship the Lord of Spirits, and this is the end of the second parable.

C.2 These *wagons,* whatever they were, were certainly not wagons as we think of them today, like something out of a western movie. These wagons sound like they were *flying on the winds*, and that they made a *lot of noise*, so much so, that it was even *noticed in heaven.* Now we see the time sequence: pillars of the earth were moved from one end to the other.

The Time sequence is the **"WRATH OF GOD".**

ISA.24:19 The *earth is utterly broken down*, the earth is clean dissolved, the *earth is moved exceedingly.*

REV.6:13 And the *stars of heaven* fell unto the earth, even as a *fig tree* casts her untimely figs, when she is *shaken of a mighty wind.*

MAT.24:32 Now learn a *parable of the fig tree;* When his branch is yet tender, and puts forth leaves, ye know that summer is nigh:

MAT.24:33 So likewise ye, when ye shall see all these things, know that it is near, even at the doors.

C.3 Notice that, whoever was in these *"wagons", ends up falling down and worshipping the Lord of spirits.*

We are not told if these men in wagons are good or evil, so we can only make an educated guess, as to whom Enoch is referring to. However due to the extreme circumstances, of the time sequence being the end of the world, as mentioned in the above verse "pillars of the earth" to me sounds like these forces were really terrified, and ended up submitting to God.

Those described in the Wagons, sound like some powerful forces are finally yielding to God's Spirit at the end of the world, as we now know it, in a very dramatic fashion. Who are these people as it does say that they are "men"?

However sometimes using the word "men" in the Book of Enoch means some type of other beings such as angels or even spirit beings. (**Enoch 17.1**: "And they took me to a place in which those who were there were like flaming fire, and when they wished, they appeared as men."

The above scenes are very unusual, as from reading the Bible, it would seem that most evil spirit being end up in the Bottomless Pit, and eventually in the Lake of Fire. The people mentioned in the above two amazing verses, seem to be "powers" who actually yield to God, at the time of the Wrath of God.

I was wondering why Enoch, who saw such incredible visions and visited so many exotic places on the earth and inside the earth and up in heaven at the throne of God. Why did he use such a seemingly plain word as "wagons" instead of say, "Flying chariots of the gods" or something of that nature? What do we think of today when we think of wagons? Let's see, we have wagon-trains and Wells Fargo type wagons, some that are large and long and some that are short. The point here is that *"wagons"* can carry "lots of people". Enoch was apparently observing some sort of *large flying craft, carrying lots of people.*

The word Wagon also conveys the idea of some sort of travelling vehicle with wheels. The word "wheels" is used many times in the Bible to describe Gods flying "wagon" which was carrying Himself and the 4 Cherubim and was actually large enough to carry a lot more people if necessary.

EZE.1:16 "The appearance of the *wheels* and their work was like unto the colour of a beryl: and *they four had one likeness*: and their appearance and their work was as it were a *wheel* in the middle of *a wheel."* (Sounds like a large UFO as in the movie, Independence Day)

EZE.10:10 And as for their appearances, they four had one likeness, as if a *wheel had been in the midst of a wheel.*

C.4 Please see Ezekiel chapters 1 & 10.to get the full picture. If you are unfamiliar with those chapters, they will amaze you. Such fantastic descriptions given of God's own *flying chariot/wagon*)

END OF THE 2ND PARABLE

C.5 END means CONCLUSION and what a conclusion, given in only 2 verses!

CHAPTER 58

1 And I began to speak the Third Parable concerning the righteous and elect.

Comments:1: I think that, the reason that Enoch wrote some of his chapters, as very short chapters, sometimes only 2-3 verses, is because they contained a lot more information and wisdom than immediately meets the eye.

Those chapters *take more study:*

PRO.1:6 To understand a proverb, and the interpretation; the words of the wise, and their dark sayings.

1TI.4:15 "Meditate upon these things, give thyself wholly unto them that thy profiting may appear to all"

C.2 In this first verse, it mentions that this is the *third parable*.

Jesus in the New Testament, also often talked in parables:

Mark 4.34 "And without a *parable* He spoke not unto them."

John 16:25 These things have I spoken unto you in proverbs: but the time cometh, when I shall no more speak unto you in proverbs, but I shall shew you plainly of the Father.

Luke 8.10 "Unto you, (His disciples) it is given to understand the meaning of the parables, but unto them (Pharisees), it is not given, to understand."

2 Blessed are ye, ye righteous and elect, for glorious shall be your lot.

And the righteous shall be in the light of the sun. And the elect in the light of eternal life. The days of their life shall be unending, and the days of the holy without number. And they shall seek the light and find righteousness with the Lord of Spirits. There shall be peace to the righteous in the name of the Eternal Lord.

C.3 Here is a modern example using the word '*lot*': 'One must be happy with one's *'lot'* in life'.

C.4 'lot' here in the following verse of Daniel 12.13 means 'garden'.

DAN.12:13 But go thou thy way till the end be: for thou shalt rest, and stand in thy *lot* at the end of the days.

DAN.12:3 And they that be wise shall shine as the brightness of the firmament; and they that turn many to righteousness as the stars for ever and ever.

REV.7:16 They shall *hunger no more*, neither thirst anymore; neither shall the sun light on them, nor any heat.

3 And after this it shall be said to the holy in heaven, that they should seek out the secrets of righteousness, the heritage of faith. For it has become bright as the sun upon earth, and the darkness is past, and there

shall be a light that never ends, and to a limit of days they shall not come. For the darkness shall first have been destroyed and the light established before the Lord of Spirits. And uprightness established for ever before the Lord of spirits.

ISA.60:1 Arise, shine; for thy light is come, and the glory of the LORD is risen upon thee.

ISA.60:2 For, behold, the darkness shall cover the earth, and gross darkness the people: but the LORD shall arise upon thee, and his glory shall be seen upon thee.

ISA.60:3 And the Gentiles shall come to thy light, and kings to the brightness of thy rising.

C.5 The time sequence is, leading up to the Millennium

CHAPTER 59

1 In those days mine eyes saw the secrets of the lightnings, and of the lights, and judgements they execute, and they lighten for a blessing or a curse as the Lord of spirits wills.

2 And there I saw the secrets of the thunder and how when it resounds above in the heaven, the sound thereof is heard, and he caused me to see the judgements executed of the earth, whether they be for well-being and blessing, or for a curse according to the word of the Lord of spirits.

And after that all the secrets of the 'lights and lightnings' were shown to me, and they lighten for blessing and for satisfying.

JOB.38:25 Who hath divided a watercourse for the overflowing of waters, or a way for the *lightning of thunder;*

JOB.38:35 Canst thou *send lightnings*, that they may go and say unto thee, '*Here we are?'*

Comment:1: *"send lightnings",* sounds like the *telephone* or *telecommunications.*

"Lights and lightnings" seem to have a lot to do with our modern society, and both electricity and telecommunications of all types.

REV.4:5 And out of the *throne* proceeded *lightnings and thunder and voices.*

C.2 *Light is also known to affect the cloud formations on the earth:*

JOB.38:24 By what way is the *light parted*, which *scatters the east wind* upon the earth?

C.3 Above it states that *'lights and lightnings'* were *shown to me,* and they *lighten for blessing and for satisfying.*

Sometimes *Lightning* is indeed dangerous and a *curse* and can kill people, start fires, and it is seen around exploding volcanoes at times. However, lightning or electricity can be channelled and used for *very good purposes*, or 'for *blessing and for satisfying'.*

Enoch could perceive these things 5000 + years ago. That is *absolutely staggering*!

CHAPTER 60

Book of Noah- a Fragment

1 In the year five hundred, in the seventh month, on the fourteenth day of the month in the life of (Noah).

In that Parable, I saw how a mighty quaking made the heaven of heavens to quake, and the host of the Most High, and the angels, a thousand thousands and ten thousand times ten thousand were disquieted with a great disquiet.

Comment:1: There was a mistake in the translation of this verse, and that is why I have put brackets around the word Noah. Why? Because this verse is clearly talking about Noah, although in the translation, the word Enoch was used

C.2 This *event* seems to be quite unique with *"mighty quaking made the heaven of heavens to quake"*. Sounds like God is angry! Another drastic event like this happened just before the *WRATH of GOD in Revelations 15.*

REV.15:8 And the *temple was filled with smoke from the glory of God*, and from *his power; and no man was able to enter into the temple, till the seven plagues of the seven angels were fulfilled.*

REV.15:4 Who shall *not fear thee, O Lord, and glorify thy name?* For thou only art holy: for all nations shall come and worship before thee; for **thy judgments** are made **manifest.**

2 And the Head of Days sat on the throne of His Glory, and the angels and the righteous stood around Him.

DAN.7:10 A fiery stream issued and came forth from before him: thousand thousand ministered unto him, and ten thousand times ten thousand stood before him: the judgment was set, and the books were opened.

3 And a great trembling seized me, and fear took hold of me, and my loins gave way. And dissolved were my reins, and I fell upon my face.

DAN.7:15 I Daniel was grieved in my spirit in the midst of my body, and the visions of my head troubled me.

4 And Michael sent another angel from among the holy ones and he raised me up, and when he had raised me up my spirit returned; for I had not been able to endure the look of this host, and the commotion and the quaking of the heaven.

DAN.10:8 Therefore I was left alone, and saw this great vision, and there remained no strength in me: for my comeliness was turned in me into corruption, and I retained no strength.

5 And Michael said unto me, "Why art thou disquieted with such a vision? Until this day lasted the day of His Mercy; and He hath been merciful and long-suffering towards those who dwell on the earth."

2 Ezdras 7.33 "And the *Most high* shall be revealed upon the *seat of Judgement*, and *compassions* shall pass away, and patience shall be withdrawn."

6 And when the day, and the power, and the punishment, and judgement come, which the Lord of Spirits hath prepared for those who worship not the righteous law, and for those who deny the righteous judgement, and those who take His name in vain. That day is prepared, for the elect a covenant, but for sinners an inquisition. When the punishment of the Lord of spirits shall rest upon them, it shall rest in order that the punishment of the Lord of Spirits may not come in vain, and it shall slay the children with their mothers and fathers. Afterwards the judgement shall take place according to His mercy and His patience.

ISA.26:10 Let *favour be shewed to the wicked,* yet will he *not learn righteousness*: in the land of *uprightness* will he *deal unjustly*, and will *not behold the majesty of the LORD.*

C.3 Even though there is going to be 1000-year reign of Christ in the Millennium, some of the wicked, who had been rebellious against God during the 7-year reign of the Anti-Christ, are even allowed to survive into the Millennium. However, at the end of the Millennium, they clearly rebel against God again, but this time are destroyed by fire from heaven.

REV.20:7 And when the thousand years are expired, Satan shall be *loosed out of his prison,*

REV.20:8 And shall go out to *deceive the nations* which are in the *four quarters of the earth, Gog, and Magog, to gather them together to battle: the number of whom is as the sand of the sea.*

REV.20:9 And they went up on the breadth of the earth, and compassed the camp of the saints about, and the beloved city: and *fire came down from God* out of heaven, and *devoured them.*

7 And on that day were two monsters parted, a female monster named Leviathan to dwell in the abysses of the ocean over the fountains of the waters.

2 Ezdras 6.49 Then thou didst keep in existence *two living creatures*; the name of one thou didst call *Behemoth* and the name of the other *Leviathan;* and thou didst separate one from the other.

8 But the male is named Behemoth who occupied with his breast a waste wilderness named Duidain, on the east of the garden where the elect

and righteous dwell, where my grandfather (Enoch) was taken up, the seventh from Adam, the first man whom the Lord of Spirits created.

9 And I besought the other angel that he should show me the might of those monsters, how they were parted on one day and cast, the one into the abysses of the sea, and the other unto the dry land of the wilderness.

BEHEMOTH & LEVIATHAN (See APPENDIX XXIV)

10 And he said unto me, "Thou son of man, herein thou dost seek to know what is hidden."

11 And the other angel who went with me and showed me what as hidden, told what is the first and the last in heaven in the height and 'beneath the earth', in the depth and at the ends of the heaven, and on the foundation of the heaven.

C.4 *"Hidden"* could not only mean *many areas of the earth and in the earth,* but also the *spirit world* as well. Enoch was privileged to have been shown the *higher* and *lower dimensions,* and what was in *control* of our *physical* universe, *hidden* in the background. Our physical world is like seeing the ornate face of an old-fashioned pocket watch. The intricate inner workings of the watch are "hidden" behind the ornate face of the watch. You can only see the hands of the watch on the surface, which is enough to tell you the time. Without the *"hidden"* inner workings, the watch simply could not function.

12 And the chambers of the winds, and how the winds are divided, and how they are weighed, and how the portals of the winds are reckoned, each according to the power of the winds, and the lights of the moon, and according to the power that is fitting; and the divisions of the stars according to their names, and how all the divisions are divided; and the thunders according to the places where they fall, and all the division that are made among the lightnings, that it may lighten, and their host that they at once obey.

C.5 *"Chambers"* Here it would indicate the *inner workings* of the winds. It also mentions *portals* again. These are not things we can observe, today in our modern world. I think Enoch was trying to get the point across that there is a *perfectly balanced control system* behind our world and universe. Even the winds and lightnings and the stars *obey* God's slightest command.

MAT.8:27 But the men marvelled, saying, 'What manner of man is this, that *even the winds* and the *sea obey him!'*

13 For the thunder has places of rest, which are assigned to it, while it is waiting for its peal; and the thunder and lightning are inseparable, and although not one and undivided, they both go together through the spirit and separate not. For when the lightning lightens, the thunder utters its voice, and the spirit enforces a pause during the peal, and divides equally between them; for the treasury of the peals is like the sand, and each one

of them as it peals is held back with a bridal, and turned back by the power of the spirit, and pushed forward according to the many quarters of the earth.

C.6 *"thunder* and *lightning* are *inseparable*, both go together *through the spirit"* Apart from this being an explanation of how lightning and thunder works, it could actually have a much deeper meaning.

If we, for a moment think allegorically of God, as *thunder,* and His Son as *lightning* and the Holy Spirit as the *Spirit of God,* then this verse, could also be stating that God, and Jesus, and the Holy Spirit, *all work together,* but *are different in appearances*, and *function,* and that they are the *ones working behind the scenes* of *all creation* along with *God's angels.*

1JN.5:7 For there are *three* that *bear record* in heaven, *the Father, the Word, and the Holy Ghost:* and *these three are one.*

14 And the spirit of the sea is masculine and strong, and according to the might of his strength he draws it back with a rein, and in like manner it is driven forward and it disperses amid all the mountains of the earth. And the spirit of the hoar-frost is his own angel, and the spirit of the hail is a good angel. And the spirit of the snow had forsaken his chambers on account of his strength. There is a special spirit therein, and that which ascends from it is like smoke, and its name is frost.

C.7 This reminds me of Disney's famous cartoon "Fantasia", showing the Frost Fairies, and Snow fairies, and other fairies from different seasons of the year. Obviously, somebody takes care of all of the nature, and as it is God, He likes to assign jobs to those under Him, including angels and perhaps even fairies (little angels). Just a thought!

C.8 Notice how many times Enoch mentions the word 'spirits' and 'angels', as working in the background, behind the physical creation.

15 And the spirit of the mist is not united with them in their chambers, but it has a special chamber; for its course is glorious both in light and darkness, and in winter and in summer and in its chamber is an angel. And the spirit of the dew has its dwelling at the ends of the heaven, and is connected with the chambers of the rain, and its course is in the winter and the summer: and its clouds and the clouds of the mist are connected, and the one gives to the other.

C.9 It is indeed, very interesting to realize, that originally God had *angels* in charge of, and caring diligently for the *mist and dew and rain.* (Unfortunately, in modern times man is messing around, and altering the weather, and it must be giving God's angels a hard time.) [See Appendix Notes])

16 And when the spirit of the rain goes forth from its chamber, the angels come and open the chamber and lead it out, and when it is diffused over

the whole earth it unites with the water on the earth, and when so ever it unites with the water on earth. For the waters are for those who dwell on the earth; for they are nourishment for the earth from the Most High who is in heaven; therefore there is a measure for the rain, and the angels take it in charge.

17 And these things I saw towards the garden of the Righteous; and the angel of peace who was with me said unto me, "These two monsters, prepared conformably to the greatness of God, shall feed..."

C.10 What do *large monsters* feed on? We have all seen paintings or pictures from the past, and dismissed them are pure fantasy, in the which sailors had claimed that their ship was attached by *giant monster sea-creatures*. However strangely enough, more and more in modern times, it is being evidenced that giant squid exist, and some creatures so big, that they can take a giant bite out of the white shark or the biggest "known" shark in the sea.

"Those who have been *destroyed by the desert*; and who have been *devoured by the beasts,* and those who have been *devoured by the fish of the sea.*"- **Enoch 61.5** (See also Appendix Notes)

CHAPTER 61

1 And I saw in those days how *long cords* were *given to those angels*, and they took to themselves wings and flew, and they went towards the *north.*

2 And I asked the angel, saying unto him, "Why have those angels taken those cords and gone off?" And he said unto me, "They have gone to measure."

EZE.40:3 And he brought me thither, and, behold, there was a man, whose appearance was like the appearance of brass, with a *line of flax* in his hand, and a *measuring reed;* and he stood in the gate.

REV.11:1 And there was given me a *reed* like unto a *rod:* and the angel stood, saying, Rise, and *measure* the temple of God, and the altar, and them that worship therein.

3 And the angel who went with me said unto me, "These shall bring the measures of the righteous, and the ropes of the righteous to the righteous, that they may stay themselves on the name of the Lord of Spirits for ever and ever."

Comment:**1**: Key word: *Measure*

A *measure* here, determines an *exact* length or distance, and in this *particular case*, what is the *exact truth* for the Righteous, that they can *hold onto*, through thick and thin in this life.

The righteous "stay themselves" on the ROCK, CHRIST JESUS.

JOH.14:6 Jesus says unto him, I am the *way,* the *truth*, and *the life*: *no man cometh unto the Father, but by me*

ACT.4:12 Neither is there *salvation* in any other: for there is *none* other *name* under heaven given among men, whereby we must be *saved*

4 The elect shall begin to dwell with the elect, and those are the measures which shall be given to faith, and which shall strengthen righteousness.

C.2 The **Elect of all time,** shall **live together in God's heavenly city**, as described in **Revelation Ch 21 & 22.**

MAT.24:31 And he shall send his angels with a great sound of a trumpet, and they shall gather together his *elect* from the four winds, from one end of heaven to the other.

JOH.14:2 In my Father's house are *many mansions*: if it were not so, I would have told you. I go to prepare a place for you.

JOH.14:3 And if I go and *prepare a place* for you, I will come again, and receive you unto myself; that where I am, there ye may be also.

REV.21:3 And I heard a great voice out of heaven saying, Behold, the *tabernacle of God* is with men, and he will dwell with them, and *they shall be his people*, and God himself shall be with them, and be their God.

5 And these measures shall reveal all the secrets of the depths of the earth, and those who have been destroyed by the desert; and who have been devoured by the beasts, and those who have been devoured by the fish of the sea.

That they return and stay themselves on the day of the Elect One. For none shall be destroyed before the Lord of Spirits, and none can be destroyed.

C.3 Looking up the word *"Elect"*, we only find this word in the Bible in the New Testament, referring to those who *believe* and have received *Jesus* as their *Saviour*. If the followers of Jesus are called the *"Elect"* in the *New Testament*, then by deduction, the *"Elect One"* mentioned many times by *Enoch*, is obviously talking about *Jesus* himself, as both the *Son of God,* and as the *Messiah*.

6 And all who dwell above in heaven, received a command and power and one voice and one light like unto fire. And that (Elect) One with their first words they blessed, and extolled and lauded with wisdom, and they were wise in utterance and in the spirit of life. And the Lord of Spirits placed the elect one on the throne of glory.

And he shall judge all the works of the holy above in heaven.

C.4 Here we clearly see, God the Father, placing His Only Begotten Son Jesus, on the *"throne of glory"*.

7 And when he shall lift up his countenance to judge their secret ways according to the word of the name of the Lord of Spirits, and their path according to the way of righteous judgement of the Lord of Spirits; then shall they all with one voice speak and bless, and glorify and extol and sanctify the name of the Lord of spirits

JOH.1:1 In the beginning was *the Word,* and the *Word was with God*, and *the Word* was God.

JOH.1:2 The *same* was in the *beginning with God.*

JOH.1:3 *All things were made by him*; and *without him (Jesus)*, was *not anything made* that was *made.*

8 And he will summon all the host of the heavens, and all the holy ones above, and the host of God, the Cherubic, Seraphim and Ophanim, and all the angels of power, and all the angels of principalities, and the Elect

One, and the powers on the earth and over the water. (**See Appendix XX**)

9 On that day shall raise one voice, and bless and glorify and exalt in the spirit of faith and in the spirit of wisdom, and in the spirit of patience, and in the spirit of mercy, and the spirit of judgement and of peace, and in the spirit of goodness, and shall all say with one voice, "Blessed is He, and may the name of the Lord of Spirits be blessed for ever and ever."

MAT.23:39 For I say unto you, Ye shall not see me henceforth, till ye shall say, 'Blessed is he that comes in the name of the Lord.'

10 All who sleep not above in heaven shall bless Him. All the holy ones who are in heaven shall bless Him, and all the elect who dwell in the garden of life, and every spirit of light who is able to bless, and glorify, and extol, and hallow Thy blessed name, and all flesh shall beyond measure glorify and bless Thy name for ever and ever.

C.5 The Old Testament *elect* used to dwell in the *"Garden of Life"* inside the earth, or also known as *"Paradise"*, or the *"Bosom of Abraham"*, until Jesus died on the cross, and descended into Hell for 3 days, in order to witness to those, who had lived and died at the time of Noah's Flood.

Jesus also went into hell, in order to fight against Satan and his forces, and as a result, took the *keys of Death & Hell* away from Satan, and took with Him all *the saints* of that time, from Adam unto the time of Christ, and *took them all up to heaven*, along with those who *repented f*rom the times from before *the Flood.*

Some of these Old Testament Saints, were actually *seen walking around* Jerusalem, and being a testimony unto many after *Christ's Resurrection*.

REV.1:18 "I am he that lives, and was dead; and, behold, I am alive for evermore, Amen; and have the *keys of hell and of death."*

MAT.27:52 "And the graves were opened; and many bodies of the saints which slept, arose,

MAT.27:53 And came out of the graves after his *resurrection*, and went into the holy city, and *appeared unto many."*

1PE.3:19 By which also he went and *preached unto the spirits in prison*;

1PE.3:20 Which sometime were *disobedient,* when once the longsuffering of God waited in the *days of Noah,* while the ark was a preparing, wherein few, that is, eight souls were saved by water.

11 For great is the mercy of the Lord of Spirits, and He is long-suffering. And all His works and all that He has created He has revealed to the righteous and elect, in the name of the Lord of Spirits.

CHAPTER 62

THE WRATH OF GOD

1 And thus the Lord commanded the kings and the mighty and the exalted, and those who dwell on the earth, and said, "Open your eyes and lift up your horns, if ye are able to recognize the Elect One."

Comments:1:

Key word: **Horn(s)**

"The kings and the mighty and the exalted" mentioned above have *horns*, which if literal, could be showing, that they are *demon kings*, and the evil rulers of the spirit world, who rule over the *kings of the earth*, from the *evil spirit world* or from the *netherworld.*

In the *Bible,* it mentions the word *horn,* but *not horns* in referring to *people.*

The word *horn* in the Bible seems to *take on a totally different meaning* than this word *horns*, that is mentioned in this *Book of Enoch*.

PSA.18:2 The LORD is my rock, and my fortress, and my deliverer; my God, my strength, in whom I will trust; my buckler, and the *horn* of my salvation, and my high tower.

JOB.16:15 I have sewed sackcloth upon my skin, and defiled my *horn* in the dust

NEW LIVING TRANSLATION OF THE BIBLE: for the word used above as "horn" **JOB 16.15** "I wear burlap to show my grief. *My pride* lies in the dust." Sometimes the word *horn* (singular) is *allegorical,* such as in *most passages* where it is *mentioned in the Bible (Job 16.15; Psalm 18.2; Ps112.9; Ps132.17; Luke1.69)*

HORN=MY PRIDE when it is speaking allegorical in the Bible.

Job speaks of Satan as the ruler over all the children of PRIDE

JOB.41:34 He beholds all high things: he is a *king* over *all* the *children of pride.*

C.2 Interestingly enough, in studying Bible prophecy, one notes that both in the Book of Daniel chapter 7, and Book of Revelations chapters 12 & 13 & 17, it does talk about horns.

In this case, allegorically talking about a ferocious Beast, with 7 heads and also with 10 horns: (Coming New World Order & Anti-Christ world leader will be the 7th head with its 10 horns)

REV.17:12 And the *ten horns* which thou saw are *ten kings*, which have received no kingdom as yet; but receive power as kings one hour with the beast (Coming Anti-Christ and his 10 Demon Kings, or at least demon-possessed physical kings)

DAN.7:7 After this I saw in the night visions, and behold a *fourth beast,* dreadful and terrible, and strong exceedingly; and it had great iron teeth: it devoured and brake in pieces, and stamped the residue with the feet of it: and it was diverse from all the beasts that were before it; and it had **ten horns.**

DAN.7:8 I considered the *horns,* and, behold, there came up among them another *little horn, (Anti-Christ),* before whom there were three of the first horns plucked up by the roots: and, behold, in this **horn** were *eyes like the eyes of man*, and a mouth speaking great things.

REV.12:3 And there appeared another wonder in heaven; and behold a *great red dragon*, having *seven heads and ten horns*, and seven crowns upon his heads.

REV.13:1 And I stood upon the sand of the sea, and saw a beast rise up out of the sea, having *seven heads and ten horns*, and upon his *horns* ten crowns, and upon his heads the name of blasphemy.

C.3 Conclusion: In this chapter of Enoch, the horns mentioned belong to ***demon kings***. Horns is sometimes talking about the "kings of the earth", as mentioned in the above verses from both Daniel and Revelations, which both mention the coming Anti-Christ world-wide kingdom, or the seventh world empire. (The 6 world empires so far, that have totally ruled the known entire world of its time in the past: 1) Egypt, 2) Assyria, 3) Babylon, 4) Medio-Persia, 5) Greece, 6) Rome) For this reason the prophets were shown the world governments of man, as ferocious ravenous monstrous beasts, and the 7th beast with 10 horns. Each of the beasts, in its time, gets worse than the one that preceded it.

Amazingly enough Enoch, saw the conclusion of these 7 world empires, and the final judgement of both the Demon Kings and the Kings of the Earth.

2 And the Lord of Spirits seated himself upon the throne of His glory. And the spirit of righteousness was poured out upon him. The word of his mouth slays all the sinners, and all the unrighteous are destroyed from before his face.

C.4 "*spirit of righteousness was poured out upon him"*

This is interesting, as we all know that God Himself is All-Powerful, All-Mighty, and Omni-present, and it is stated that even though He is surrounded by thousands of people, "He doesn't need a counsellor". However, God, obviously chooses, to listen to others, and He especially likes to pass down responsibility, to those around Him, showing that He both loves them and trusts them.

We traditionally, have the image that God *always has "the spirit of righteousness". The above verse "spirit of righteousness was poured out upon him",* gives the impression that *someone else*, or some other being or angel, was responsible for pouring out this "righteousness upon God Himself" on this special occasion. *Who could be counted worthy enough to do that?*

I believe it *very likely* that it is the *Holy Spirit herself*, who is the one who is pouring out this *spirit of righteousness* upon God.

Remember that God the Father and God the Son and God the Holy Spirit are different from each other, and have different attributes, and yet totally agree in One.

Maybe "righteousness" is a special attribute of the Holy Spirit herself, who is also known as WISDOM in Proverbs 8, and she is both female, and God's wife.

So who better to give God one of *her* attributes, when He needs them more than ever for this occasion of the **WRATH OF GOD.**

C.5 "*The word of his mouth* slays all the sinners"

I would like to reiterate that when Enoch talks about 'sinners', he is actually talking about '*totally incorrigible degenerates*', not the word sinners as used so generally in modern times.

REV.19:15 And out of his mouth goes a sharp sword, that with it he should smite the nations: and he shall rule them with a rod of iron: and he treads the winepress of the fierceness and wrath of Almighty God.

REV.19:21 And the remnant were slain with the sword of him that sat upon the horse, which sword proceeded out of his mouth:

2TH.1:8 In *flaming fire taking vengeance* on them that know not God, and that obey not the gospel of our Lord Jesus Christ:

3 And there shall stand up in that day all the kings and the mighty, and the exalted and those who hold the earth, and they shall see and recognize how he sits on the throne of his glory, and righteousness is judged before him, and no lying word is spoken before him. Then shall pain come upon them as on a woman in travail, and she in pain is bringing forth.

C.6 'No lying word is spoken before Him'. The Bible does not speak well of *LIARS:*

REV.21:27 And there shall in no wise enter into it anything that defiles, neither whatsoever worketh abomination, or *makes a lie*: but they which are written in the Lamb's book of life.

REV.22:15 For without are dogs, and sorcerers, and whoremongers, and murderers, and idolaters, and whosoever loveth and *makes a lie.*

1JN.2:22 Who is a *liar* but he that denies that *Jesus is the Christ?* He is *antichrist, that denies the Father and the Son.*

1JN.2:23 Whosoever *denies the Son*, the same *hath not the Father:* He that acknowledges the *Son hath the Father also.*

From the above verses we are obviously talking about very evil people, who *perpetually LIE*, and *fabricate lies* as a profession. This class of people, such the *great MERCHANTS* of the earth, who deceive nations for gain, and who have no conscience at all about their deceptions, LIES and cheating, and resultant terrible suffering of the poor, whom they cheat, rob, murder and subjugate, in order to gain even more power & wealth, but most of all total control.

REV.18:23 For thy *merchants* were the *great men* of the earth; for by thy *sorceries* were all nations *deceived.*

C.7 In the not too distant future, starting with the Kings of the earth, *"no lying word"* is spoken before God.

In the coming *Millennium or the Golden Age*, of Christ's 1000 years reign on earth, no-one will be able to get away with *LYING!* Sounds good, doesn't it. Everyone will have to learn to be honest.

4 And one portion shall look on the other, and they shall be terrified, and they shall be downcast of countenance and pain shall seize them, when they see that Son of Man sitting on the throne of His glory. And the kings and the mighty and all who possess the earth shall bless and glorify and extol him who rules over all, who was hidden.

C.8 It states in the **Book of Enoch 68.4** that the *"fallen angels do, as if they were the Lord".*

Isn't this also how the Elite today, like to think that they are *'invincible'* & that *'they rule the planet'* behave: That they won't be held to account, for all their heinous iniquities and diabolical abominations?

In this above verse, finally they *are brought to account*, and they see and recognize each other, and simply can't believe what is happening to them-*Judgement by Christ on His throne.*

5 For from the beginning the Son of Man was hidden. And the Most High preserved him in the presence of His might, and revealed him to the elect. And the congregation of the elect and holy shall be sown, and all the elect shall stand before him on that day.

C.9 The truth about Jesus being the Son of God, and One of the Trinity, as some call them, was hidden for thousands of years. In the Apocryphal book 2nd Ezdras, God talked about His Son the Messiah.

In the *Book of Daniel 7*, it clearly mentions *two beings together,* God the Father and God the Son.

DAN.7:13 I saw in the night visions, and, behold, one like the *Son of man (Jesus)* came with the clouds of heaven, and came to the *Ancient of days*, and they brought him near before him.

DAN.7:14 And there was given him dominion, and glory, and a kingdom, that all people, nations, and languages, should serve him: *his dominion is an everlasting dominion*, which shall not pass away, and *his kingdom that which shall not be destroyed.*

ACT.7:56 And said, Behold, I see the heavens opened, and the *Son of man* standing on the *right hand of God.*

C.10 The religious Jews are famous for quoting *"The Lord are God is One God".* However, when one looks at the original Hebrew, it uses the plural form- 'Elohim', and actually says "*The Lords are Gods, are one God*".

REV.19:19 And I saw the beast, and the kings of the earth, and their armies, gathered together to make war against him *(Jesus)* that sat on the horse, and against his army.

REV.19:20 And the beast was taken, and with him the false prophet that wrought miracles before him, with which he deceived them that had received the 'mark of the beast', and them that worshipped his image. These both were cast alive into a lake of fire burning with brimstone.

REV.19:21 And the remnant were slain with the sword of him that sat upon the horse, which sword proceeded out of his mouth: and all the fowls were filled with their flesh.

REV.20:10 And the Devil that deceived them was cast into the lake of fire and brimstone, where the beast and the false prophet are, and shall be tormented day and night for ever and ever.

C.11 Satan has always been trying to minimize the 'Saviour' and 'Messiah' 'Jesus Christ', even though there are at least 300 prophecies about Jesus, hundreds to yet thousands of years, before his birth, in the Bible alone, not to mention the apocryphal books, some of which also prophecy about Jesus, as the coming Messiah. Satan has always hated Jesus with a vengeance, because Satan always thought that he himself, should be God.
So, Satan inspires people to lie, and negate the truth about Jesus as the true Saviour, and as the Messiah.
Satan also knows, that it will be *Jesus* who eventually *defeats him.*

Stephen, the 1st martyr of the early church really nailed this topic in his railing address to the Pharisees, who had him killed immediately afterwards, for his exposure of their hypocritical traditions and laws, just like they did Jesus.

ACT.7:52 'Which of the prophets have not your fathers persecuted?' 'And they have slain them which shewed before of the *coming of the Just One*; of whom ye have been now the *betrayers* and *murderers'*

ACT.7:53 'Who have *received the law* by the *disposition of angels,* and have *not* kept it.'

Think of this verse for a moment: Stephen was stating that many of the laws which the Jews held to 2000 years ago, were actually not given to them by God, but by the '*disposition of angels',* or in other words, from 'fallen angels' and demons.
Jesus Himself said, "Ye by your *traditions* have made the *laws of God* of none effect." - **MAR.7:13**
Jesus was saying to them, that it was much more important having *mercy and*

compassion on the people, than being so judgemental and trying to keep so many ridiculous laws.

Jesus stated, that there were *only two laws*:

MAT.22:37-40: 'Thou shalt love the Lord thy God with all thy heart, and with all thy soul, and with all thy mind.' And the second is like unto it, 'Thou shalt love thy neighbour as thyself.' 'On these two commandments hang all the law and the prophets.'

JOH.1:17 For the law was given by Moses, but grace and truth came by Jesus Christ.

6 And all the kings and the mighty and exalted and those who rule the earth shall fall down before him on their faces, and worship and set their hope upon that Son of Man, and petition him and supplicate for mercy at his hands; nevertheless that Lord of Spirits will so press them, that they shall hastily go forth from His presence, and their faces shall be filled with shame, and the darkness grow deeper on their faces, and he will deliver them to the angels for punishment to execute vengeance on them because they have oppressed His children and His elect.

7 And they shall be a spectacle for the righteous and for His elect. They shall rejoice over them, because the wrath of the Lord of spirits rests upon them, and His sword is drunk with their blood. And the righteous and elect shall be saved on that day, and they shall never thenceforth see the face of the sinners and unrighteous.

REV.19:19 And I saw the beast, and the kings of the earth, and their armies, gathered together to make war against him that sat on the horse, and against his army.

REV.19:20 And the beast was taken, and with him the false prophet that wrought miracles before him, with which he deceived them that had received the mark of the beast, and them that worshipped his image. These both were cast alive into a lake of fire burning with brimstone.

REV.19:21 And the remnant were slain with the sword of him that sat upon the horse, which sword proceeded out of his mouth: and all the fowls were filled with their flesh.

8 And the Lord of spirits will abide over them, and with that Son of Man, shall they eat, and lie down and rise up for ever and ever. And the righteous and elect shall have risen from the earth, and ceased to be of downcast countenance; and they shall have been clothed with garments of glory; and these shall be garments of life from the Lord of Spirits; and your garments shall not grow old, nor your glory pass away before the Lord of Spirits.

REV.7:14 And I said unto him, Sir, you know. And he said to me, "These are they which came out of great tribulation, and have washed their robes, and made them white in the blood of the Lamb.

REV.7:15 Therefore are they before the throne of God, and serve him day and night in his temple: and he that sits on the throne shall dwell among them.

REV.7:16 They shall hunger no more, neither thirst anymore; neither shall the sun light on them, nor any heat.

REV.7:17 For the Lamb (Jesus) which is in the midst of the throne shall feed them, and shall lead them unto living fountains of waters: and God shall wipe away all tears from their eyes."

CHAPTER 63

1 In those days shall the mighty and the kings who possessed the earth implore Him to grant them a little respite from His angels of punishment to whom they were delivered, that they might fall down and worship before the Lord of spirits, and confess their sins before Him.

Comment:1: *'mighty and the kings who possessed the earth'.* It is indeed going to be a very severe judgement for the rulers of the world under the coming *demon-possessed Anti-Christ*, not to mention the fallen angels, and their sons the former giants, who are now the disembodied spirits (demons) who work behind the scenes, to empower and inspire the 'mighty and the kings who possess the earth.'

C.2 It is interesting to note that at present the fallen angels '*act as if they were the Lord'*, and they blind themselves to what ultimately is coming their way- *terrible judgement.* Imagine having to pay for every single crime that they have committed over the past 6000 plus years. I sure wouldn't want to be in their boots. It always amazes me how that the biggest bullies are also the biggest cowards, when it comes to 'facing the music' for their crimes. When we consider the amount of devilish crimes committed on this planet over the past 6000 years, and that most of those crimes were inspired by devils and demons, then they are certainly *headed for the deep fry!*

REV.14:10 The same shall drink of the wine of the wrath of God, which is poured out without mixture into the cup of his indignation; and he shall be *tormented with fire and brimstone* in the presence of the holy angels, and in the presence of the Lamb (Jesus).

C.3 The beauty of accepting Jesus as our saviour, is that we don't have to pay for our sins, as Jesus washes them away.

1JN.1:9 If we confess our sins, he is faithful and just to forgive us our sins, and to cleanse us from all unrighteousness.

1JN.1:10 If we say that we have not sinned, we make him a liar, and his word is not in us.

C.4 Satan, along with the fallen angels were very dumb to have rejected Jesus, even before the creation of the world, which is the reason why they can't be forgiven, until they yield to God.

C.5 Satan and his entourage of evil spirits spend a lot of their time trying to dissuade the peoples of the earth from believing in Jesus, & in particular, *because He is the Word of God* and the ultimate nemesis of both Satan, and all of his evil powers and followers.

2 And they shall bless and glorify the Lord of spirits and say, "Blessed is the Lord of Spirits, and the Lord of kings, and the Lord of the mighty and the Lord of the rich, and the Lord of glory and the Lord of wisdom;

and splendid in every secret thing is Thy power from generation to generation, and Thy glory for ever and ever. Deep are thy secrets and innumerable, and thy righteousness is beyond reckoning."

REV.19:16 And he hath on his vesture and on his thigh a name written, KING OF KINGS, AND LORD OF LORDS.

3 We have now learnt that we should glorify and bless the Lord of Kings and Him who is king over kings: And they shall say, "Would that we had rest to glorify and give thanks, and confess our faith before His glory; and now we long for a little rest, but find it not. We follow hard upon and obtain it not. Light has vanished from before us, and darkness is our dwelling-place for ever and ever."

REV.14:11 "And the smoke of their torment ascends up for ever and ever: and they have no rest day nor night, who worship the beast and his image, and whosoever receives the mark of his name."

4 For we have not believed before Him, not glorified the name of the Lord of Spirits, nor glorified our Lord. But our hope was in the sceptre of our kingdom and in our glory. And in the day of our suffering and tribulation He saves us not, and we find no respite for confession. That our Lord is true in all His works, and in His judgements and His justice, and His judgements have no respect of persons. And we pass away from before His face on account of our works, and all our sins are reckoned up in righteousness. Now they shall say unto themselves, "Our souls are full of unrighteous gain, but it does not prevent us from descending from the midst thereof into the burden of Sheol." *[1]

5 And after that their faces shall be filled with darkness, and shame before that Son of Man, and they shall be driven from His presence, and the sword shall abide before his face in their midst.

6 Thus spoke the Lord of Spirits, "This is the ordinance and judgement with respect to the mighty and the kings and the exalted and those who possess the earth before the Lord of Spirits."

C.6 *[1] Sheol (Hebrew word): The grave & Hell, or unseen state:

DEU.32:22 'For a fire is kindled in mine anger, and shall burn unto the lowest hell, and shall consume the earth with her increase, and set on fire the foundations of the mountains'.

2SA.22:6 The sorrows of hell compassed me about; the snares of death prevented me.

JOB.11:8 It is as high as heaven; what canst thou do? deeper than hell; what canst thou know.

JOB.26:6 Hell is naked before him, and destruction hath no covering.

PSA.9:17 The wicked shall be turned into hell, and all the nations that forget God.

PSA.16:10 For thou wilt not leave my soul in hell; neither wilt thou suffer thine Holy One to see corruption.

PSA.18:5 The sorrows of **hell** compassed me about: the snares of death prevented me.

PSA.55:15 Let death seize upon them, and let them go down quick into hell: for wickedness is in their dwellings, and among them.

PSA.86:13 For great is thy mercy toward me: and thou hast delivered my soul from the lowest hell.

PSA.116:3 The sorrows of death compassed me, and the pains of hell gat hold upon me: I found trouble and sorrow.

PSA.139:8 If I ascend up into heaven, thou art there: if I make my bed in hell, behold, thou art there.

PRO.5:5 Her feet go down to death; her steps take hold on hell.

PRO.7:27 Her house is the way to hell, going down to the chambers of death.

PRO.9:18 But he knows not that the dead are there; and that her guests are in the depths of hell.

PRO.15:11 Hell and destruction are before the LORD: how much more then the hearts of the children of men?

PRO.15:24 The way of life is above to the wise, that he may depart from hell beneath.

PRO.23:14 Thou shalt beat him with the rod, and shalt deliver his soul from hell.

PRO.27:20 Hell and destruction are never full; so the eyes of man are never satisfied.

ISA.5:14 Therefore hell hath enlarged herself, and opened her mouth without measure: and their glory, and their multitude, and their pomp, and he that rejoices, shall descend into it.

C.7 Talking about Satan:

ISA.14:9 Hell from beneath is moved for thee to meet thee at thy coming: it stirs up the dead for thee, even all the chief ones of the earth; it hath raised up from their thrones all the kings of the nations.

ISA.14:15 Yet thou shalt be brought down to hell, to the sides of the pit.

ISA.28:15 Because ye have said, 'We have made a covenant with death, and with hell are we at agreement; when the overflowing scourge shall pass through, it shall not come unto us: for we have made lies our refuge, and under falsehood have we hid ourselves'

ISA.28:18 'And your covenant with death shall be disannulled, and your agreement with hell shall not stand; when the overflowing scourge shall pass through, then ye shall be trodden down by it.'

ISA.57:9 And thou went to the king with ointment, and didst increase thy perfumes, and didst send thy messengers far off, and didst debase thyself even unto hell.

EZE.31:16 I made the nations to shake at the sound of his fall, when I cast him down to hell with them that descend into the pit: and all the trees of Eden, the choice and best of Lebanon, all that drink water, shall be comforted in the nether parts of the earth.

EZE.32:21 The strong among the mighty shall speak to him out of the midst of hell with them that help him: they are gone down, they lie uncircumcised, slain by the sword.

EZE.32:27 And they shall not lie with the mighty that are fallen of the uncircumcised, which are gone down to hell with their weapons of war: and they have laid their swords under their heads, but their iniquities shall be upon their bones, though they were the terror of the mighty in the land of the living.

AMO.9:2 Though they dig into hell, thence shall mine hand take them; though they climb up to heaven, thence will I bring them down.

JON.2:2 And said, I cried by reason of mine affliction unto the LORD, and he heard me; out of the belly of hell cried I, and thou heard my voice.

HAB.2:5 Yea also, because he transgresses by wine, he is a proud man, neither keeps at home, who enlarges his desire as hell, and is as death, and cannot be satisfied, but gathers unto him all nations, and heaps unto him all people:

C.8 These two *chapters 62 & 63*, happen at the ***Judgement Seat of Christ***, which happens *after the **Wrath of God**,* and right before the ***Golden Age of Peace*** of the ***Millennial Kingdom of CHRIST*** **on earth.**

CHAPTER 64

1 And other forms I saw hidden in that place. I heard the voice of the angel saying, "These are the angels who descended to the earth, and revealed what was hidden to the children of men and seduced the children of men into committing sin."

Comment:1: *Angels are famous for changing their forms or appearances.* Satan is known to have originally been in a somewhat angelic form before being turned into a reptilian snake form*1. Satan has also been depicted as a great 7-headed red dragon*2, and also as the huge sea monster Leviathan*3. Of course, he and other evil fallen angels like him, are not bound to these forms.

2CO.11:14 And no marvel; for Satan himself is transformed into an angel of light.

*1 **GEN.3:1** Now the *serpent* was more subtle than any beast of the field which the LORD God had made. And he said unto the woman, 'Yea, hath God said, Ye shall not eat of every tree of the garden?'

*2 **REV.12:3** And there appeared another wonder in heaven; and behold a great red dragon, having seven heads and ten horns, and seven crowns upon his heads.

*3 **JOB.41:34** He beholds all high things: he is a king over all the children of pride.

C.2 Was Satan, the real father of Eve's first-born Cain?

The angels that originally rebelled, degenerated more and more over time into despicable forms. I think there is plenty of evidence on this planet of very strange looking creatures, seen by different peoples through time, created originally by these fallen angels, who can change their form at will.

There *are those who believe* that because of Adam and Eve's original disobedience of eating the fruit from the tree of the knowledge of good and evil, that this immediately gave the Devil the upper hand, and that later on, he *disguised himself as Adam*, unbeknownst to Eve, and made love with her, and the *Devil thus fathered Cain and introduced his evil seed into humanity, which was his intention all along, in the attempt to destroy the 'seed of the woman' or the descendants of Adam and Eve, and the promised coming Messiah.*

GEN.3:15 And I will put enmity between thee and the woman, and between thy seed and her seed; it shall bruise thy head, and *thou shalt bruise his heel.*

C.3 This would indeed explain the extreme negative behaviour of Cain's slaying his brother Abel for seemingly nothing. Cain seemed to have the spirit of Rage, which is demonic.

1JN.3:12 Not as Cain, who *was of that wicked one*, and slew his brother. And wherefore slew he him? Because his own works were evil, and his brother's righteous.

ANTIQUITIES OF THE JEWS BK 1. CH 2 (CONCERNING CAIN): 'He augmented his household substance with much wealth, by _raping_ and _violence_; he excited his acquaintance to procure pleasures and spoils by robbery, and became a great leader of men into wicked courses. He also introduced a change in that way of simplicity wherein men lived before; and was the author of measures and weights.' And whereas they lived innocently and generously while they knew nothing of such arts, he changed the world into _cunning craftiness_.

C.4 Was Cain the very first of the Merchants? Was Cain actually born of Satan?)

C.5 N.B. "Women ought to *keep their heads covered* because of *the angels.*" Even in Paul's time, he was *warning women of the dangers of deceptive shape-shifter angels*, who liked to *seduce women* and *trick them into evil perversions.*

1CO.11:10 For this cause ought the woman to have *power on her head* because of the angels.

C.6 If Satan could put enough of *his seed* either directly through himself or alternatively through his fallen angels, among mankind, he figured that 'no righteous seed would remain' and that all of humanity would thus be destroyed and none left fort Jesus to safe when He came to the earth. Satan almost succeeded right before the Great Flood as only 8 souls out of billions survived! Well that was Satan's plan, but as you can see his plan has utterly failed to stop the Messiah Jesus, from having been born. No matter what Satan attempts to do, he will *ultimately totally fail* and have to how-tow to Jesus in the end.

C.7 In doing research on this interesting topic, it has been the belief of many, for thousands of years that Satan, being the Great Deceiver, and the most subtle of creatures, beguiled Eve to eat the fruit from the Tree of the knowledge of Good and Evil.

To beguile also apparently can mean to *seduce.*

Later on, as Eve had already been led astray, by her to sin of deliberately blinding herself to God's Word, which had warned Adam and Eve that 'ye shall surely die', Eve was now in a state of unbelief. So, Satan took advantage of Eve, by disguising himself as Adam, in some unguarded moment.

C.8 It is also my conviction, that *Adam and Eve were teenagers*, and as such were sometimes spontaneous, hasty or even erratic in their actions, due to lack of experience and maturity. Perhaps Adam was one day off 'doing his own thing', while Eve was obviously left alone to ponder.

That's when the Devil seized his opportunity, as he *wanted to plant his seed into humanity*, in order to destroy the woman's seed, which was *destined to bring forth the Messiah and the Saviour of all mankind.* Satan wanted to pre-empt things from the very beginning, and stop the salvation of all mankind, so he disguised himself in the form of a beguiling Adam, & unbeknownst to both Eve and Adam, became the father of their very first son.

C.9 It is very shocking to think that the very first child born on this planet was a murderer, and as God Himself said, 'You have killed your brother for nought'. In studying this very interesting subject further it is clear that some people are indeed born as the Devil's children. Jesus made that very clear in His talk to the Pharisees who also ended up murdering Him:

JOH.8:37 I know that ye are Abraham's seed; but ye seek to kill me, *because my word hath no place in you.*

JOH.8:44 *Ye are of your father the devil*, and the lusts of your father ye will do. *He was a murderer from the beginning*, and abode not in the truth, because there is *no truth in him*. When he speaks a lie, he speaks of his own: for he is a liar, and the father of it.

C.10 SATAN WAS THE FIRST TO FALL, OF GOD'S ANGELS:

LUK.10:18 And he said unto them, I beheld Satan as lightning fall from heaven.

Perhaps Satan's initial beguiling, and later seducing Eve, gave the rest of the fallen angels their inspiration to do the same!

C.11 Later in time, eventually, one third of the angels of God fell; the Bible specifically dates that time as in the days of Jared or around 500 years after creation. The angels of God started falling, and started seducing the women on earth and cohabiting with them, procreating, and bring forth giants.

As mentioned before the angels didn't all fall at the same time. In time the women themselves learned to be seductive, and they deliberately wanted to attract more angels to fall.

C.12 Thus, God's Judgement of the Great Flood, which was actually caused, by the original *disobedience of Adam and Eve, under Satan's influenced*, & subsequently *the fallen angels meddling in human affairs.*

CHAPTER 65

1 And in those days Noah saw the earth that it had sunk down and its destruction was nigh; and he arose from thence and went to the "ends of the earth" and cried aloud to his grandfather Enoch, and Noah said three times with an embittered voice, "Hear me, hear me, hear me".

Comment::**1**: How was Noah physically able to travel to the ends of the earth? To travel, in his time to the "ends of the earth", must have been quite an undertaking, in order to find his great-grandfather Enoch who had already been "translated to the Garden of Eden", according to the Jewish Book of Jubilees. In the absence of modern transportation, how did people travel long distances before the Flood? Are we right about that assumption, or were there 'Portals'*1 in existence back then?

Jubilees 4.23 "And he (Enoch) was taken from amongst the children of men, and we (angels of God) conducted him into the garden of Eden in majesty and honour, and behold there he writes down the condemnation and judgement of the world, and all the wickedness of the children of men."

C.2 Secondly, *where is this specific location of the "ends of the earth"?*

It would appear that Noah must have been taken there by the angels, or by the Spirit of God in order to talk to Enoch, as Noah was to be the next most important vessel of the Lord God at that time, and it was necessary at some point for Enoch to pass on his books, that he had written in the Garden of Eden to Noah, who took the books with him on the Ark. (Book of Enoch 68.1 "And after that my grandfather Enoch gave me the teaching of all the secrets in the Book in the Parables, which had been given to him...")

There is evidence in the Bible, that when someone is desperate in prayer and is strong in the Lord's spirit, that their physical body can be moved from one place to another on a very special occasion. This is exactly what happened to Philip in the book of Acts.

ACT.8:26 And the angel of the Lord spoke unto Philip, saying, 'Arise, and go toward the south unto the way that goes down from Jerusalem unto Gaza, which is desert'.

ACT.8:29 Then the Spirit said unto Philip, 'Go near, and join thyself to this chariot.'

ACT.8:39 And when they were come up out of the water, the "*Spirit of the Lord" caught away Philip*, that the eunuch saw him no more: and he went on his way rejoicing.

C.3 Philip was later found at Antioch, about 200 miles away from where he had been witnessing to the eunuch.

CAVE OF MAKHPELAH

C.4 *What if some of the traditions from the Jewish Zohar are true?* According to this mystical book of the Zohar, Abraham bought a cave to bury Sarah, his wife in Makhpelah, only to find that within the cave, was another cave, and a passageway leading down into the earth, and that below the cave on the inner surface of the earth was the garden of Eden. Was that cave *some sort of 'Portal'* from the outer earth to the inner earth? If that was the case maybe, it wasn't so difficult after all for Noah to visit Enoch at the "ends of the earth" Maybe he only needed to travel to Makhpelah.

Here are some quotes about the Zohar, from a modern Jewish writer and investigator: "There is an Inner Earth and the Garden of Eden is at the centre of the Earth hundreds of miles down, directly underneath the Cave of Makhpelah." The astounding proclamation is stated ever so clearly in the Zohar and in other ancient sources. "The Garden of Eden is thus accepted by our Sages as a physical domain deep inside Inner Earth. Yet, just as the Garden is located there, so are there other domains, even the physical location of Gehinnom (Hell). These are not places of myth or the repose of the souls in the afterlife. They are accepted as being physical inhabited domains, whose inhabitants very much interact with us on a regular basis. They know all about us." (* See **Appendix** for more details on this strange story of Abraham and Sarah.)

2 And I said unto him, "Tell me what it is that is falling out on the earth, that the earth is in such evil plight and shaken, lest perchance I shall perish with it?"

C.5 Why would Enoch who had already been translated, and was in the Garden of Eden writing down his books, make such a statement as to say. "lest perchance I shall *perish* with it?"

If Enoch had already *died*, then surely, he would not have made such a statement? There have been possibly three people whom we know lived in the times of the Bible, who never physically died: 1stly Enoch, 2ndly Elijah and thirdly Moses.

3 And thereupon there was a great commotion, on the earth, and a voice was heard from heaven, and I fell on my face.

REV.4:1 After this I looked, and, behold, a door was opened in heaven: and the first voice which I heard was as it were of a trumpet talking with me; which said, 'Come up hither, and I will shew thee things which must be hereafter.'

4 And Enoch my grandfather came and stood by me, and said unto me, "Why hast thou cried unto me with a bitter cry and weeping?"

5 And a command has gone forth from the presence of the Lord concerning those who dwell on the earth that their ruin is accomplished, because they have learnt all the secrets of the angels, and all the violence of the Satans, and all their powers, the most secret ones, and all the power of those who practice sorcery, and the power of witchcraft, and the power of those who make molten images for the whole earth.

Jubilees:5.6 "And against the (Fallen) angels whom He had sent upon the earth,

He was exceedingly wroth, and He gave commandment to root them out of their dominion, and He bade us (angels) to bind them in the depths of the earth."

Jubilees 5.9 "And He sent His sword into their midst (Giants, the sons of the fallen angels) that each should slay his neighbour, and they began to slay each other till they all fell by the sword and were destroyed from the earth."

6 And how silver is produced from dust of the earth, and how soft metal originates in the earth. For lead and tin are not produced from the earth like the first; it is a fountain that produces them, and an angel stands therein, and that angel is pre-eminent.

C.6 The only fountain that comes to mind is a volcanic fountain of boiling liquid metals. It certainly would have to be very hot for the lead and tin to be coming out of a fountain. I have just studied about volcanoes, and was pleasantly surprised, to see that it mentions lead and many metals and even diamonds are that are formed by volcanic activity.

7 And after that my grandfather Enoch took hold of me by the hand and raised me up, and said unto me, "Go, for I have asked the Lord of Spirits as touching this commotion on the earth."

8 And he said unto me, "Because of their unrighteousness their judgement has been determined upon and shall not be withheld by Me for ever. Because of their sorceries which they have searched out and learnt, the earth and those who dwell upon it shall be destroyed. And they, they have no place of repentance for ever, because they have shown them what was hidden and they are the damned; but as for thee, my son, the Lord of Spirits knows that thou art pure, and guiltless of this reproach concerning the secrets."

C.7 'And they, they have no place of repentance for ever'-This referring to the fallen angels.

Jubilees 5.2 "And lawlessness increased on the earth and all flesh corrupted its way, alike men and cattle and beasts and birds and everything that walks on the earth- all of them corrupted their ways and their orders and they began to devour each other, and lawlessness increased on the earth and every imagination of the thoughts of all men was thus evil continually."

9 And He has destined thy name to be among the holy and will preserve thee amongst those who dwell on the earth and has destined thy righteous seed both for kingship and for great honours. And from thy seed shall proceed a fountain of the righteous and holy without number forever.

C.8 *The Genealogy of Luke chapter 3.23-38,* shows a line of the Kings of Judah going back from Christ Jesus to King David to Abraham to Noah to Enoch and back all the way to Adam: I have deliberately compressed 15 verses in only one verse. The dots between names that follow indicate many generations in between. I only mention the most notable persons mentioned here in this genealogy.

LUK.3:23-38 And Jesus himself began to be about thirty years of age, being (as was supposed) the son of Joseph, which was the son of Heli,...... which was the son of (King) David,........ which was the son of ....Jacob, which was the son of Isaac, which was the son of Abraham, ...which was the son of Noah....son of Methuselah, which was the son of Enoch which was the son of Jared...... which was the son of Adam, *which was the son of God.*

CHAPTER 66

1 And after that he showed me the angels of punishment who are prepared to come and let loose all the powers of the waters which are beneath in the earth, in order to bring judgement and destruction on all who abide and dwell on the earth.

2 And the Lord of Spirits gave commandments to the angels who were going forth, that they should not cause the waters to rise but should hold them in check; for those angels were over the power of the waters.

Comment:1: These angels were in charge of the waters. As with many other things mentioned in this Book of Enoch, God is totally in control of everything that happens in His creation, and has angels in charge of everything, from the lightning to the seas and fountains of waters. Contrary to the teachings of modern science, happenings on earth are not just random, but perfectly controlled and perfectly timed by God and His agents.

ROM.1:20 For the invisible things of him from the creation of the world are clearly seen, being understood by the things that are made, even his eternal power and Godhead; so that they are without excuse.

3 And I, (Noah) went away from the presence of Enoch.

CHAPTER 67

1 And in those days the word of God came unto me, and He said unto me, "Noah, thy lot has come up before Me, a lot without blame, a lot of love and uprightness."

2 And now the angels are making a wooden building and when they have completed that task, I will place My hand upon it and preserve it. And there shall come forth from it the seed of life, and a change will set in so that the earth shall not remain without inhabitant.

Comment:1: According to the Bible and other Jewish books, God Himself commanded Noah to build the Ark. In this above verse, it would appear that in actuality, it was the angels that built the Ark or at first, seemingly so?

Or is there something we are missing here? Let's imagine for a moment that we are architects. In order for a large sophisticated structure to be build, such as say, a modern Ocean Liner, it would take lots of initial drawings, trial and error, testing, until the original design on paper was perfect.

Planning, Consolidation & Substantiation

Then the experts in different fields, would first be consulted in the building project, and finally the actual managers of manual labourers would have to be advised. The ship would not be slapped together in a big hurry, but it would be a long-term project. We have seen, so far, from the Book of Enoch, that there is a spiritual world behind the physical. It could be that the verse above, is talking about the design and preparation stage for the coming ARK, that Noah would be eventually be commanded to build by God Himself. How could God have given very specific plans and details as to how to build that great Ark, unless the plans had already been systematically drawn up well in advance. I propose, that God gave the initial research and planning job, to some of his angels. It is always the case, that before we see something substantiated in the physical realm, it has already been done or made somewhere in either the good or evil spiritual realms.

Another point is, that Noah was ordered to build the Ark, and as he build it, it was supposed to be a testimony to all, that God would soon bring the judgement of the flood. If mankind had seen angels building a large Ark, they would have run away in terror, as they had already had too much trouble with "fallen angels". So, we can be fairly sure, that it was indeed Noah who ended up building the Ark as a testimony to all of God's coming judgments.

GEN.6:13 And God said unto Noah, 'The end of all flesh is come before me; for the earth is filled with violence through them; and, behold, I will destroy them with the earth'.

GEN.6:14 Make thee an Ark of gopher wood; rooms shalt thou make in the ark, and shalt pitch it within and without with pitch.

GEN.6:15 And this is the fashion which thou shalt make it of: The length of the ark shall be three hundred cubits, the breadth of it fifty cubits, and the height of it thirty cubits.

GEN.6:16 A window shalt thou make to the ark, and in a cubit shalt thou finish it above; and the door of the ark shalt thou set in the side thereof; with lower, second, and third stories shalt thou make it.

3 And I will make fast thy seed before me for ever and ever, and I will spread abroad those who dwell with thee: it shall not be unfruitful on the face of the earth, but it shall be blessed and multiply on the earth in the name of the Lord.

GEN.9:1 And God blessed Noah and his sons, and said unto them, 'Be fruitful, and multiply, and replenish the earth.'

GEN.8:17 Bring forth with thee every living thing that is with thee, of all flesh, both of fowl, and of cattle, and of every creeping thing that creeps upon the earth; that they may breed abundantly in the earth, and be fruitful, and multiply upon the earth.'

C.2 God's original commandment to firstly Adam and Eve, and then also to Noah & his sons, right after the Flood was: "To be fruitful and multiply". See how modern man, has corrupted this law. There have been over 1 Billion abortions, since abortions were allowed in the USA, in the early 60's. **(Book of Enoch 69.12** "And the fifth (fallen angel) was name Kasdeja; this is he who showed the children of men all the wicked smitings of spirits and demons, and the *smitings of the embryo in the womb*, that it may pass away." (See **Appendix** for more on this topic.)

4 And He will imprison those angels, who have shown unrighteousness, in that burning valley which my grandfather Enoch had formerly shown to me in the west among the mountains of gold and silver and iron and soft metal and tin.

DAN.2:45 Forasmuch as thou saw that the stone was cut out of the mountain without hands, and that it brake in pieces *the iron, the brass, the clay, the silver, and the gold;* the great God hath made known to the king what shall come to pass hereafter: and the dream is certain, and the interpretation thereof sure.

5 And I saw that valley in which there was a great convulsion and a convulsion of waters. And when all this took place, from that fiery molten metal and from the convulsion thereof in that place, there was produced a smell of sulphur, and it was connected with those waters, and that valley of the angels, who had led astray mankind beneath that land.

C.3 This verse is obviously talking about the "lake of fire" inside the earth. It mentions the smell of sulphur typical of volcanoes and the verse specifically states where all the activity is going on.. *'beneath that land'.*

6 And through its valleys proceed streams of fire, where these angels are punished who had led astray those who dwell upon the earth. But those waters shall in those days serve for the kings and the mighty and the exalted, and those who dwell on the earth, for the healing of the body, but for the punishment of the spirit; now their spirit is full of lust, that they may be punished in their body, for they have denied the Lord of spirits, and see their punishment daily, and yet believe not in His name.

C.4 It is very interesting to know that it is true that today many wealthy people seek out sulphur baths, or ancient volcanic Roman baths, as the sulphur has a healing quality for the body. These verses would seem to indicate that the old seemingly dead volcanoes will one day come back to life and be both the punishment of wicked men on earth who used to bath in these waters, and more importantly, the fallen angels will be punished inside the earth in the inner circle of the lake of fire. One other interesting detail concerning SULPHUR, is that those on earth who claim to have met "aliens", or been kidnapped by aliens and taken to subterranean chambers below the earth, which I call mere "demons masquerading as aliens", that they often report noticing the smell of sulphur coming from these underground beings.

7 And in proportion as the burning of their bodies becomes severe, a corresponding change shall take place in their spirit for ever and ever; for before the Lord of spirits, none shall utter an idle word. For the judgement shall come upon them, because they believe in the lust of their body and deny the Spirit of the Lord.

1JN.2:15 Love not the world, neither the things that are in the world. If any man loves the world, the love of the Father is not in him.

1JN.2:16 For all that is in the world, the lust of the flesh, and the lust of the eyes, and the pride of life, is not of the Father, but is of the world.

1JN.2:17 And the world passes away, and the lust thereof: but he that doeth the will of God abides for ever.

8 And those same waters will undergo a change in those days; for when those angels are punished in these waters, these water-springs shall change their temperature, and when the angels ascend, this water of the springs shall change and become cold.

9 And I heard Michael answering and saying, "This judgement wherewith the angels are judged is a testimony for the kings and the mighty who possess the earth, because the waters of judgement minister to the healing of the body of the kings and the lust of their body; therefore, they will not see and will not believe that those waters will change and become a fire which burns for ever."

C.5 *Satan, the King Empires,* and his *fallen angels* have been responsible for all of man's world empires. Daniel 2 mentioned 5 of the empires including the LAST coming Anti-Christ Empire. All were symbolized as different METALS. Finally, it states in Daniel 2, that the Lord will arise to destroy the Anti-Christ Empire and the remnant of all these past 7 empires, and He Himself shall set up an everlasting kingdom that shall never be destroyed or pass away. According to the Book of Enoch all metals will be banned from the earth in the Coming Millennial Kingdom of Christ; as METALS have been behind nearly all WEAPONS of WAR. One day all of man's gold and silver and weapons of metal will be a testimony against him, as it will also be a testimony against the angels which are bound in this above-mentioned valley of fire and Brimstone.

GAL.6:7 Be not deceived; God is not mocked: for whatsoever a man soweth, that shall he also reap.

ISA.2:20 In that day a man shall cast his idols of silver, and his idols of gold, which they made each one for himself to worship, to the moles and to the bats;

REV.6:15 And the kings of the earth, and the great men, and the rich men, and the chief captains, and the mighty men, and every bondman, and every free man, hid themselves in the dens and in the rocks of the mountains;

REV.6:16 And said to the mountains and rocks, 'Fall on us, and hide us from the face of him that sits on the throne, and from the wrath of the Lamb'

REV.6:17 For the great day of his wrath is come; and who shall be able to stand?

CHAPTER 68

1 And after that, my grandfather (great-grandfather) Enoch gave me the teaching of all the secrets in the book in the Parables, which has been given to him, and he put them together for me in the words of the book of Parables.

2 And on that day Michael answered Raphael and said, "The power of the spirit transports and makes me to tremble because of the severity of the judgement of the secrets, the judgement of the angels; who can endure the severe judgement which been executed, and before which they melt away?"

3 And Michael answered again, and said to Raphael, "Who is he whose heart is not softened concerning it, and whose reins are not troubled by the word of judgement that has gone forth upon them because of those who have thus led them out?"

Comments:1: Even the angels of God are shocked at the severity of God's Judgments on the 'fallen angels', but can you really blame God for being so severe, when the fallen angels had literally totally messed up and destroyed nearly all of the peoples on the earth?

Back then, even the angels of God, could not have foreseen the long-term terrible results of all the rebellion, violence and perversion caused by 'Satan' and his 'band of fallen angels' and demonic powers and entities.

Because of the 'fallen angels' rebellion and evil ways, their offspring the giants and other monstrous hybrids, roamed the earth for centuries, causing absolute havoc prior to the Great Flood.

After the giants all killed each other in battle, then their spirits were the origins of the demons, who have subsequently tormented the peoples of the earth ever since.

If it wasn't for the protection of God's good angels, and God's direct intervention upon occasion, this world would have been totally destroyed by Satan, his fallen angels, and their sons the demons, thousands of years ago.

God has thwarted every major move of these evil entities to destroy all of mankind.

However, in the future, God's Wrath will be upon the earth again, as it was at the time of the Flood and for the same reason: Those same entities will have totally taken over the world again, and brought on the total enslavement of all of mankind with the infamous 'Mark of the Beast of Revelations Chapter 13, under the control of the coming Anti-Christ, who becomes none other than Satan himself trying to rule the earth with disastrous consequences.

After the Rapture, and God has taken all of his saved children home to Heaven, then comes the Wrath of God of Revelations chapter 16, which is the 2nd Judgement.

4 And it came to pass when he stood before the Lord of Spirits, Michael said thus to Raphael, "I will not take their part under the eye of the Lord; for the Lord of Spirits has been angry with them, because they do as if they were the Lord. Therefore all that is hidden shall come upon them for ever and ever; for neither angel nor man shall have his portion in it, but alone they have received their judgement for ever and ever."

C.2 Talking about the fallen angels: '**they do as if they were the Lord'**. What could this be talking about? One only has to study ancient mythology from all around the world, to see that behind ancient mythology there were some basic truths to the ancient myths, and resultant religions. So many of them describe what they saw as gods which had powers, and could fly upon flying vessels. Hundreds and hundreds of accounts showing the powers of the fallen angels, who indeed masqueraded to man, as if they were God himself, when in reality they are but powerful spiritual deceivers, who are still deceiving mankind today. (**See Appendix XIII: MYTHOLOGY & THE FALLEN ANGELS**)

This deception will increase in these Last Days according to 2 Thessalians 2.

2TH.2:3 Let no man deceive you by any means: for that day shall not come, except there come a *falling away first*, and that man of sin (the Anti-Christ or false Messiah) be revealed, the son of perdition;

2TH.2:4 Who opposes and exalts himself above all that is called God, or that is worshipped; so that he as God sits in the temple of God, shewing himself that he is God.

2TH.2:8 And then shall that Wicked (Satan) be revealed, whom the Lord shall consume with the spirit of his mouth, and shall destroy with the brightness of his coming:

2TH.2:9 Even him, whose coming is after the working of Satan with all power and signs and lying wonders,

2TH.2:10 And with all deceivableness of unrighteousness in them that perish; because they received not the love of the truth, that they might be saved.

2TH.2:11 And for this cause God shall send them strong delusion, that they should believe a lie:

2TH.2:12 That they all might be damned who believed not the truth, but had pleasure in unrighteousness.

CHAPTER 69

1 And after this judgement they shall terrify (be terrified) and make them to tremble, because they have shown this (the hidden secrets of heaven) to those who dwell on the earth.

Comment:1: The first 200 fallen angels *were terrified* because they were the ones who taught evil to those on the earth, before the Great Flood. The ones *terrifying* them *were* other angels of God's punishment. Now finally, they *were* judged and totally lost their 'high and mighty position' in pretending to be 'great gods' over mankind.

C.2 When one thinks about it, this does explain how different advanced civilizations existed before the Great Flood, including Atlantis, Lemuria and the Land of Mu. Unfortunately, all of man's advanced technology, (taught to man by fallen angels), only ended up killing mankind with terrible wars, that went on between the above-mentioned powerful kingdoms.

C.3 These advanced civilizations became descendants of the 'gods' who liked to appear as powerful 'gods and rulers' over the rest of mankind, all around the world. Many were honoured as 'gods' because they had flying vehicles, and had strange powers.

C.4 No wonder that God had to bring the Great Flood as:

GEN.6:4 There were giants in the earth in those days; and also after that, when the sons of God came in unto the daughters of men, and they bare children to them, the *same became mighty men which were of old, men of renown.*

GEN.6:5 And God saw that the wickedness of man was great in the earth, and that *every imagination of the thoughts of his heart was only evil continually.*

2 And behold the names of those angels and these are their names: the first is Samjaza, and the second Artaquifa, and third Armen, the fourth Kokabel, the fifth Turael, the sixth Rumjal, the seventh Danjal, the eighth Neqael, the ninth Baraqel, the tenth Azazel, the eleventh Armaros, the twelfth Batarjal, the thirteenth Busasejal, the fourteenth Turel, and the sixteenth Simapesiel, the seventeeth Jetrel, the eighteenth Tumael, the nineteenth Turel, the twentieth Rumarl. *

3 And these are the chiefs of their angels and their names, and their chief ones over hundreds and over fifties and over tens.

4 The name of the first Jeqon; that is, the one who led astray all the sons of God, and brought them down to the earth, and led them astray through the daughters of men. And the second was named Asbeel; he imparted to the holy sons of God evil counsel, and led them astray so that defiled their bodies with the daughters of men.

And the third was Gadreel; he it is who showed the children of men all the blows of death, and he led astray Eve, and showed the weapons of death to the sons of men, the shield and coat of mail, and the sword for battle, and all the weapons of death to the children of men. And from his hand they have proceeded against those who dwell on the earth from that day and for evermore.

REV.6:4 And there went out another horse that was red (The 2nd Horseman of WAR, red like fire and blood): and power was given to him that sat thereon to take peace from the earth, and that they should kill one another: and there was given unto him a great sword.

REV.6:8 And I looked, and behold a pale horse (The 4th Horseman of Death): and his name that sat on him was Death, and Hell followed with him. And power was given unto them over the fourth part of the earth, to kill with sword, and with hunger, and with death, and with the beasts of the earth.

C.5 This nasty character Gadreel, who sounds like Satan himself, actually taught mankind all kinds of weapons of warfare. No wonder God judged these fallen angels and bound the first 200 of them deep down in the earth. They were totally reprobate.

5 And the fourth was named Penemue; he taught the children of men the "bitter and the sweet", and he taught them all the secrets of this wisdom; and he instructed mankind in writing with ink and paper, and thereby many sinned from eternity to eternity and unto this day.

ECC.12:12 And further, by these, my son, be admonished: of making many books there is no end; and much study is a weariness of the flesh.

ECC.12:13 Let us hear the conclusion of the whole matter: Fear God, and keep his commandments: for this is the whole duty of man.

ECC.12:14 For God shall bring every work into judgment, with every secret thing, whether it be good, or whether it be evil.

C.6 What is the "bitter and the sweet" mentioned here? Is it talking about all kinds of herbs, meats used in potions for use in sorcery or in healings; and the summoning of evil spirits or alternatively the secret to driving away bad spirits as known in eastern religions.

A good example of "bitter and the sweet" is found in the Apocryphal Book of Tobias: "Then the angel said unto him, Take the fish and open the fish and take the heart and liver, and the gall (bitter) ..6.7 touching the heart and liver, if a devil or an evil spirit trouble any, we must make a smoke thereof before the man or the woman, and the party shall be no more vexed. 6.8 As for the gall, it is good to anoint a man that hath "whiteness in his eyes" (a type of blindness), and he shall be healed"

6 For men were not created for such a purpose, to give confirmation to their good faith with pen and ink. For men were created exactly like the angels, to the intent that they should continue pure and righteous, and death which destroys everything, could not have taken hold of them, but through this their knowledge they are perishing, and through this power it is consuming me.

GEN.3:6 And when the woman saw that the tree (Of the knowledge of Good and Evil) was good for food, and that it was pleasant to the eyes, and a tree to be desired to make one wise, she took of the fruit thereof, and did eat, and gave also unto her husband with her; and he did eat.

GEN.3:17 And unto Adam he said, 'Because thou hast hearkened unto the voice of thy wife, and hast eaten of the tree, of which I commanded thee, saying, 'Thou shalt not eat of it: cursed is the ground for thy sake; in sorrow shalt thou eat of it all the days of thy life'.

GEN.3:22 And the LORD God said, Behold, the man is become as one of us, to know good and evil: and now, lest he put forth his hand, and take also of the tree of life, and eat, and live for ever…

C.7 Most of Man's so-called knowledge of the Sciences and Medicine, is very often based on only half-truths at best, and thus most of what mankind has invented, since the beginning of time has been EVIL. As Jesus stated: "You can judge a tree by its fruit", and the fruit of man constantly "picking fruits" from the "tree of the knowledge of both Good and Evil", has mostly been Evil inventions continually.

7 And the fifth was name Kasdeja; this is he who showed the children of men all the wicked smitings of spirits and demons, and the smitings of the embryo in the womb, that it may pass away, and the smitings of the soul, the bites of the serpent, and the smitings which befall through the noontide heat, the son of the serpent named Tabaat; and this is the task of Kasbeel, the chief of the oath, which showed to the holy ones when he dwelt high above in glory, and its name is Biqa.

C.8 Kasdeja: this character was a particularly nasty fallen angel who also taught how to '*do away with unborn defenceless babies inside the womb*'. What a monster. Unfortunately, his influence is abounding on the earth today, when one considers 1,000,000,000 babies have been deliberately aborted since the early sixties!

C.9 He also taught the 'smitings of spirits and demons'& 'the smitings of the soul' This sounds like the kind of problem mentioned to Noah by his sons and grandsons after the Great Flood as mentioned in the Book of Jubilees:

Jubilees 10.1-2 The unclean demons began to lead astray the children of the sons of Noah, and to make them to err and destroy them. And the sons of Noah came to Noah their father and they told him concerning the demons which were leading astray and *blinding and slaying* his son's sons.

8 This angel requested Michael to show him the hidden name, that he might enunciate it the oath, so that those might quake before that name an oath who revealed all that was in secret to the children of men. And this is the power of this oath, for it is powerful and strong, and he placed this oath Akae in the hand of Michael.

9 And these are the secrets of his oath… And they are strong through his oath. And the heaven was suspended before the world was created, and for ever. And through it the earth was founded with water, and from the secret recesses of the mountains come beautiful waters. From the creation of the world and unto eternity. And through that oath the sea was created and its foundation He set for it the sand against the time of its anger. And it dare not pass beyond it from creation of the world unto eternity.

10 And through the oath are the depths made fast, and abide and stir not from their place from eternity unto eternity; and through that oath the sun and moon complete their course, and deviate not from their course, and deviate not from their ordinance from eternity to eternity. And through that oath the stars complete their course, and He calls them by their names, and they answer Him from eternity to eternity.

11 And in like manner the spirits of the water, and of the winds, and of all *zephyrs*, and their paths from all the quarters of the winds. And there are preserved the voices of the thunder and the light of the lightnings and there are preserved the chambers of the hail and the chambers of the hoarfrost, and the chambers of the mist, and the chambers of the rain and dew.

C.10 *Zephyrs* = "holy spirits" or those sent by the HOLY SPIRIT of God.

1KI.19:12 'And after the earthquake a fire; but the LORD was not in the fire: and after the fire a still small voice.'

PRO.8:30 Then I, (The Holy Spirit, in feminine form), was by him, as one brought up with him: and I was daily his delight, *rejoicing always before him*. The Holy Spirit has also been known as the "Wild Wind of God"

PRO.9:3 She (Wisdom=HOLY SPIRIT) hath sent forth her maidens (Other female spirits sent by the Holy Spirit Herself)

12 And all these believe and give thanks before the Lord of Spirits, and glorify Him with all their power, and their food is in every act of thanks-

giving; they thank and glorify and extol the name of the Lord of Spirits for ever and ever. And this oath is mighty over them and through it they are preserved and their paths are preserved, and their course is not destroyed. And there was great joy amongst them, and they blessed and glorified and extolled, because the name of that Son of Man had been revealed unto them.

13 And he sat on the throne of his glory and the sum of judgement was given unto the Son of Man, and he caused many sinners to pass away and be destroyed from of the face of the earth. Those who have led the world astray with chains shall they be bound, and in their assemblage-place of destruction shall they be imprisoned, and their works vanish from the face of the earth.

14 And henceforth there shall be nothing corruptible, for the Son of Man has appeared, and has seated himself on the throne of his glory and all evil shall pass away before his face, and the word of that Son of Man shall go forth and be strong before the Lord of Spirits. This is the third Parable of Enoch.

C.11 Keyword: *THE OATH*

What oath is this actually talking about that even Satan wanted to talk to Michael the archangel about? What NAME was HIDDEN. Notice how this verse mentions that Heaven (spirit world) existed before the creation of the earth and physical universe.

The secret here is that a lot went on before the creation in the spiritual realm and to cut a long story short: There came a day in Heaven when God came to present His Son (The Son of Man mentioned here) to all the angels and beings and peoples in Heaven and the rest of the Spirit World. God announced that this Son of Man (Jesus) was to become His only begotten Son, and for all to believe in Him. This is the tragic moment when Satan rebelled against God and decided against all counsel of those in heaven to rebel and go his own way. I have read that the Name of Jesus and the Name Joshua and Yahweh are all linked together. The Word *LOGOS* mentioned in John chapter 1.1 is also mentioned in the book of creation of Genesis 1.1, I won't go into the details of that right now as that would involve many other essays, but please check these things out for yourselves. You will be amazed want you will find out!

1JN.2:22 Who is a liar but he that denies that Jesus is the Christ? He is antichrist, that denies the Father and the Son.

C.12 The important point I want to bring out is that Satan was talking to Michael about the OATH. Why? He obviously hadn't fully understood what the OATH meant.

I believe that the Oath was originally made by God Himself when Satan rebelled. God realized with the Fall of His very top Archangel, that if He couldn't trust Satan, then, who could He really trust in Heaven and the greater Spirit world, when they were "put to the test"? It was then, that God made an Oath, that He would create another Reality. (The physical Dimension) He did this in order to test all of His creation to see if people would still believe in God and Jesus and His Holy Spirit, if they couldn't actually see Him and had to believe in Him by faith.*

It is clear that when God originally presented Jesus to those in Heaven, that a lot of things concerning Him were still hidden, as they are today. It is very possible that God was testing the people in Heaven to see, if they had faith to believe, when much was hidden from them they didn't know the whole picture concerning God's Son. Sadly, Satan and one third of the angels of God rebelled! I think that Satan rebelling was sort of a very premature decision by him being impatient to begin with.

REBELLION against God makes angels and humans BLIND spiritually speaking, and one mistake leads to yet another and another and down a very slippery path it leads down to Hell and the Lake of Fire for some.

In the not too distant future, Jesus will return in the 2nd coming and ALL shall see Him and we who have seen in a glass darkly will begin to see things very clearly concerning this Son of Man who will be ruling this physical universe.

PRO.13:13 Whoso despises the word shall be destroyed: but he that fears the commandment shall be rewarded.

JOH.1:1 In the beginning was the Word, and the Word was with God, and the Word was God.

JOH.1:2 The same was in the beginning with God.

JOH.1:3 All things were made by him; and without him was not anything made that was made.

PRO.14:14 The backslider in heart shall be filled with his own ways:

C.13 "Clearly Satan was destroyed by rejecting the Son of God before creation, and insanity took tight hold on him. Scriptures tell us that the Son of God is the Word of God and by Him everything in this physical realm was created. Satan was so blind that he simply didn't even recognize Jesus on earth in such a humble form of God Himself as part of the Trinity."

1JN.2:2 And he (Jesus) is the propitiation for our sins: and not for ours only, but also for the sins of the whole world.

1JN.2:5 But whoso keeps his Word (Jesus), in him verily is the love of God perfected: hereby know we that we are in him.

CHAPTER 70

1 And it came to pass after this that his name during his lifetime was raised aloft to that Son of Man and to the Lord of Spirits from amongst those who dwell on the earth; and he was raised aloft on the chariots of the spirit and his name vanished among them.

Comment:1: This sounds like the First coming of Christ and of His subsequent Ascension up to Heaven.

"His name vanished" among them. Could this possibly mean that after Jesus death, the Jewish nation minimized the Name of Jesus, and in fact in modern times, the name of Jesus has become a curse word instead of a word of blessing & honour & majesty and might. Sadly, the Pharisees' rejection of Jesus as the Messiah, has indeed led millions of people astray from the TRUTH, and damned countless souls to hell.

MAR.16:19 So then after the Lord had spoken unto them, he was received up into heaven, and sat on the right hand of God.

JOH.14:6 Jesus said unto him, I am the way, the truth, and the life: no man cometh unto the Father, but by me.

ACT.4:12 Neither is there salvation in any other: for there is none other name under heaven given among men, whereby we must be saved

2 And from that day I was no longer numbered amongst them; and he set me between the two winds, between the North and the West, where the angels took cords to measure for me the place for the elect and righteous.

3 And there I saw the first fathers and the righteous who from the beginning dwell in that place.

CHAPTER 71

1 And it came to pass after this that *my spirit was translated**, and it ascended into the heavens, and I saw the holy sons of God. They were stepping on flames of fire; their garments were white, and their faces shone like snow. And I saw two streams of fire, and the light of that fire shone like hyacinth, and I fell on my face before the Lord of Spirits.

C.1 *Translated:

HEBREWS.11:5 "By faith Enoch was *translated* that he should not see death; and was not found, because God had translated him: for before his translation he had this testimony, that he pleased God."

Jasher.36 "And it was upon the seventh day that Enoch ascended into heaven in a whirlwind, with horses and chariots of fire"

Jubilees 4.23 "And he was taken from amongst the children of men, and we (angels of God) conducted him into the Garden of Eden in majesty and honour…"

(Related: Enoch 12.1; Jasher Chapters 3-4; Jubilees 4.17-23)

2 And the angel Michael one of the archangels seized me by my right hand, and lifted me up and led me forth into all the secrets, and he showed me all the secrets of righteousness. And he showed me all the secrets of the ends of the heaven, and all the chambers of the stars and all the luminaries. Whence they proceed before the face of the holy ones.

3 And he *translated* my spirit into the heaven of heavens, and I saw there as it were a structure built of crystals, and between those crystals tongues of living fire; and my spirit saw the girdle which girt that house of fire and on its four sides were streams of live fire, and they girt that house.

4 And round about were Seraphim, Cherubic and Ophannim. And these are they who sleep not and guard the throne of His Glory; and I saw the angels who could not be counted, a thousand thousand, and ten thousand times ten thousand encircling the house: And Michael and Raphael and Gabriel and Phanuel and the holy angels who are above the heavens, go in and out of that house.

C.2 Who are the [1]***Seraphim,*** [2]***Cherubic and*** [3]***Ophannim?***

The key to understanding the [1]Seraphim is in Isaiah's description, "The Seraphim stood *above* Him." (Isa 6:2) The Seraphim are the two living creatures covering the throne from above, while the [2]Cherubim are the four living creatures covering the throne from beneath and the sides. The Seraphim are two in number and were seen by Isaiah as above the throne of God.

The Cherubim are four in number, seen in Revelation 4 and are always around the throne. In Ezekiel Chapters1 & 10, The [3]Ophannim is another name for *'living wheels' or a wheel within a wheel.* These 3 types of beings are seen together and concern the throne of God.

That is quite a study in itself, which you can read more details of in the Appendix.

(*See **Appendix XXI** concerning **Seraphim, Cherubic and Ophannim**)

5 And they came forth from that house, and Michael and Gabriel, Raphael and Phanuel, and many holy angels without number; and with them the Head of Days, his head white and pure as wool, and His raiment indescribable.

6 And I fell upon my face, and my whole body became relaxed, and my spirit was *transfigured**; and I cried with a loud voice, ...with the spirit of power, and blessed and glorified and extolled. And these blessings which went forth out of my mouth were well pleasing before that Head of Days.

C.3 CHRIST was also transfigured, and what is noteworthy, is that it happened quite some time before His actual physical death. He was met by Moses and Elias on the mountain where he was transfigured, where they talked to Jesus of His coming death:

MAT.17:2 And was transfigured before them: and his face did shine as the sun, and his raiment was white as the light.

MAR.9:2 And after six days Jesus taketh with him Peter, and James, and John, and leads them up into an high mountain apart by themselves: and he was transfigured before them.

MAR.9:3 And his raiment became shining, exceeding white as snow; so as no fuller on earth can white them.

MAR.9:4 And there appeared unto them Elias with Moses: and they were talking with Jesus.

C.4 Note how that Enoch was transfigured as was also Moses. Only a few people throughout Bible times were actually transfigured like Christ.

7 And that Head of Days came with Michael and Gabriel, Raphael and Phanuel, thousands and ten thousand of angels without number.

[Lost passage wherein the Son of Man was described as accompanying the Head of Days, and Enoch asked one of the angels (as in Enoch chapter 46.2) concerning the Son of Man as to who he was]

DAN.7:13 I saw in the night visions, and, behold, one like the Son of man came with the clouds of heaven, and came to the Ancient of days, and they brought him near before him.

8 And he (the angel) came to me and greeted me with his voice and said unto me, "This is the Son of Man, who is born unto righteousness; and righteousness abides over him, and the righteousness of the Head of Days forsakes him not." And he said unto me, "He proclaims unto thee peace in the name of the world to come; for from hence has proceeded peace since the creation of the world; and so shall it be unto thee for ever and ever."

9 And all shall walk in His ways since righteousness never forsakes him: with Him will be their dwelling-places, and with him their heritage, and they shall not be separated from him for ever and ever and ever.

JOH.14:1 Let not your heart be troubled: ye believe in God, believe also in me.

JOH.14:2 In my Father's house are many mansions: if it were not so, I would have told you. I go to prepare a place for you.

JOH.14:3 And if I go and prepare a place for you, I will come again, and receive you unto myself; that where I am, there ye may be also.

10 And so there shall be length of days with the Son of Man; and the righteous shall have peace and an upright way in the name of the Lord of Spirits for ever and ever.

CHAPTER 72

The Book of the Courses of the Heavenly Luminaries

The book of the courses of the Luminaries of heaven, the relations of each, according to their courses, their dominion and their seasons, according to their names and places of origin, and according to their months, which Uriel, the holy angel, who was with me, who is their guide, showed me; and he showed me all their laws exactly as they are, and how it is with regard to all the years of the world and unto eternity, till the new creation is accomplished which endures unto eternity.

Comment:1: I think that the word '*new creation*' is the interesting expression here. It wasn't until we got the Books of Jubilees 1500 BC & Isaiah in around 700 BC and then the Book of Revelations in around 90 AD, that the writers even talked about the NEW CREATION. What is absolutely both amazing, and wonderful, as a believer, reading the Book of Enoch, is that it is plain obvious that URIEL was, and is a real angel of God, who did indeed reveal the secrets of the courses of the Luminaries of heaven to Enoch over 5000 years ago. Note, that it is also the same angel, URIEL, who visited Ezra in 500 BC and gave him the "hidden" or "for the illuminated" Book of II EZDRAS.

2 And this is the first law of the luminaries the luminary the Sun has its rising in the eastern portals of heaven, and its setting in the western portals of the heaven.

And I saw six portals in which the sun rises, and six portals in which the sun sets and the moon rises and sets in these portals, and the leaders of the stars and those whom they lead; six in the east and six in the west, and all following each other in accurately corresponding order; also many windows to the right and left of these portals.

C.2 Enoch's description of the luminaries, or the sun the moon and stars is certainly very strange to those of us in modern times, and seemingly very odd to the science of modern astronomy that we have all been taught. It would seem that Enoch is indicating here in this chapter that the Earth, is the centre of the universe and that all the luminaries or stars and constellations all revolve around the earth. What are both these portals and many windows, which we obviously cannot see today? I would venture a guess to say that they are probably dimensional gates and windows.

In investigating the earth "being at the centre of the universe" theory, one finds that ancient civilizations all believed that the earth is in the centre of the universe. This also seems to be born out in the creation Book of Genesis:

GEN.1:10 And God called the dry land Earth; and the gathering together of the waters called he Seas: and God saw that it was good. (The 3rd Day of Creation)

GEN.1:14 And God said, Let there be lights in the firmament of the heaven to divide the day from the night; and let them be for signs, and for seasons, and for days, and years. (The 4th Day of Creation)

C.3 According to the Bible the earth was created before the Sun and the Moon and the Stars

As I have mentioned before the word Portals is a very difficult word in this particular text to pin down in physical terms, as it is not something that we can observe in modern times; but we should not be closed minded as scientists. It would seem that the original creation was in fact much more fantastic and beautiful than it is today in modern times.

From our limited perspective in this physical universe, we see only the face of the great watch of the universe. However, I think that Enoch was shown the inner workings of this great watch of both the space and time continuum, or perhaps more accurately stated the dimensions both above and below this physical one, and thus it looked very different to Enoch than to us in modern times, and he could actually observe what forces are behind this physical realm and how it is all controlled like a perfectly synchronized watch.

3 And first there goes forth the great luminary, named the Sun, and his circumference is like the circumference of the heaven, and he is quite filled with illuminating and heating fire. The chariot on which he ascends, the wind drives, and the sun goes down from the heaven and returns through the north, in order to reach the east and is so guided that he comes to the appropriate portal and shines in the face of heaven.

PSA.19:6 His going forth is from the end of the heaven, and his circuit unto the ends of it: and there is nothing hid from the heat thereof.

C.4 This sounds like one of those archaic mythological paintings of the sun being carried in a chariot and blown around the universe by the solar winds. We have all seen pictures like that, but perhaps as mentioned above, Enoch was actually seeing and observing the inner workings of the massive watch of this physical universe, so of course it is not going to make much sense to us today. As scientific minded persons, we must not immediately have the attitude that this is just the writings of a simple person in ancient times, who didn't know any better, lest we be like the guy who stated that he did not believe that London existed, simply as he personally had never seen it!

The following verses 4-20 for the rest of this chapter, show both the orbits of the sun and the positions and timings of the sun's rising each day of a 30-day month in ascending progression. Using a basis of 30 days in the month would give 360 days in the year. This is exactly the same measurements given in both the prophetic Books of Daniel and Revelations of 360 day/year. We in modern times count $365^{1/4}$ days in a year. What if we are wrong, and that the solar year of 360 days is right? This would mean that we are seriously in error in many of our calculations about astronomy. This all seems to be mentioned in the Book of Jubilees 1.13, that exactly this would happen.

Book of Jubilees 1.13 "And they will forget all My law and all My commandments and all My judgements, and will go astray as to new moons and sabbaths, and festivals and jubilees and ordinances."

Book of Jubilees 6.34 "They will go wrong as to all the order of years"

Book of Jubilees 6.36 "For there will be those who will assuredly make observations of the moon. How it disturbs the seasons, and comes in from year to year ten days too soon".

4 In this way he rises in the first month in the great portal, which is the fourth of those six portals in the cast. And in that fourth portal from which the sun rises in the first month are twelve window-openings, from which proceed a flame when they are opened in their season.

5 When the sun rises in the heaven, he comes forth through the fourth portal thirty mornings in succession, and sets accurately in the fourth portal in the west of the heaven. And during this period the day becomes daily longer and the night nightly shorter to the thirtieth morning.

6 On that day the day is longer than the night by a ninth part, and the day amounts exactly to ten parts, and the night to eight parts. And the sun rises from that fourth portal, and sets in the fourth and returns to the fifth portal of the east thirty mornings, arises from it and sits in the fifth portal.

7 And then the day becomes longer by two parts and mounts to eleven parts, and the night becomes shorter and mounts to even parts. And it returns to the east and enters into the sixth portal, and rises and sets in the sixth portal one and thirty mornings on account of its sign.

8 On that day the day becomes longer than the night, and the and becomes double the night, and the day becomes twelve parts, and the night is shortened and becomes six parts. And the sun mounts up to make the day shorter and the night longer, and the sun returns to the east and enters into the sixth portal, and rises from it and sets thirty mornings.

9 And when thirty mornings are accomplished, the day decreases by exactly one part, and becomes eleven parts, and the night seven. And the sun goes forth from that sixth portal into the west, and goes to the east and rises in the fifth portal for thirty mornings, and sets in the west again in the fifth western portal.

10 On that day the day decreases by two parts, and amounts to ten parts and the night to eight parts. And the sun does forth form that fifth portal and sets in the fifth portal of the west, and rises in the fourth portal from

one and thirty mornings on account of its sign, and sets in the west.

11 On that day the day is equalized with the night, and the night amounts to nine parts and the day to nine parts. And the sun rises from that portal and sets in the west, and returns to the east and rises thirty mornings in the third portal and sets in the west in the third portal.

12 And on that day the night becomes longer than the day, and the night becomes longer than night, and day shorter than day til the thirtieth morning, and the night amounts exactly to ten parts and the day to eight parts.

13 And the sun rises from that third portal and sets in the portal in the west and returns to the east, and for thirty mornings rises in the second portal in the east, and in like manner sets in the second portal in the west of the heaven.

14 And on that day the night amounts to eleven parts and the and to seven parts.

And the sun rises on that day from that second portal and sets in the west in the second portal, and returns to the east into the first portal for one and thirty mornings, and sets in the first portal in the west of the heaven. And on that day the night becomes longer and amounts to the double the day: and the night amounts to exactly twelve parts and the day to six.

15 And the sun has therewith traversed the divisions of his orbit and turns again on those divisions of his orbit, and enters that portal thirty mornings and sets also in the west opposite it. And on that night has the night decreased in length by a ninth part, and the night has become eleven parts and the day seven parts.

C.5 Observation: Did I just read that right? After studying at university many years ago, that the earth actually revolves around the sun, then the question I would ask here is, if "*his orbit*," is implying that the sun is orbiting something else, then what is it orbiting, if it is not the earth, especially when it also gives the exact time sequences in days and months and years? Here in the Book of the Luminaries, by Enoch, however, does it seem to indicate that the Sun actually orbits around the earth, or in scientific terms the sun is **GEO-CENTRIC** rather than **HELIO-CENTRIC**? (See **APPENDIX XIX** for more details)

16 And the sun has returned and entered into the second portal in the east, and returns on those his divisions of his orbit for thirty mornings, rising and setting. And on that day the night decreases in length, and the night amounts to ten parts and the day to eight.

17 And on that day the sun rises from that portal, and sets in the west, and returns to the east, and rises in the third portal for one and thirty mornings, and sets in the west of heaven. On that day the decreases and amounts to nine parts, and the day to nine parts, and the night is equal to the day and the year is exactly as to its days three hundred and sixty four.

Jubilees 6.32 "And command the children of Israel that they observe the years according to this reckoning-three hundred and sixty-four days, and these will constitute a complete year…33 But if they do not observe them according to this commandment, they will disturb all their seasons and the years will disturb the season and the years will be dislodged.."

C.6 This is interesting that well before the Flood or around 5000 years ago, Enoch recorded the year as being supposedly 364 days long. By the time of Moses, 3400 years ago, the year was supposedly reckoned by God Himself, as being 364 days long. So why has man in modern times changed the years to 365 ¼ days, which God, predicted that if the length of the year were changed, that it would cause havoc! Now, wait a minute, I thought that God had everything in His universe under perfect control, and absolute precision and timing to the split second?

C.7 According to modern astronomers however, there are no absolutes (life is random), & the length of the year does change! Something about how we are affected by the gravitation of the planets as the earth travels thorough space and blah blah blah. Wow! Sounds like Astronomical Fakery *, where the scientist make it all up as they go along, and the TRUTH is as former president of the USA arrogantly stated, "The truth is whatever I say it is". How many things in science are actually incomplete or even deliberate lies.

C.8 The truth be said, man's constant disobedience to God, and His laws is really putting us all in greater and greater dangers as the time goes by. All because of the arrogance of man's so-called scientific knowledge, which amount to nothing but foolishness in the eyes of God. The timing of the year is the precision of God's watch of the universe.

C.9 It would seem that man has again messed around with the timing of the years, for whatever reason! One Jewish website that I just visited, stated that before the flood there were 360 days in the year. A nice number just like 360 degrees in a circle.

As I stated in the introduction to my book, that I suspected that someone had tampered with the dates in some of the Apocryphal Books. I personally suspect that the 364 days mentioned in the Book of Enoch and the Book of Jubilees has been deliberately altered for whatever reason.

If you study the Book of the Luminaries what does it actually say for the most part. It states that there are 30 days to each month. Therefore 12 times 30 =360 days. Only one verse states 364 days. It would appear that that verse (Enoch 72.17) is out of context with all the other verses in the Book of Luminaries. The prophetic year mentioned above, quoted in both the Books of

Revelations and Daniel are what were also called the lunar year. However, when one looks up the official lunar year today it is not anymore 360 days but around 354 days. Some important people have tampered with the days of the year for whatever motive.

If it is true that the earth is actually the centre of the universe as suggested by both the Bible and the Book of Enoch, then to true observers in astronomy, our first satellite is the moon. So the calculation of the year, according to the orbits of the moon would be the most logical and easiest to accurately measure and thus the original 360 days/the year and not the 365.25 days/year that we have now!

C.10 In my opinion, Man's science idols, will end up destroying him, because most of mankind's leaders and scientists do not take the Word of God seriously. (*See Astronomical Fakery in the Appendix of this book)

18 And the length of the day and of the night, and the shortness of the day and of the night arise, through the course of the sun these distinctions are made. So it comes that its course becomes daily longer, and its course nightly shorter.

19 And this is the law and the course of the sun and his return as often as he returns sixty times and rises, for ever and ever; and that which rises is the great luminary, and is so named according to its appearance, according as the Lord commanded.

20 As he rises, so he sets and decreases not, and rests not, but runs day and night, and his light is sevenfold brighter than that of the moon; but as regards size they are both equal (in appearance).

C.11 The following is an accurate description of this Book of the Luminaries as given in the Book of Jubilees from the angels of God's Presence to Moses:

Jubilees 4.17 "Enoch was the first among men who learnt writing and knowledge and wisdom and who wrote down the signs of heaven according to the order of their months in a book, that men might know the seasons of the years according to the order of their separate months….and made known to men days of the years, and set in order the months and recounted the Sabbaths of the years as we (angels) made them known to him"

C.12 The angels themselves stated here in the Book of Jubilees, that they are the same angels that instructed Enoch.

CHAPTER 73

1 And after this law I saw another dealing with the smaller luminary, which is named the moon; and her circumference is like the circumference of the heaven, and her chariot in which she rides is driven by the wind, and light is given to her in measure.

2 And her rising and setting change every month; and her days are like the days of the sun, and when her light is uniform (i.e. full) it amounts to the seventh part of the light of the sun; and thus she rises; and her first phase in the east comes forth on the thirtieth morning and on that day she becomes visible, and constitutes for you the first phase of the moon on the thirtieth day together with the sun in the portal where the sun rises.

3 And one half of her goes forth by a seventh part, and her whole circumference is empty without light, with the exception of one seventh part of it, and the fourteenth part of her light; and when she receives one seventh part of the half of her light amounts to one seventh part and the half thereof.

4 And she sets with the sun, and when the sun rises, the moon rises with him and receives the half part of one part of the light, and in that night in the beginning of her morning [in the commencement of the lunar day] the moon sets with the sun, and is invisible that night with the fourteenth parts and half of one of them.

5 And she rises on that day with exactly a seventh part, and comes forth and recedes from the rising of the sun, and in her remaining days she becomes bright in the remaining thirteen parts.

CHAPTER 74

1 And I saw another course, a law for her, and how according to that law she performs her monthly revolution.

2 And all these Uriel, the holy angel who is the leader of them all, showed me, and their positions, and I wrote down their positions as he showed them to me, and I wrote down their months as they were, and the appearance of their lights till fifteen days were accomplished.

3 In single seventh parts she accomplishes all her light in the east, and in single seventh parts accomplishes all her darkness in the west; and in certain months she alters her settings, and in certain months she pursues her own peculiar course.

4 In two months the moon sets with the sun; in those two middle portals the third and fourth. She goes forth for seven days, and turns about and returns again through the portal where the sun rises, and accomplishes all her light; and she recedes from the sun, and in eight days enters the sixth portal from which the sun goes forth.

5 And when the sun goes forth from the fourth portal she goes forth seven days, until she goes forth from the fifth and turns back again in seven days into the fourth portal and accomplishes all her light; and she recedes and enters into the first portal in eight days.

6 And she returns again in seven days into the fourth portal from which the sun goes forth. Thus, I saw their position, how the moon rose and the sun set in those days.

7 And if five years are added together the sun has an overplus of thirty days, and all the days which accrue to it for one of those five years, when they are full amount to 364 days. And the over plus of the sun and of the stars amounts to six days; in 5 years, 6 days every year come to 30 days; and the moon falls behind the sun and stars to the number of 30 days.

8 And the sun and the stars bring in all the years exactly, so that they do not advance or delay their position by a single day unto eternity; but complete the years with perfect justice in 364 days.

9 In 3 years there are 1092 days, and in 5 1820 days, so that in 8 years there are 2912 days; for the moon alone the days amount in 3 years to 1062 days, and in 5 years she falls 50 days behind. And in 5 years there are 1770 days, so that for the moon the days in 8 years amount to 2832 days.

10 For in 8 years she falls behind to the amount of 80 days, all the days she falls behind in 8 years are 80; and the year is accurately completed in conformity with their world-stations and the stations of the sun, which rise from the portals which the sun rises and sets 30 days.

CHAPTER 75

1 And the leaders of the heads of thousands, who are placed over the whole creation and over all the stars, have also to do with the four intercalary days, being inseparable from their office, according to the reckoning of the year, and these render service on the four days which are not reckoned in the reckoning of the year.

2 And owing to them men go wrong therein, for those luminaries truly render service on the world-stations, one in the first portal, one in the third portal of the heaven, one in the fourth portal and one in the sixth portal, and the exactness of the year is accomplished through its separate three hundred and sixty four station.

3 For the signs and the times and the years and the days the angel Uriel showed to me, whom the Lord of glory that set for ever over all the luminaries of the heaven, in the heaven and in the world, that they should rule on the face of the heaven and be seen on the earth, and be leaders for the day and the night, the sun, moon and stars, and all the ministering creatures which make their revolution in all the chariots of the heaven.*

GEN.1:14 And God said, 'Let there be lights in the firmament of the heaven to divide the day from the night; and let them be for signs, and for seasons, and for days, and years.'

Comments:1: God stated here that the stars are for signs and seasons. The whole universe that is rotating around the earth acts also in controlling the 12 STAR SIGNS, and administer different characters to those who are born on the earth, in order to bring perfect diversity. Astrology is a real science after all and up until a hundred years ago Astrology and Astronomy were combined and not separate sciences.

4 In like manner twelve doors Uriel showed me, open in the circumference of the sun's chariot in the heaven, through which the rays of the sun break forth; and from them is wrath diffused over the earth, when they are open at their appointed seasons. And for the winds and the spirit of the dew when they are opened, standing open in the heavens at the ends.

5 As for the twelve portals in the heaven, at the ends of the earth, out of which go forth the sun, moon, and stars, all the works of heaven in the east and in the west. There are many windows open to the left and right of them, and one window at its appointed season produces warmth, corresponding to those doors from which the stars come forth

according as He has commanded them, and wherein they set corresponding to their number,

6 And I saw chariots in the heaven, running in the world, above those portals win which revolve that never set; and one is large than all the rest, and it is that that makes its course through the entire world.

C.2 I believe that Enoch was seeing the workings of the constellations and the stars, sun and moon and what effects they had upon mankind. *'Wrath is diffused over the earth, when they are open at their appointed seasons'* Exactly as Astrology teaches today. How each of us is born under a certain Sun Star Sign which is influenced by the moon and stars. The fact that peoples' lives have been affected by the stars in the heavens is very evident. Well, the fact is, Enoch could actually see the effects of these heavenly bodies on future events upon both the earth and its peoples.

GEN.1:14 And God said, 'Let there be lights in the firmament of the heaven to divide the day from the night; and let them be *for signs, and for seasons, and for days, and years*'

JDG.5:20 'They *fought from heaven*; the *stars in their courses* fought against Sisera.'

C.3 This is an outstanding verse, which was showing that king Sisera couldn't win in his fight against Israel, as both Heaven and the stars, were fighting against him. He was a King of the Amalekites and enemy of Israel, who ended up being killed by a woman called Jael, the wife of Nahum who drove a long nail right through his head while he slept. (Judges 4.21)

CHAPTER 76

1 And at the ends of the earth I saw twelve portals open to all the quarters of the heaven, from which the winds go forth and blow over the earth. Three of them are open on the face (i.e. the east) of the heavens, and therein the west, and three on the right (i.e. the south) of the heaven, and three on the left (i.e. the north). And the three first are those of the east, and three are of the north, and three of the south, and three of the west.

Comment:1: Twelve Portals, but what exactly are these portals? According to my current understanding something is wrong with the directions mentioned in verse 1. How can it state 'on the right (i.e. the south)

2 Through four of these come winds of blessing and prosperity, and from those eight come hurtful winds; when they are sent, they bring destruction on all the earth and on the water upon it, and on all who dwell thereon, and on everything which is in the water and on the land.

3 And the first wind from those portals, called the east wind, comes forth through the first portal which in the east, inclining towards the south; from it come desolation, drought, heat and destruction. And through the second portal in the middle comes what is fitting, and from it there some rain and fruitfulness and prosperity and dew; and through the third portal which lies toward the north come cold and drought.

4 And after these come forth the south winds through three portals; through the first portal of them inclining to the east comes forth a hot wind. And through the middle portal next to it there come forth fragrant smells, and dew and rain, and prosperity and health. And through the third portal lying to the west come forth dew and rain, locusts and desolation.

REV.9:3 And there came out of the smoke *locusts* upon the earth: and unto them was given power, as the scorpions of the earth have power.

5 And after these the north winds: from the seventh portal in the east come dew and rain, locusts and desolation. And from the middle portal come in a direct direction health and rain and dew and prosperity; and through the third portal in the west come cloud and hoar-frost and snow and rain and dew and locusts.

REV.16:12 And the sixth angel poured out his vial upon the great river Euphrates; and the water thereof was dried up, that the way of the *kings of the east* might be prepared.

6 And after these four are the west winds; through the first portal adjoining the north come forth dew and hoar-frost, cold and snow and frost. And from the middle portal come forth dew and rain, and prosperity, and blessing; through the last portal which adjoins the south come forth drought and desolation and burning and destruction.

C.2 "first portal adjoining the north" sounds like countries in the Northern Hemisphere. (Scandinavia, Russia and Canada.)

"middle portal" sounds like the mid-section of the earth. (USA, UK GERMANY, & the wealthy nations)

"last portal" sounds like the Southern Hemisphere. (Australia)

C.3 At different seasons come forth blessings of rain and at other seasons curses, such as drought in the hot summers of arid countries, such as Northern Africa, India, the Middle-East.

7 And the twelve portals of the four quarters of the heaven are therewith completed, and all their laws and all their plagues and all their benefactions have I shown to thee, my son Methuselah.

C.4 In this case, the 12 Portals bring the 12 months of the year, & the 4 Seasons of Winter, Spring, Summer & Autumn.

CHAPTER 77

1 And in the first quarter is called the east, because it is the first; and the second, the south, because the Most High will descend there, yea, there in quite a special sense will He who is blessed for ever descend. And the west quarter is named the diminished, because there all the luminaries of the heaven wane and go down.

Comment:1: 'And the second, the south, because the *'Most High will descend there'*. This has to be the 2nd Coming of Christ, when He will descent from Heaven and land on Mount Zion in Israel.

2 And the fourth quarter, named the north is divided into three parts; the first of them is for the dwelling of men; and the second contains seas of water, and the abysses and forests and rivers and darkness and clouds; and the third part contains The Garden of Righteousness.

C.2 Here the fourth quarter is describing more than what is on the outer surface of the earth. It seems to be mentioning three parts, which contain both the outer earth and the inner-earth, and it is notable that the outer earth and inner earth do connect in the North, where the North Pole should be, but isn't. Also, according to Jewish Zohar traditions, as mentioned before, the Garden of Eden is situated inside the Hollow Earth.

3 I saw seven high mountains higher than all the mountains which are on the earth; and thence comes forth hoar-frost, and days seasons and years pass away. I saw seven rivers on the earth larger than all the rivers; one of them coming from the west pours its waters into the Great Sea; and these two come from the north to the sea and pour their waters into the Erythraean Sea in the East, and two into the Great Sea and discharge themselves there and some say; into the desert.

C.3 Today in modern times, the Erythraean Sea is listed as the sea between Saudi Arabia and India. But is that the original location of that sea as mentioned by Enoch. After the Flood, and after everything on earth and in the earth had presumably been destroyed. Once man started spreading out again on the earth, he would have had to re-name all the new countries that now existed and all the seas and rivers and mountains etc. It is a big possibility that they would have drawn from names they used to know existed on the earth before the flood. For this reason we do not know where the original Erythraean sea, was before the Flood. Personally, from the description given above, I believe it likely that it was one of the INNER WORLD seas originally, as this chapter also mentions the Garden of Righteousness or the Garden of Eden This chapter also mentions that the topography of the mountain ranges is higher than any mountains on earth, as Enoch puts it. Obviously, he is describing a hidden realm, such as the INNER EARTH.

4 Seven great islands I saw in the sea, and in the mainland; two in the mainland and five in the Great Sea.

C.4 Could this be describing the 7 great islands of Atlantis?

C.5 This description does not sound like any lands we know on the outer surface. This chapter would seem to answer the age old question which I also mentioned in the introduction to this book. Many tens of thousands or even millions of people have believed in the hollow Earth throughout the ages. One of the main questions has been: Did Adam and Eve stay inside the earth after being driven from the Garden of Righteousness/ Eden or did God immediately put them on the Outer surface of the earth where we currently live to day? Alternatively did Noah in the Ark and his family of 8 souls migrate inadvertently to the outer surface at the time of the Flood. From what I have studied of the Book of Enoch and other Apocrypha books, I believe it more likely that man started to live on the outer surface after the Flood, and I will explain in details why, in the APPENDIX of this book.*

C.6 Concerning the earth being hollow, I read a very interesting book some time ago about a guy taking a trip down to Hell and back. Here are some interesting details from that book called 'Journey to Gragau by Alan Trenholm. I believe that the following book explains that cities were build inside the earth before the Great Flood and not outside. As far-fetched as it might initially seem, in the book *'Journey to Gragau'* we see a guy called Travis, taking a trip down to Hell. In chapter 2, he travels through a portal while riding a horse, through the 'outer surface of the earth', Suddenly, a 'clammy cold hand' grabs holds of his leg, as he rides down into hell. It nearly scared the living days light out of him, and happened *just before* he reached the INNER EARTH. The explanation given by Elatia (his spirit guide), is what gives it all away. She states that before the flood, people lived inside the earth, when she explained about the "rock people" who were spirits from before the Flood, who were buried in the rubble of their former cities, and imprisoned there, in the strata of the earth, close to the inner earth, because they didn't honour God; but honoured themselves, and their cities, often built at the price of human blood and sacrifice.

C.7 There is apparently, a physical dimension going down to the centre of the earth, and also at a slightly lower dimension, also parallel to the physical one, also going down to hell. The difference between the two, being that when Alan was travelling down to hell he was in his spirit on a spirit trip. And presumably his physical body was asleep on the earth, back in his bed. He said that on his spirit trip he was riding through a tunnel straight down through the strata of the earth, until he reached the inner surface of the earth, where he stated there was an *'inner sun'* to his surprise. From this account in chapter 1 and 2 of his brilliant book 'Journey to Gragau', one also is given the clue that buildings were originally built on the INNER SURFACE of the planet millennia before man lived on the outer surface, which probably didn't happen until after the Flood.

C.8 This could also explain why much of the Book of Enoch, the topography of the earth as described by Enoch sounds most of the time, like he was talking about an earth very different than what we see today and probably he is describing mostly the INNER EARTH. I believe that he also visited the uninhabited outer surface of the earth as well, & Heaven itself; as well as the lower dimensions of both Hell and the Lake of fire.

C.9 I highly recommend this book by Alan Trendholm about hell, the Lake of fire, demons and fallen angels, as it gives an amazing amount of insightful information about the lower worlds and the future of our planet.

CHAPTER 78

1 And the names of the sun are the following: the first Orjares, and the second Tomas; and the moon has four names: the first name is Asonja, the second Ebla, the third Benase, and the fourth Erae.

Comment:1: Why do the sun and the moon have so many names? If you know, please let me know?

2 These are the two great luminaries; their circumference is like the circumference of the heaven, and the size of the circumference of both is alike. In the circumference of the sun there are seven portions of light which are added to it more than to the moon, and definite measures it is transferred till the seventh portion of the sun is exhausted.

C.2 In appearance, the sun and the moon appear as the same size.
Think how amazing that really is for God to create the sun and the moon to 'appear' to us as being the same size, when in reality the sun is millions of times larger than the earth. The distance from the earth to the moon is only around 150,000 miles. Distance from the earth to the sun is around 93,000,000 miles. So the sun is circa 12,000 times further away from the earth than the moon. All this amazing information, and yet the sun and the moon appear as the same size, so that we can enjoy watching 'eclipses.' *Such a precise miracle of creation.*

3 And they set and enter the portals of the west, and make their revolution by the north, and come forth through the eastern portals on the face of the heaven; and when the moon rise one-fourteenth part appears in the heaven; the light becomes full in her; on the fourteenth day she accomplishes her light.

4 And fifteen parts of light are transferred to her till the fifteenth day when their light is accomplished, according to the sign of the year, and she becomes fifteen parts, and the moon grows by fourteen parts; and in her waning the moon decreases on the first day to fourteen parts of her light, on the second to thirteenth parts of light, on the third to twelve, on the fourth to eleven, on the fifth to ten, on the sixth to nine, on the seventh to eight, on the eighth to seven, on the sixth to six, on the tenth to five, on the eleventh to four, on the twelve to three, on the thirteenth to two, on the fourteenth to the half of seventh, and all her remaining light disappears wholly on the fifteenth; and in certain months has twenty-nine days and one twenty-eight.

5 And Uriel showed me another law: when light is transferred to the moon, and on which side it is transferred to her by the sun. During all the

period during which the moon is growing in her light, she is transferring it to herself when opposite the sun during fourteen days and when she is illuminated throughout, her light is accomplished full in the heaven.

6 And on the first day she is called the new moon, for on that day the light rises upon her. She becomes full moon exactly on the day when the sun sets in the west, and from the east she rises at night, and the moon shines the whole night through till the sun rises over against her and the moon is seen over against the sun.

7 On the side whence the light of the moon comes forth, there again she wanes till all the light vanishes and all the days of the month are at an end, and her circumference is empty, void of light. And there three months she makes of thirty days, and at her time she makes three months of twenty-nine days, in the which she accomplishes her waning in the first period of time, and in the first portal for one hundred and seventy-seven days.

8 And in the time of her going out she appears for three months of thirty days.

At night she appears like a (man) for twenty days each time, and by day she appears like the heaven, and there is nothing else in her save her light.

C.3 The word (man) is obviously out of place

CHAPTER 79

1 And now my son, I have shown thee everything, and the law of all the stars of the heaven is completed. And he showed me all the laws of these for every day, and for every season of bearing rule, and for every year, and for its going forth, and for the order prescribed to it every month and every week.

2 And the waning of the moon which takes place in the sixth portal; for in this sixth portal her light is accomplished, and after that there is the beginning of the waning. And the waning which takes place in the first portal in its season, till one hundred and seventy-seven days are accomplished; reckoned according to weeks, twenty-five weeks and two days.

3 She falls behind the sun and the order of the stars exactly five days in the course of one period, and when this place which you see has been traversed. Such is the picture and sketch of every luminary which Uriel the archangel, who is their leader, showed me.

Comment: Strange descriptions here, which are indeed difficult for us to understand in modern times, as we simply *cannot see the portals.*

CHAPTER 80

1 And in those days the angel Uriel answered and said to me, "Behold, I have shown thee everything, Enoch, and I have revealed everything to thee that thou see this sun and this moon, and the leaders of the stars of the heaven, and all those who turn them, their tasks, and times and departures."

2 And in the days of the sinners the years shall be shortened; and their seed shall be tardy on their lands and fields, and all things on the earth shall alter, and shall not appear in their time: and the rain shall be kept back and the heaven shall withhold it

MAT.24:22 'And except those days should be shortened.'

3 And in those times the fruits of the earth shall be backwards. The fruits of the trees shall be withheld in their time; and the moon shall alter her order, and not appear at her time; and those days the sun shall be seen and he shall journey in the evening other extremity of the great chariot in the west; and shall shine more brightly than accords with the order of light.

II Ezdras 8.50 "For many miseries will affect those who inhabit the world in the last times, because they have walked in great pride".

JOEL.2:30 And I will shew wonders in the heavens and in the earth, blood, and fire, and pillars of smoke. (Nuclear war?)

JOEL.2:31 The sun shall be turned into darkness, and the moon into blood, before the great and terrible day of the LORD come.

4 And many chiefs of the stars shall transgress their order.* And these shall alter their orbits and tasks, and not appear at the seasons prescribed to them; and the whole order of the stars shall be concealed from sinners; and thoughts to those on the earth shall err concerning them, and they shall be altered from all their ways, yea they shall err, and take them to be gods; and evil shall be multiplied upon them and punishment shall come upon them so as to destroy all.

JOEL.2:10 The earth shall quake before them; the heavens shall tremble: the sun and the moon shall be dark, and the stars shall withdraw their shining:

MAT.24:29 Immediately after the tribulation of those days shall the sun be darkened, and the moon shall not give her light, and the stars shall fall from heaven, and the powers of the heavens shall be shaken.

REV.6:13 And the stars of heaven fell unto the earth, even as a fig tree casts her untimely figs, when she is shaken of a mighty wind.

REV.6:14 And the heaven departed as a scroll when it is rolled together; and every mountain and island were moved out of their places.

II Ezdras 5.4 "You shall see (the world) thrown into confusion after the third period; and the sun shall suddenly shine forth at night, and the moon during the day."

II Ezdras 5.5 "blood shall drip from wood, and the stone shall utter his voice; the peoples shall be troubled, and the stars shall fall."

Comment:1: Stars are often representative of angels. Black hole stars representative of fallen angels.*

CHAPTER 81

1 And he said unto me, "Observe Enoch, these heavenly tablets, and read what is written thereon, and mark every individual fact; and I observed the heavenly tablets and read everything which was written thereon and understood everything, and read the book of all the deeds of mankind, and of all the children of flesh that shall be upon the earth to the remotest generations."

Comment:1: Here it is stating that the angel of God is showing the entire history of the world to Enoch and mentioning all the main events that will happen on the earth from the beginning of the creation unto the New Heaven and the New Earth. An entire panorama of 7000 Years of world history.

Jubilees 6.30 "Thus it is engraved and ordained on the ***heavenly tablets***"

2 And forthwith I blessed the great Lord the King of glory for ever, in that He has made all the works of the world, and I extolled the Lord because of His patience, and blessed Him because of the children of men. And after that I said: "Blessed is the man who dies in righteousness and goodness, concerning whom there is not a book of unrighteousness written, and against whom no day of judgment shall be found."

3 And those seven holy ones brought me and placed me on the earth before the door of my house, and said unto me, "Declare everything to thy son Methuselah, and show to all thy children that no flesh is righteous in the sight of the Lord, for He is their Creator. One year we will leave thee with thy son, till thou give thy last commands, that thou mayest teach they children and record it for them, and testify to all thy children; and in the second year, they shall take thee from their midst."

C.2 These 7 holy ones are the 7 angels of the 'Presence of God'

4 Let thy heart be strong, for the good shall announce righteousness to the good: the righteous with the righteous shall rejoice, and shall offer congratulations to one another; but sinners shall die with the sinners and the apostate do down with the apostate; and those who practice righteousness shall die on account of the deeds of men, and be taken away on account of the doings of the godless. And in those days they ceased to speak to me, and I came to my people, blessing the Lord of the world.

MAT.24:22 And except those days should be shortened there should no flesh be saved: but for the elect's sake those days shall be shortened.

CHAPTER 82

1 And now my son Methuselah, all these things I am recounting to thee, and writing down for thee, and I have revealed to thee everything, and given thee books concerning all these; so preserve, my son Methuselah, the books from thy fathers hand, and see that thou deliver them to the generations of the world.

2 I have given Wisdom to thee and to thy children, and thy children that shall be to thee, that they may give it to their children for generations. This wisdom that passes their thought, and those who understand it shall not sleep, but listen with the ear thereof better than good food.

Comment:1: God is stating here for the record that the Book of Enoch and all that it contains was given to Enoch by God himself, and that it is to be passed on to Methuselah and his sons and to all generations. Thus the books ended up being taken on the Ark with Noah at the time of the Great Flood, which happened 500 years after Enoch had been translated.

JOB.23:12 Neither have I gone back from the commandment of his lips; I have esteemed the words of his mouth more than my necessary food.

JOH.6:27 Labour not for the meat which perishes, but for that meat which endures unto everlasting life, which the Son of man shall give unto you: for him hath God the Father sealed.

JOH.6:63 It is the spirit that quickens; the flesh profits nothing: the words that I speak unto you, they are spirit, and they are life.

3 Blessed are all the righteous, blessed are all those who walk in the way of righteousness and sin not as the sinners, in the reckoning of all their days in which the sun traverses the heaven entering into and departing from the portals for thirty days with the heads of thousands of the order of the stars, together with the four which are intercalated, which divide the four portions of the year, which lead them and enter with them four days.

4 Owing to them men shall be at fault and not reckon them in the whole reckoning of the year; yea, men shall be at fault, and not recognize them accurately. For they belong to the reckoning of the year and are truly recorded for ever, one in the first portal and one in the third, and one in the fourth, and one in the sixth, and the year is completed in three hundred and sixty-four days.

5 And the account thereof is accurate and the recorded reckoning thereof exact; for the luminaries, and months and festivals, and years

and days had Uriel shown and revealed to me to whom the Lord of the whole creation of the world hath subjected the host of heaven; and he had power over night and day in the heaven to the light to give light to men. The sun, moon and stars, and all the powers to the heaven which revolve in the circular chariots

C.2 Here Enoch could be stating that the sun, moon and stars revolve around the earth in circular obits. He also stated several times that the year has 364 days. He states that the account thereof is accurate and the recorded reckoning thereof exact. Enoch states that because men will deduce the wrong number of days to the year that it will cause pandemonium.

In modern times, we all accept that there are 365 1/4 days in the year. So what went wrong between Enoch's & Moses times, who both stated the same number of days to the year as 364 days?

Enoch states that blessed are the righteous, who calculate the correct number of days in the year.

As mentioned before the prophetic year given in the Bible in both the books of Daniel and Revelation gives 360 days to the year. A perfect number like the 360 degrees in the circle.

The expert on this subject was the late David Flynn, who uncovered the ancient "absolute mathematics". I remember that in his book, the number 360 is a very special number. Find out about the hidden ancient knowledge or Prisca Sapientia *as written about so well in David Flynn's excellent and mind-boggling book of mathematical secrets, called "Temple in the Centre of Time"* Here is a simple quote from that book:

"The physical dimensions of both the Earth and the moon are based on 2,520 (=7 x 360), and 360."

C.3 This hidden knowledge of absolute constants in mathematics was revealed unto Moses, by God Himself on Mount Sinai. Apparently even the distance to the sun and the diameter of the sun is dependent on these absolute numbers, not to mention the whole rest of the creation out there including the other planets and stars etc.

(See the **Appendix XVI** to know more of this fantastic subject.)

6 And these are the orders of the stars, which set in their places, and their seasons and festivals and months, and these are the names of those who lead them who watch that they enter at their times, in their orders, in their seasons, in their months, in their periods of dominion, and in their positions.

7 Their four leaders who divide the four parts of the year enter first; and after them the twelve leaders of the orders who divide the months; and for the three hundred and sixty days three are heads over thousands who divided the days; and for the four intercalary days there are the leaders

which sunder the four parts of the year.

C.4 This verse, in contradiction to the others above states that there are 360 days in the year, with 12 months and 4 seasons

See in the *Appendix how all ancient civilizations counted 12 months of 30 days, or 360 days to the year. Who changed the number of the days in the year and why? See the Appendix to see *"There are Absolutes" and how man has deliberately corrupted God's creation including Mathematics and Astronomy. Why? This is because, the whole creation, along with its exact timing & precision in the orbits of the sun, the moon and the stars, proves the existence of God. Therefore ungodly scientists and leaders, led by Satan, try to get rid of the Absolute, God Himself.

8 And these heads over the thousands are intercalated between leader and leader, each behind a station, but their leaders the division. And these are the names of the leaders who divide the fourth Helemmelek, and Melejal, and Narel, and the names of those who lead them: Adnarel and Ijasusael, and Elomeel.

9 These three follow the leaders of the orders, and there is one that follows the three leaders of the orders of the stations that divide the four parts of the year. In the beginning of the year Melkejal rises first and rules, who is named Tamaini and sun, and all the days of his dominion whilst he bears rule are ninety-one days.

C.5 Here we are clearly being told that God has special angels who take care of the 4 seasons.

10 And these are the signs of the days which are to be seen on earth in the days of his dominion; sweat, and heat and calms; and all the trees bear fruit, and leaves are produced on all the trees, and the harvest of wheat, and the rose-flowers, and all the flowers which come forth in the field, but the trees of the winter season become withered.

11 And these are the names of the leaders which are under them: Berkael, Zelebsel, and another who is added a head of a thousand, called Hiujasph; and the days of the dominion of this leader are at an end. The next leader after him is Helemmelek, whose name is the shining sun, and all the days of this light are ninety-one days.

C.6 Enoch here seems to be saying that it is the responsibility of thousands of God's angels to both guard and guide the constant and consistent pathway of the sun in order for us to have the 4 seasons of the year!

C.7 What is really shocking is that God told Enoch that man should not alter the number of the days of the year. It is not only stated to Enoch in the book of the Luminaries, but also much later in time to Moses by the same angel Uriel. However, man does not respect the absolute order of the absolute maths of creation and tries to alter it, by telling us lies, for example. We are told that there are 365 1/4 days in the year, but *is this really the case*?

ECC.12:13 Let us hear the conclusion of the whole matter: Fear God, and keep his commandments: for this is the whole duty of man.

ECC.12:14 For God shall bring every work into judgment, with every secret thing, whether it be good, or whether it be evil.

12 And these are the signs of his days on the earth; glowing heat and dryness, and the trees ripen their fruits and produce all their fruits ripe and ready, and the sheep pair and become pregnant, and all the fruits of the earth are gathered in and everything that is in the fields, and the winepress; these things take place in the days of his dominion.
13 These are the names and the orders, and the leaders of those heads of thousands; Gidaijal. Keel and Heel, and the name of the head of a thousand which is added to them, Asfael; and the days of his dominion are at an end.

CHAPTER 83

The Dream Visions

1 And now my son Methuselah, I will show thee all my visions which I have seen, recounting them before thee: Two visions I saw before I took a wife and the one was quite unlike the other: the first when I was learning to write: the second before I took thy mother, when I saw a terrible vision. And regarding them I prayed to the Lord.

Comment:1: This is a synopsis of the following chapters 83-90. The first vision-dream is covered in chapters 83-84. The 2nd dream-vision is covered from chapters 85-90.

2 I had laid me down in the house of my grandfather Mahalalel, when I saw a vision how the heaven collapsed and was borne off and fell to the earth; and when it fell to earth was swallowed up in the great abyss, and mountains were suspended upon mountains, and hills sank down on hills, and high trees were rent from their stems, and hurled down and sunk in the abyss.

C.2 This sounds like a prediction of the coming Great Flood, but could also being talking about the end of the world in the time of the Wrath of God as well.

If, it is true, that the earth is actually hollow and the crust of the earth is only a few hundred miles thick, then Enoch seeing "mountains were suspended upon mountains, and hills sank down on hills" "hurled down and sunk in the abyss". The inner surface of the earth, apparently has high volcanic mountains higher than those on the outer surface.

With a total devastation of the crust of the earth perhaps indeed the outer surface mountains and hills will collapse onto the inner earth mountains and hills in at least some places as the crust of the earth becomes totally unstable, as it would seem to indicate in this dream-vision of Enoch's.

"Heaven collapsed and was borne off and fell to the earth" is probably talking about the fact that there used to be protective layers of waters "around the earth" and "under the inner surface of the earth" in pre-flood times, which all fell from the sky to the earth in the time of Noah.

ISA.24:1 Behold, the LORD makes the earth empty, and makes it waste, and turns it upside down, and scatters abroad the inhabitants thereof.

ISA.24:3 The land shall be utterly emptied, and utterly spoiled: for the LORD hath spoken this word.

ISA.24:4 The earth mourns and fades away, the world languishes and fades away, the haughty people of the earth do languish.

ISA.24:5 The earth also is defiled under the inhabitants thereof; because they have transgressed the laws, changed the ordinance, broken the everlasting covenant.

ISA.24:6 Therefore hath the curse devoured the earth, and they that dwell therein are desolate: therefore the inhabitants of the earth are burned, and few men left.

3 And thereupon a word fell into my mouth, and I lifted up my voice to cry aloud, and said, "The earth is destroyed." And my grandfather Mahalalel waked me as I lay near him, and said unto me, "Why dost thou cry so, my son, and why dost thou make such lamentation?"

4 And I recounted to him the whole vision which I had seen, and he said unto me, "A terrible thing hast thou seen, my son, and of grave moment is thy dream-vision as to the secrets of all the sin of the earth: it must sink into the abyss and be destroyed with great destruction."

ISA.24:19 The earth is utterly broken down, the earth is clean dissolved, the earth is moved exceedingly.

ISA.24:20 The earth shall reel to and fro like a drunkard, and shall be removed like a cottage; and the transgression thereof shall be heavy upon it; and it shall fall, and not rise again.

ISA.24:21 And it shall come to pass in that day, that the LORD shall punish the host of the high ones that are on high, and the kings of the earth upon the earth.

ISA.24:22 And they shall be gathered together, as prisoners are gathered in the pit, and shall be shut up in the prison, and after many days shall they be visited.

ISA.24:23 Then the moon shall be confounded, and the sun ashamed, when the LORD of hosts shall reign in mount Zion, and in Jerusalem, and before his ancients gloriously.

5 And now, my son, arise and make petition to the Lord of glory, since thou art a believer, that a remnant may remain on earth. My son, from heaven all this will come upon the earth, and upon the earth there will be great destruction. After that, I arose and prayed and implored and besought and implored, and wrote down my prayer for the generations of the world, and I will show everything to thee, my son Methuselah.

6 And when I had gone forth below and seen the heaven, and the sun rising in the east, and the moon setting in the west, and a few stars, and the whole earth, and everything as He had known it is the beginning then I blessed the Lord of judgement and extolled Him because He had made the sun to go forth from the windows of the east, and he ascended and rose on the face of the heaven, and set out and kept traversing the path shown unto him.

C.3 Notice how it states: 'the sun to go forth from the *windows* of the *east*'. What is that actually talking about? Are there windows in the sky, which we cannot see, because they are invisible to us, but were visible to Enoch?

CHAPTER 84

1 And I lifted up my hands in righteousness and blessed the Holy and Great One, and spoke with the breath of my mouth, and with the tongue of flesh, which God has made for the children of the flesh of men, that they should speak therewith, and He gave them breath and a tongue and a mouth that they should speak therewith.

Comment: Enoch is stating that he is still alive as a physical being, as he states *'with a tongue of flesh',* talking about himself, so he can't yet be a spirit in this chapter. On this occasion is giving his books over to this son Methuselah. In various chapters it seems that Enoch is being translated, but he doesn't get completely translated until a later chapter. *

C.2 One thing I would like to state here for the record, is that the Book of Enoch is amazing, and has so many details in it, that one cannot understand it by just skimming through it quickly. This book has to be meditated upon and should be read various times prayerfully, as it is very deep in content. Only those who are the most interested in knowing the truth behind this book will be able to wade through these incredible waters of knowledge and wisdom that have been all but hidden during the past 1000 years or so.

LUK.1:53 He hath filled the hungry with good things; and the rich he hath sent empty away.

2 "Blessed be thou, O Lord King. Great and mighty Thy greatness, Lord of the whole creation of the heaven. King of Kings and God of the whole world, and thy power and kingship and greatness abide for ever and ever, and throughout all generations Thy dominion; and all the heavens are Thy throne for ever, and the whole earth Thy footstool for ever and ever.

3 For thou hast made and Thou rules (over) all things, and nothing is too hard for Thee. Wisdom departs not from the place of Thy throne, nor turns away from thy presence. You know and see and hear everything, and there is nothing hidden from Thee. And now the angels of Thy heavens are guilty of trespass and upon the flesh of men abides Thy wrath until the great day of judgement.

4 And now, O God and Lord and Great King, I implore thee and beseech Thee to fulfil my prayer, to leave me a posterity on earth, and not destroy all the flesh of man, and make the earth without inhabitant, so that there should be an eternal destruction; and now, my Lord destroy from the earth the flesh which has aroused thy wrath, but the flesh of righteousness and uprightness establish as a plant of the eternal seed, and hide not

Thy face from the prayer of Thy servant, O Lord."

CHAPTER 85

1 And after this I saw another dream, and I will show the whole dream to thee me son. And I Enoch lifted up my voice and spoke to my son Methuselah, "To thee, my son will I speak. Here my words, incline thine ear to the dream-like vision of thy father."

1TI.4:15 Meditate upon these things; give thyself wholly to them; that thy profiting may appear to all.

Comment:1: This Second Vision gives an account from the creation to the end of all things from chapters 85-90. It is a parable in the which the people are sheep or other animals depending on their nature or character.

2 Before I took thy mother Edna, I saw in a vision on my bed, and behold a bull came forth from the earth, and that bull was white; and after it came forth a heifer, and along with this came forth two bulls, one of them black and the other red.

3 And that black bull gored the red one and pursued him over the earth, and thereupon I could no longer see that red bull; but that black bull grew and that heifer went with him, and I saw that many oxen proceeded from him which resembled and followed him.

4 And that cow, that first one, went from the presence of that first bull in order to seek that red one, but found him not, and lamented with great lamentation over him and sought him. And I looked till that first bull came to her and quieted her, and from that time onward she cried no more.

5 And after that she bore another white bull, and after him she bore many bulls and black cows. And I saw in my sleep that white bull likewise grow and become a great white bull, and from him proceeded many white bulls, and they resembled him. And they began to beget many white bulls which resembled him, one following the other, even many.

C.2 This allegorical story is counting the story of mankind from the beginning using animals for the different persons, according to their character. In these first five verses we see the story of mankind, starting with Adam and Eve, then Cain and Abel, and subsequent generations of peoples represented by the white Bull. White colour to indicate that they had not yet been polluted by the fallen angels and their procreation with human women.

CHAPTER 86

1 And again I saw with mine eyes as I slept, and I saw heaven above, and behold a star fell from heaven, and it arose and ate and pastured amongst those oxen. And after that I saw the large and the black oxen, and behold they all changed their stalls and pastures, and their cattle, and began to live with each other.

LUK.10:18 And he said unto them, I beheld Satan as lightning fall from heaven

REV.12:4 And his tail drew the third part of the stars of heaven, and did cast them to the earth

2 And again I saw in the vision, and looked towards the heaven, and behold I saw many stars descend and cast themselves down from heaven to that first star, and they became bulls amongst those cattle and pastured with them amongst them.

And I looked at them and saw, and behold they let out their privy members, like horses, and began to cover the cows of the oxen, and they all became pregnant and bare elephants, camels, and asses.

Comment:1: A story showing how the angels of God came down from heaven following that first fallen star, and they started to corrupt mankind by lying with the women and fathering strange children, which turned out to be giants. Illustrated well here in this story as the progeny no longer merely being white (good) bulls, but now elephants, camels and asses. These new creatures were generally much bigger.

3 And all the cattle feared them and were affrighted at them, and (they) began to bite with their teeth, and to devour and to gore with their horns; and they began, moreover, to devour those oxen; and behold all the children of the earth began to tremble and quake before them and to flee from them.

C.2 These new beasts were no ordinary cattle, as they started to devour the other cattle. It mentions that they had horns, and sounds like they were demonic.

In the real world in pre-flood times, the giants started eating mankind.

CHAPTER 87

1 And again I saw how they began to gore each other and to devour each other, and the earth began to cry aloud.

2 And I raised mine eyes again to heaven, and I saw in the vision, and behold there came forth from heaven beings who were like white men; and four went forth from that place and three with them.

Comment: Sounds like 4 angels plus another 3 making 7 angels in white. These 7 angels, are the 7 angels of God's Presence.

3 And those three that had last come forth grasped me by the hand and took me up, away from the generations of the earth, and raised me up to a lofty place, and showed me a tower raised high above the earth, and all the hills were lower.

4 And one said unto me, "Remain here till thou see everything that befalls those elephants, and asses, and the stars and the oxen, and all of them."

CHAPTER 88

1 And I saw one of those four who had come forth first, and he seized that first star, which had fallen from the heaven, and bound it hand and foot and cast it into the abyss; now that abyss was narrow and deep, and horrible and dark.

2 And one of them drew a sword, and gave it to those elephants and camels and asses; then they began to smite each other, and the whole earth quaked because of them.

3 And as I was beholding in the vision, lo, one of those four, who had come forth stoned them from heaven, and gathered and took all the great stars whose privy members were like those of horses and bound them all hand and foot, and cast them in an abyss of the earth.

CHAPTER 89

1 And one of those four went to that white bull and instructed him in secret, without his being terrified; he was born a bull and became a man, and built himself a great vessel and dwelt thereon; and three bulls dwelt with him in that vessel and they were covered in.

Comment:1: Interpretation: Noah and his 3 sons and the Ark and subsequent Great Flood.

2 And again, I raised mine eyes towards heaven and saw a lofty roof, with seven water torrents thereon, and those torrents flowed with much water into an enclosure. And I saw again, and behold fountains were opened on the surface of that great enclosure, and that water began to swell and rise upon the surface, and I saw that enclosure till all its surface was covered with water.

3 And the water, the darkness, and the mist increased upon it; and as I looked at the height of that water, that water had risen above the height of that enclosure, and was streaming over that enclosure, and it stood upon the earth; and all that cattle of that enclosure were gathered together until I saw how they sank and were swallowed up and perished in that water.

4 But that vessel floated on the water, while all the oxen and elephants and camels and asses sank to the bottom with all the animals, so that I could no longer see them, and they were not able to escape, but perished and sank into the depths.

C.2 A perfect description of Noah's Ark with all the animals aboard.

5 And again I saw in vision till the water torrents were removed from that high roof, and the chasms of the earth were levelled up and other abysses were opened. Then the water began to run down into these, till the earth became visible; but that vessel settled on the earth, and the darkness retired and light appeared.

6 But that white bull which had become a man came out of that vessel, and the three bulls with him, and one of those three was white like that bull, and one of them was red as blood, and one black; and that white bull departed from them.

C.3 The three bulls were Shem, Ham and Japheth.

7 And they began to bring forth beasts of the field and birds, so that there arose different genera: lions, tigers, wolves, dogs, hyenas, wild

boars, foxes, squirrels, swine, falcons, vultures, kites, eagles, and ravens; and among them was born a white bull.

C.4 This white bull was Abraham. The fact that many different animals are now mentioned, shows that after the Flood, as before it, there was again interference in the genetic blood-line of mankind by the fallen angels with the intent to try and stop the blood-line of Abraham and corrupt it, so that the prophesied Messiah could not arise from Abraham's lineage.

8 And they began to bite one another; but that white bull, which was born amongst them begat a wild ass and a white bull with it, and the wild asses multiplied; but that bull which was born from him begat a black wild boar and a white sheep ; the former begat many boars, but that sheep begat twelve sheep.

C.5 This is the interpretation: Wild ass: *Ishmael*; White bull: *Isaac*; Black wild boar: *Esau;* white sheep: *Jacob.* The *12 Sheep* are the *12 sons of Jacob*, which became the *12 tribes of Israel*

The many *wild boars* are the *sons of Esau*.

9 And when those sheep had grown, they gave up one of them to the asses, and those asses again gave up that sheep to the wolves, and that sheep grew up among the wolves; and the Lord brought the eleven sheep:- to live with it and to pasture with it among the wolves; and they multiplied and became many flocks of sheep.

C.6 Jacobs sons sell their brother Joseph to the Ishmaelites who then sold him as a slave to the Egyptians.

GEN.46:3 And he said (to Jacob), I am God, the God of thy father: fear not to go down into Egypt; for I will there make of thee a great nation:

GEN.37:27 Come, and let us sell him to the Ishmaelites *(asses)*, and let not our hand be upon him; for he is our brother and our flesh. And his brethren were content.

GEN.37:28 Then there passed by Midianites*(asses)* merchantmen; and they drew and lifted up Joseph out of the pit, and sold Joseph to the Ishmaelites for twenty pieces of silver: and they brought Joseph into Egypt.

C.7 Interpretation: (*Egyptians=Wolves*)

10 And the wolves began to fear them, and they oppressed them until they destroyed their little ones, and they cast their young into a river of much water: but those sheep began to cry aloud on account of their little ones, and to complain unto their Lord.

EXO.1:8 Now there arose up a new king over Egypt, which knew not Joseph.

EXO.1:11 Therefore they did set over them taskmasters to afflict them with their burdens. And they built for Pharaoh treasure cities, Pithom and Raamses.

11 And a sheep which had been saved from the wolves fled and escaped to the wild asses; and I saw the sheep how they lamented and cried and besought their Lord with all their might, till that Lord of the sheep descended at the voice of the sheep from a lofty abode, and came to them and pastured them.

C.8 'And a sheep': = Moses); 'wolves': = the Egyptians

EXO.2:15 Now when Pharaoh heard this thing, he sought to slay Moses. But Moses fled from the face of Pharaoh, and dwelt in the land of Midian (*Midianites=wild asses*)

EXO.3:2 And the angel of the LORD appeared unto him (Moses) in a flame of fire out of the midst of a bush: and he looked, and, behold, the bush burned with fire, and the bush was not consumed.

EXO.3:8 And I am come down to deliver them out of the hand of the Egyptians, and to bring them up out of that land unto a good land and a large, unto a land flowing with milk and honey; unto the place of the Canaanites, and the Hittites, and the Amorites, and the Perizzites, and the Hivites, and the Jebusites.

12 And He called that sheep which had escaped the wolves that it should admonish when not to touch the sheep; and the sheep went to the wolves according the word of the Lord, and another sheep met it and went with it, and the two went and entered into the assembly of the wolves, and spoke with them and admonished them not to touch the sheep from henceforth.

C.9 'Another sheep' =Aaron: **EXO.5:1** And afterward Moses and Aaron went in, and told Pharaoh, Thus, says the LORD God of Israel, 'Let my people go, that they may hold a feast unto me in the wilderness.'

13 And thereupon I saw the wolves, and how they oppressed the sheep exceedingly with all their power, and the sheep cried aloud. And the Lord came to the sheep and they began to smite those wolves; and the wolves began to make lamentation; but the sheep became quiet and forthwith ceased to cry out.

EXO.7:20 And Moses and Aaron did so, as the LORD commanded; and he lifted up the rod, and smote the waters that were in the river, in the sight of Pharaoh, and in the sight of his servants; and all the waters that were in the river were turned to blood.

EXO.7:21 And the fish that was in the river died; and the river stank, and the Egyptians could not drink of the water of the river; and there was blood throughout all the land of Egypt.

14 And I saw the sheep till they departed from amongst the wolves.

EXO.12:41 And it came to pass at the end of the four hundred and thirty years, even the (very) same day it came to pass, that all the hosts of the LORD went out from the land of Egypt.

But the eyes of the wolves were blinded, and those wolves departed in pursuit of the sheep with all their power. And the Lord of the sheep went with them, as their leader, and all his sheep followed Him; and his face as dazzling and glorious and terrible to behold.

15 But the wolves began to pursue those sheep till they reached a sea of water; and that sea was divided, and the water stood on this side and that before their face, and their Lord led them and placed Himself between them and the wolves.

EXO.14:9 But the Egyptians pursued after them, all the horses and chariots of Pharaoh, and his horsemen, and his army, and overtook them encamping by the sea, beside Pihahiroth, before Baalzephon.

16 And as those wolves did not yet see the sheep, they proceeded into the midst of the sea, and the wolves followed the sheep, and those wolves ran after them into that sea. And when they saw the Lord of the sheep, they turned to flee before His face, but the sea gathered itself together, and became as it had been created, and the water swelled and rose till it covered those wolves.

EXO.14:21 And Moses stretched out his hand over the sea; and the LORD caused the sea to go back by a strong east wind all that night, and made the sea dry land, and the waters were divided.

17 And I saw till all the wolves who pursued those sheep perished and were drowned; but the sheep escaped from that water and went forth into a wilderness, where there was no water and no grass; and they began to open their eyes and to see; and I saw the Lord of the sheep pasturing them and giving them water and grass, and that sheep going and leading them.

EXO.14:27 And Moses stretched forth his hand over the sea, and the sea returned to his strength when the morning appeared; and the Egyptians fled against it; and the LORD overthrew the Egyptians in the midst of the sea.

EXO.14:28 And the waters returned, and covered the chariots, and the horsemen, and all the host of Pharaoh that came into the sea after them; there remained not so much as one of them.

18 And that sheep ascended to the summit of that lofty rock and the Lord of the sheep sent it to them. And after that I saw the Lord of the sheep who stood before them, and His appearance was great and terrible

and majestic, and all those sheep saw Him and were afraid before His face.

C.10 'Summit of a lofty rock'=(Mount Sinai)

EXO.19:3 And Moses went up unto God, and the LORD called unto him out of the mountain, saying, 'Thus shalt thou say to the house of Jacob, and tell the children of Israel';

EXO.34:29 And it came to pass, when Moses came down from mount Sinai with the two tables of testimony in Moses' hand, when he came down from the mount, that Moses wist not that the skin of his face shone while he talked with him.

19 And they all feared and trembled because of Him, and they cried to that sheep with them which was among them, "We are not able to stand before our Lord or behold Him"; and that sheep which led them again ascended to the summit of that rock, but the sheep began to be blinded and to wander from the way which he had showed them, but that sheep wot not thereof.

EXO.32:1 And when the people saw that Moses delayed to come down out of the mount, the people gathered themselves together unto Aaron, and said unto him, Up, make us gods, which shall go before us; for as for this Moses, the man that brought us up out of the land of Egypt, we wot not what is become of him.

20 And the Lord of the sheep was wrathful exceedingly against them, and that sheep discovered it, and went down from the summit of the rock, and came to the sheep, and found the greatest part of them blinded and fallen away; and when they saw it they feared and trembled at its presence, and desired to return to their folds.

21 And that sheep took other sheep with it, and came to those sheep which had fallen away, and began to slay them; and the sheep feared its presence, and thus that sheep brought back those sheep that had fallen away, and they returned to their folds.

EXO.32:28 And the children of Levi did according to the word of Moses: and there fell of the people that day about three thousand men.

22 And I saw in this vision till that sheep became a man and built a house for the Lord of the sheep, and placed all the sheep in that house. And I saw till this sheep which had met that sheep which led them fell asleep: and I saw till all the great sheep perished and little ones arose in their place, and they came to a pasture, and approached a stream of water.

EXO.25:9 According to all that I shew thee, after the pattern of the tabernacle (A large tent=House of God, in the wilderness), and the pattern of all the instruments thereof, even so shall ye make it.

EXO.40:38 For the cloud of the LORD was upon the tabernacle by day, and fire was on it by night, in the sight of all the house of Israel, throughout all their journeys.

23 Then that sheep, their leader which had become a man, withdrew from them and fell asleep, and all the sheep sought it and cried over it with a great crying. And I saw till they left off crying for that sheep and crossed that stream of water, and there arose the two sheep as leaders in the place of those had led them and fallen asleep.

C.11 Interpretation: 'That sheep, their leader': *Moses;* 'fell asleep' means: *died;* 'two sheep as leaders': Joshua & Caleb

JOS.1:1 Now after the death of Moses the servant of the LORD it came to pass, that the LORD spake unto *Joshua* the son of Nun, Moses' minister, saying,

JOS.1:2 Moses my servant is dead; now therefore arise, go over this Jordan, thou, and all this people, unto the land which I do give to them, even to the children of Israel.

24 And I saw till the sheep came to a goodly place, and a pleasant and glorious land, and I saw till those sheep were satisfied; and that those stood amongst them in the pleasant land. And sometimes their eyes were opened, and sometimes blinded, till another sheep arose and led them and brought them all back and their eyes were opened.

JOS.21:43 And the LORD gave unto Israel all the land which he swore to give unto their fathers; and they possessed it, and dwelt therein.

JOS.21:44 And the LORD gave them rest round about, according to all that he swore unto their fathers: and there stood not a man of all their enemies before them; the LORD delivered all their enemies into their hand.

25 And the dogs and foxes and wild boars began to devour those sheep till the Lord of sheep raised up another sheep, a ram from their midst which led them; and that ram began to butt on either side those dogs, foxes, and wild boars till he had destroyed them all.

C.12 The "**Lord of the Sheep**": Jesus is the Lord of the sheep:

JOH.10:11 I am the good shepherd: the good shepherd giveth his life for the sheep

26 And that sheep whose eyes were opened saw that ram, which was amongst the sheep, till it forsook its glory and began to butt those sheep, and trampled upon them, and behaved itself unseemly; and the Lord of the sheep sent the lamb to another lamb and raised it to being a ram and leader of the sheep instead of that ram which forsaken his glory.

C.13 'And that sheep whose eyes were opened' This was King David 'Forsook its glory and began to butt those sheep'. This was King Saul.

27 And it went to it and spoke to it alone, and raised it to being a ram, and made it the prince and leader of the sheep but during all these things those dogs oppressed the sheep; and the first ram pursued that second ram, and that second ram arose and fled before it; and I saw till those dogs pulled down the first ram.

C.14 King Saul first trained David in his court, whilst the dogs (the Philistines) persecuted Israel. Saul turned against David and sought to kill him. David fled into the wilderness. King Saul was then killed in battle because of the Philistines.

1SA.16:21 And David came to Saul, and stood before him: and he loved him greatly; and he became his armour bearer.

1SA.18:8 And Saul was very wroth, and the saying displeased him; and he said, 'They have ascribed unto David ten thousands, and to me they have ascribed but thousands: and what can he have more but the kingdom?'

1SA.31:4 Then said Saul unto his armour bearer, 'Draw thy sword, and thrust me through therewith; lest these uncircumcised come and thrust me through, and abuse me.' But his armour bearer would not; for he was sore afraid. Therefore, Saul took a sword, and fell upon it.

28 And that second ram arose and led the little sheep. And those sheep grew and multiplied; but all the dogs, and foxes, and wild boars feared and fled before it, and that ram butted and killed the wild beasts and those wild beasts had no longer any power among the sheep, and robbed them no more of ought.

C.15 'Second ram arose and led the little sheep'- King David

29 And that ram begat many sheep, and fell asleep; and a little sheep became a ram in its stead, and became prince and leader of those sheep; and that house became great and was built for those sheep: and a tower lofty and great was built on the house of the Lord of the sheep, and that house was low, but the tower was elevated and lofty, and the Lord of the sheep stood on that tower and offered a full table before Him.

C.16[1] 'A little sheep'-This was Solomon, the youngest of David's sons and the least likely to have been made king.

1KI.2:12 Then sat Solomon upon the throne of David his father; and his kingdom was established greatly.

[2] 'A tower lofty and great was built on the house of the Lord of the sheep'- Solomon was the one who built the Temple for the Lord.

30 And again I saw those sheep that they again erred and went many ways, and forsook that their house and the Lord of sheep called some

from amongst the sheep, and sent them to the sheep, but the sheep began to slay them. And one of them was saved and was not slain, and it sped away and cried aloud over the sheep; and they sought to slay it, but the Lord of the sheep saved it from the sheep, and brought it up to me and caused it to dwell there.

MAT.23:34 Wherefore, behold, I send unto you prophets, and wise men, and scribes: and some of them ye shall kill and crucify; and some of them shall ye scourge in your synagogues, and persecute them from city to city:

31 And many other sheep He sent to those sheep to testify unto them and lament over them; and after that I saw that when they forsook the house of the Lord, and His tower, they fell away entirely, and their eyes were blinded; and I saw the Lord of the sheep who He wrought much slaughter amongst them in their herds until those sheep invited that slaughter and betrayed His place.

ACT.7:52 Which of the prophets have not your fathers persecuted? And they have slain them which shewed before of the coming of the Just One; of whom ye have been now the betrayers and murderers:

32 And He gave them over into the hands of the lions and tigers, and wolves, and hyenas, and into the hand of the foxes, and to all the wild beasts, and those wild beasts began to tear in pieces those sheep; and I saw that He forsook that house and their tower and gave them all into the hand of the lions to tear and devour them, into the hand of all the wild beasts.

C.17 After King David and Solomon reigned and the Kingdom of Israel was divided into two, with 12 tribes in the north, called Israel, and 2 in the south called Judah. It wasn't but a few hundred years later, as predicted by the prophet Isaiah, that the northern kingdom of Israel, was taken into captivity by Assyria, the 2nd world empire, around 720 BCE

ASSYRIA as symbolized by a type of ***large wild cat.***

Babylon, the 3rd world Empire, was symbolized by a **LION**. Babylon under Nebuchadnezzar totally devastated Israel, and razed Jerusalem and the temple to the ground in 589BC)

DAN.7:4 "The first was like a lion, and had eagle's wings"

Medio-Persia, the 4th World empire took over in 538 BCE

Medio-Persia, the 4th World empire was symbolized by a RAM, with two horns (Media and Persian) in Daniel chapter 8.

DAN.8:4 I saw the ram pushing westward, and northward, and southward; so that no beasts might stand before him, neither was there any that could deliver out of his hand; but he did according to his will, and became great.

C.18 Alexander the Great and the Grecian empire, the 5th world empire, took over the world in 333 BCE

Alexander the Great's Grecian Empire, was symbolized by a **HE-GOAT** with a notable large horn (Alexander) in Daniel chapter 8.)

DAN.8:5 And as I was considering, behold, an he goat came from the west on the face of the whole earth, and touched not the ground: and the goat had a notable horn between his eyes

Julius Caesar and the **Romans** and the 6th world empire conquered the world in around 43 BCE

Rome symbolized by a ravenous monstrous Beast much worse than all the ones who had preceded it! **Rome** also had the symbol of the **Wild Eagle**.

DAN.7:7 After this I saw in the night visions, and behold a fourth beast (Rome), dreadful and terrible, and strong exceedingly; and it had great iron teeth: it devoured and brake in pieces, and stamped the residue with the feet of it: and it was diverse from all the beasts that were before it; and it had ten horns.

All these **5 WORLD EMPIRES**, one after another, **symbolized by ferocious wild beasts**, by both Enoch, and the prophet Daniel, and other prophets, which totally subjugated Israel between 720 BCE and 70 AD, when Israel was totalled decimated by the Romans, and the 'Diaspora' occurred, and Israel ceased to exist as a nation for almost 2000 years until 1948.

33 And I began to cry aloud with all my power, and to appeal to the Lord of the sheep, and to represent Him in regard to the sheep that they were devoured by all the wild beasts; but He remained unmoved, though He saw it, and rejoiced that they were devoured and swallowed and robbed, and left them to be devoured in the hand of all the beasts.

C.19 The Romans finally totally destroyed Israel as a nation in 70 AD, just as Jesus had predicted 40 years earlier in 30 AD.

MAR.13:1 And as he went out of the temple, one of his disciples said unto him, Master, see what manner of stones and what buildings are here!

MAR.13:2 And Jesus answering said unto him, you see these great buildings? There shall not be left one stone upon another, that shall not be thrown down.

MAT.23:38 Behold, your house is left unto you desolate.

34 And He called seventy shepherds, and cast those sheep to them that might pasture them, and He spoke to the shepherds and their companions: "Let each individual of you pasture the sheep henceforth, and everything that I shall command you that do ye; and I will deliver them over unto you duly numbered, and tell you which of them are to be destroyed, and them destroy ye." And He gave over unto them those sheep.

C.20 It is difficult to know who these *70 shepherds* described long ago by Enoch were. However, it is interesting that there were 70 members of the SANHEDRIN which had absolute control over Israel at the time of Christ. Apparently, many of them were false shepherds according to Jesus' own words:

MAT.23:13 But woe unto you, scribes and Pharisees, hypocrites! For ye shut up the kingdom of heaven against men: for ye neither go in yourselves, neither suffer ye them that are entering to go in.

Perhaps originally God had commanded the Sanhedrin to be good shepherds over Israel, but they went astray, after slaying their own prophets and then their own Saviour, as Jesus related to them exactly, and also in a parable.

MAT.21:35 And the husbandmen took His (God's) servants, and beat one, and killed another, and stoned another.

MAT.21:36 Again, he sent other servants more than the first: and they did unto them likewise.

MAT.21:37 But last of all he sent unto them His Son, (Jesus) saying, 'They will reverence my son.'

MAT.21:38 But when the husbandmen saw the son, they said among themselves, 'This is the heir; come, let us kill him, and let us seize on his inheritance'.

35 And He called another and spoke unto him; "Observe and mark everything that the shepherds will do to those sheep; for they will destroy more of them than I have commanded them; and every excess and the destruction which will be wrought through the shepherds, record how many they devour according to my command, and how many according to their own command, and how many according to their own caprice: record against every individual shepherd all the destruction he effects.

36 And read out before me by number how many they destroy, and how many they deliver over for destruction, that I may have this as a testimony against them, know every deed of the shepherds, that I may comprehend and see what they do, whether or not they abide by my command which I have commanded them.

37 But they shall not know it, and thou shalt not declare it to them, nor admonish them, but only record against each individual all the destruction which the shepherds effect in his time and lay it before me."

38 And I saw till those shepherds pastured in their season, and they began to slay, and to destroy more than they were bidden, and they delivered those sheep into the hands of the lions; and the lions and tigers ate and

devoured the greater part of those sheep, and the wild boars ate along with them; and they burnt that tower and demolished that house.

39 And I became exceedingly sorrowful over that tower because that house of the sheep was demolished, and afterwards I was unable to see if those sheep entered that house; and the shepherds and their associates delivered over those sheep to all the wild beast, to devour them, and each one of them received in this time a definite number; it was written by the other in a book how many each of them destroyed of them.

40 And each one slew and destroyed many more than was prescribed; and I began to weep and lament to account of those sheep; and thus in the vision I saw that one who wrote how he wrote down every one that was destroyed by those shepherds, day by day and carried up and laid down and showed actually the whole book to the Lord of the sheep-even everything that they had done, and all that each one of them had made away with, and all that they had given over to destruction.

41 And the book was read before the Lord of the sheep, and He took the book from his hand and read it and sealed it and laid it down.

42 And forthwith I saw how the shepherd pastured for twelve hours, and behold three of those sheep turned back, and came and entered and began to build up all that had fallen down of that house; but the wild boars tried to hinder them, but they were not able.

C.21 Zerubbabel, Ezra & Nehemiah were good shepherds who did rebuild Jerusalem in around 454 BCE.

EZR.6:3 In the first year of Cyrus the king the same Cyrus the king made a decree concerning the house of God at Jerusalem, Let the house be built, the place where they offered sacrifices, and let the foundations thereof be strongly laid; the height thereof threescore cubits, and the breadth thereof threescore cubits;

NEH.4:18 For the builders, everyone had his sword girded by his side, and so built. And he that sounded the trumpet was by me.

43 And they began again to build as before, and they reared up that tower, and it was named the high tower; and they began again to place a table before the tower, but all the bread on it was polluted and not pure.

44 And as touching all this the eyes of those sheep were blinded so that they saw not, and the eyes of the shepherds likewise; and they delivered them in large numbers to their shepherds for destruction, and they trampled the sheep with their feet and devoured them.

45 And the Lord of the sheep remained unmoved till all the sheep were

dispersed over the field and mingled with them, and they did not save them out of the hands of the beasts.

C.22 The ones mentioned in these verses, seem to be those trying to rebuild the Temple, or to keep the customs of the temple, but were themselves destroyed in their attempts to do this, because they were not pure.

MAT.27:51 And, behold, the veil of the temple was rent in twain from the top to the bottom; and the earth did quake, and the rocks rent;

MAT.15:6 Thus have ye made the commandment of God of none effect by your tradition.

C.23 This could be referring to the times immediately after the crucifixion of Christ in the period of 40 years up until the total destruction of Israel as a nation. Because, the Pharisees killed the true Saviour of Israel, Jesus, then their future attempts to keep the temple pure failed, and eventually they lost the temple, their capital city, and indeed their entire country, to the destruction done by the Romans, under general Titus in 70 AD. All because of rebellion against God and His true prophets, and finally their own Messiah.

46 And this one who wrote the book carried it up, and showed it and read it before the Lord of the sheep, and implored Him on their account, and besought Him to their account as he showed Him all the doings of the shepherds, and gave testimony before Him against all the shepherds. And he took the actual book and laid it down beside Him and departed.

CHAPTER 90

1 And I saw till that in this manner thirty-five shepherds undertook the pasturing of the sheep, and they severally completed their periods as did the first; and others received them into their hands, to pasture them for their period, each shepherd in his own period.

2 And after that I saw in my vision all the birds of the heaven coming, the eagles, vultures, the kites, the ravens; but the eagles led all the birds; and they began to devour those sheep, and pick out their eyes and to devour their flesh.

Comment:1: Could the fact that the eagles led all the birds signify that this period of time is during the Roman Empire, whose symbol was clearly the eagle?

3 And the sheep cried out because their flesh was being devoured by the birds, and as for me I looked and lamented in my sleep over that shepherd who pastured the sheep.

4 And I saw until those sheep were devoured by the dogs and eagles and kites and they left neither flesh or skin or sinew remaining on them till only their bones stood there; and their bones to fell to the earth and the sheep became few.

PSA.22:16 For dogs have compassed me: the assembly of the wicked have enclosed me: they pierced my hands and my feet.

PSA.22:12 Many bulls have compassed me: strong bulls of Bashan have beset me round.

PSA.22:13 They gaped upon me with their mouths, as a ravening and a roaring lion.

C.2 This sounds like it could be the very climax of the destruction of Israel in 70 AD, when a million Israelites were slain, and 100,000 were crucified in the hills around Jerusalem. Those that were not slain were driven abroad upon the face of the earth. Why did all this terrible judgment happen? What had happened exactly 40 years before, when an innocent man, by the name of Jesus, was about to be crucified on a cross near Jerusalem?

MAT.27:24 When Pilate saw that he could prevail nothing, but that rather a tumult was made, he took water, and washed his hands before the multitude, saying, I am innocent of the blood of this just person: see ye to it.

MAT.27:25 Then answered all the people, and said, His blood be on us, and on our children.

C.3 God did not let Israel get away with crucifying His only Begotten Son, Jesus! But 40 years after they had crucified the Son of God, the Romans came and slaughtered the Israelites like never before because of their *not honouring their own Messiah* when He visited them.

5 And I saw until the twenty-three had undertaken the pasturing and completed in their several periods fifty-eight times

But behold lambs were born by those white sheep, and they began to open their eyes and to see, and to cry to the sheep.

6 Yea, they cried to them, but they did not hearken to what was said to them, but were exceedingly deaf and their eyes were very exceedingly blinded.

And I saw in vision how the ravens flew upon those lambs and took one of those lambs, and dashed the sheep in pieces and devoured them.

7 And I saw till horns grew upon those lambs and the ravens cast down their horns; and I saw till there sprouted a great horn of one of those sheep, and their eyes were opened

C.4 Here arises a great leader of the sheep

And it looked at them and the eyes were opened, and it cried to the sheep, and the rams saw it and all ran to it.

8 And notwithstanding all this whose eagles and vultures and ravens and kites still kept tearing the sheep, and swooping down upon them and devouring them; still the sheep remained silent, but the rams lamented and cried out.

And those ravens fought and battles with and sought to lay low its horn, but they had no power over it.

And I saw till the shepherds and eagles and those vultures and kites came, and they cried to the ravens and that they should break the horn of that ram, and battled and fought with it, and it battled with them and cried that its help might come.

9 And I saw till that man, who wrote the names of the shepherds and carried up into the presence of the Lord of the sheep.

10 And I saw till the Lord of the sheep came unto them in wrath, and all who saw Him fled, and they all fell into His shadow from before His face.

11 All the eagles and vultures and ravens, and kites were gathered together, and there came with them all the sheep of the field, yea they all came together, and helped each other to break that horn of the ram.

C.5 Could this RAM with the Big Horn(s), possibly be talking about the two End-time prophets, which the soon-coming Anti-Christ government (New World Order) and all their forces cannot kill?

REV.11:3 And I will give power unto my two witnesses, and they shall prophesy a thousand two hundred and threescore days, clothed in sackcloth.

REV.11:5 And if any man will hurt them, fire proceeds out of their mouth, and devours their enemies: and if any man will hurt them, he must in this manner be killed.

12 And I saw that man who wrote the book according to the command of the Lord, till he opened that book concerning the destruction which those twelve last shepherds had wrought, and that they had destroyed much more than their predecessors, before the Lord of the sheep.

13 And I saw till the Lord of the sheep came unto them and took in His hand the staff of His wrath, and smote the earth, and the earth clave asunder, and all the beast and all the birds of the heaven fell from amongst those sheep, and were swallowed up in the earth and it covered them.

C.6 This sounds like the time of **ARMAGEDDON & THE WRATH OF GOD**

REV.19:17 And I saw an angel standing in the sun; and he cried with a loud voice, saying to all the fowls that fly in the midst of heaven, Come and gather yourselves together unto the supper of the great God;

REV.19:18 That ye may eat the flesh of kings, and the flesh of captains, and the flesh of mighty men, and the flesh of horses, and of them that sit on them, and the flesh of all men, both free and bond, both small and great.

REV.19:19 And I saw the beast, and the kings of the earth, and their armies, gathered together to make war against him that sat on the horse, and against his army.

REV.19:20 And the beast was taken, and with him the false prophet that wrought miracles before him, with which he deceived them that had received the mark of the beast, and them that worshipped his image. These both were cast alive into a lake of fire burning with brimstone.

REV.19:21 And the remnant were slain with the sword of him that sat upon the horse, which sword proceeded out of his mouth: and all the fowls were filled with their flesh.

ISA.24:17 Fear, and the pit, and the snare, are upon thee, O inhabitant of the earth.

ISA.24:19,18 The earth is utterly broken down, the earth is clean dissolved, the earth is moved exceedingly; and the foundations of the earth do shake.

ISA.24:20 The earth shall reel to and fro like a drunkard, and it shall fall, and not rise again.

14 And I saw till a great sword was given to the sheep and the sheep

proceeded against all the beasts of the field to slay them, and all the beast and the birds of heaven fled before their face.

REV.19:11 And I saw heaven opened, and behold a white horse; and he that sat upon him was called Faithful and True, and in righteousness he doth judge and make war.

REV.19:14 And the armies which were in heaven followed him upon white horses, clothed in fine linen, white and clean.

REV.19:8 And to her was granted that she should be arrayed in fine linen, clean and white: for the fine linen is the righteousness of saints.

15 And I saw till a throne was erected in the pleasant land, and the Lord of the sheep sat Himself thereon, and the other took the sealed books and opened those books before the Lord of the sheep.

C.7 After Armageddon and the wrath of God comes the 1000-year MILLENNIUM and the Reign of CHRIST with all of HIS RESURRECTED SAINTS:

REV.20:4 And I saw thrones, and they sat upon them, and judgment was given unto them: and I saw the souls of them that were beheaded for the witness of Jesus, and for the word of God, and which had not worshipped the beast, neither his image, neither had received his mark upon their foreheads, or in their hands; and they lived and reigned with Christ a thousand years.

C.8 At the end of the Golden age of the Millennium, comes the final Battle of Gog and Magog and then we have the final judgement of the GREAT WHITE THRONE JUDGMENT

REV.20:11 And I saw a great white throne, and him that sat on it, from whose face the earth and the heaven fled away; and there was found no place for them.

REV.20:12 And I saw the dead, small and great, stand before God; and the books were opened: and another book was opened, which is the book of life: and the dead were judged out of those things which were written in the books, according to their works.

16 And the Lord called those men the seven first white ones (angels) and commanded that they should bring (them) before Him, beginning with the first star which led the way, all the stars whose privy members were like those of horses, and they brought them all before Him.

C.9 The "first star" was Semjaza. (Book of Enoch 6.7)

17 And He said to that man who wrote before Him, being one of those seven white ones, and said unto him, "Take those seventy shepherds to whom I delivered the sheep, and who taking them on their own authority slew more that I commanded them."

MAT.23:2 Saying The scribes and the Pharisees sit in Moses' seat:

MAT.23:3 All therefore whatsoever they bid you observe, that observe and do; but do not ye after their works: for they say, and do not.

C.10 Let's take a look at the laws of Moses, for which there were 27 counts of capital punishment. The question is how many times have the so-called religious leaders, such as the Pharisees of Jesus time used the letter of the law to slay people, just as they did the Messiah, Jesus Christ.

The religionists have always used the laws of Moses in the wrong spirit and more for the interests of financial gain and power and not for the concern of the people (sheep).

Think also how many people were slaughtered in the Catholic INQUISITION. People burnt at the stake for the slightest error. Surely these 70 shepherds acted more like demons than humans. This is why when Jesus came, He came and did away with the laws of Moses, stating:1) "Thou shalt love the Lord they God with all of thy heart and mind and strength" 2) Love they neighbour as thyself. He then stated: "upon these two laws hang all the laws and the prophets." Jesus showed that the original spirit behind the law was intended to protect people, and not to enslave them as it ended up doing. Religionists today have caused untold number of wars and incessant slaughter of the poor and innocent, for financial gain in their support of the Merchants of the earth.

18 And behold they were all abound, I saw, and they all stood before Him.

19 And the judgement was held over the stars, and they were judged and found guilty, and went to the place of condemnation, and they were cast into an abyss, full of fire and flaming, and full of pillars of fire.

20 And those seventy shepherds were judged and found guilty, and they were cast into that fiery abyss.

21 And I saw at that time how a like abyss was opened in the midst of the earth, full of fire, and they brought those blinded sheep, and they were all judged and found guilty, and cast into this fiery abyss, and they burned; now the abyss was to the right of the house. And I saw those sheep burning and their bones burning.

C.11 The above story of the 70 Shepherds, does not end well for all of the false shepherds of all the false religions of man.

NB. Common sense would dictate that: Any religion that encourages the killing of innocent people for financial gain, is not of God, but is Satanic in nature.

22 And I stood up to see till they folded up that old house; and carried off all the pillars, and all the beams, and ornaments of the house were at the same time folded up with it, and they carried it off and laid it in a place in the south of the land.

23 And I saw till the Lord of the sheep brought a new house greater and loftier than that first, and set it up in the place of the first which had been folded up: all its pillars were new, and its ornaments were new and larger than those of the first, the old one which He had taken away, and all the sheep were within it.

C.12 God is replacing the infinitesimally small temples of man's religions, with His Amazingly large Crystal Pyramid City, which is 1500 miles long, wide & high.

REV.21:16 And the city lies foursquare, and the length is as large as the breadth: and he measured the city with the reed, twelve thousand furlongs (=1500 miles). The length and the breadth and the height of it are equal.

REV.21:2 And I John saw the Holy City, New Jerusalem, coming down from God out of heaven, prepared as a bride adorned for her husband.

REV.21:22 And I saw no temple therein: for the Lord God Almighty and the Lamb are the temple of it.

REV.21:3 And I heard a great voice out of heaven saying, Behold, the tabernacle of God is with men, and he will dwell with them, and they shall be his people, and God himself shall be with them, and be their God.

24 And I saw all the sheep which had been left, and all the beasts of the earth, and all the birds of the heavens, falling down, and doing homage to those sheep and making petition to and obeying them in everything.

DAN.2:44 And in the days of these kings shall the God of heaven set up a kingdom, which shall never be destroyed: and the kingdom shall not be left to other people, but it shall break in pieces and consume all these kingdoms, and it shall stand for ever.

DAN.7:22 Until the Ancient of days came, and judgment was given to the saints of the Most High; and the time came that the saints possessed the kingdom

DAN.7:27 And the kingdom and dominion, and the greatness of the kingdom under the whole heaven, shall be given to the people of the saints of the Most High; whose kingdom is an everlasting kingdom, and all dominions shall serve and obey him.

25 And therefore those three who were clothed in white and had seized my hand and the hand of that ram also seizing hold of me, they took up and set me down in the midst of those sheep before the judgement took place.

C.13 'those three who were clothed in white'= (angels)

26 And those sheep were all white and their wool was abundant and clean.

27 And all that had been destroyed and dispersed, and all the beasts of

the field, and the birds of the heaven assembled in that house, and the Lord of the sheep rejoiced with great joy, because they were all good and had returned to His house.

28 And I saw till they laid down the sword, which had been given the sheep, and they brought it back into the house, and it was sealed before the presence of the Lord, and all the sheep were invited into that house, but it held them not.

C.14 The NEW HOUSE of the HEAVENLY CITY mentioned in Revelation 21-22

PSA.2:9 Thou shalt break them with a rod of iron; thou shalt dash them in pieces like a potter's vessel.

REV.2:26 And he that overcomes, and keeps my works unto the end, to him will I give power over the nations:

REV.2:27 And he shall rule them with a rod of iron; as the vessels of a potter shall they be broken to shivers: even as I received of my Father.

29 And the eyes of them all were opened, and they saw the good, and there was not one among them that did not see,

30 And I saw that that house was large and broad and very full. And I saw that a white bull was born, with large horns and all the beasts of the field and all the birds of the air feared him and made petition to him all the time.

31 And I saw till all their generations were transformed, and they became white bulls; and the first among them became a lamb, and the lamb became a great animal and had great black horns on his head; and the Lord of the sheep rejoiced over it and over all the oxen.

C.15 Most people, and peoples will come to acknowledgement of the truth in the end.

32 And I slept in their midst; and I awoke and saw everything.

This vision which I saw while I slept, and I awoke and blessed the Lord of Righteousness and gave Him glory.

33 Then I wept with a great weeping and my tears stayed not till I could no longer endure it; when I saw, they flowed on account of what I had seen; for everything shall come and be fulfilled, and all the deeds of men in their order were shown to me.

34 On that night I remembered the first dream and because of it I wept and was troubled-because I had seen the vision.

C.16 UNIVERSAL RECONCILIATION.

Eventually, most people will come to acknowledge God, and submit to His authority. Many and probably most of those in Hell, will repent, and all those who those who will unfortunately go through the Lake of Fire will be forcibly altered and purified. That is the whole purpose of Hell and the Lake of Fire: to cleanse and to purify and then make whole again.

REV.20:14 And death and hell were cast into the lake of fire. This is the second death.

C.17 Eventually God's entire original creation will be restored to its original perfection and without sin anymore. Even the beasts of the field and the birds together with the sheep and cattle will all learn to get on together in the end.

Notice the following two verses: 1) Those type of people thrown in the Lake of Fire:

REV.20:15 And whosoever was not found written in the book of life was cast into the lake of fire.

REV.21:27 And there shall in no wise enter into it (The Heavenly City) anything that defiles, neither whatsoever worketh abomination, or makes a lie: but they which are written in the Lamb's book of life.

Then, those who in the next chapter eventually come to live outside the Heavenly City. It would seem to be the same category of people.

REV.22:15 For without (The Heavenly City) are dogs, and sorcerers, and whoremongers, and murderers, and idolaters, and whosoever loveth and makes a lie.

C.18 All evil creatures and beings, once they have served their punishment, will be forgiven and have some sort of happy existence, without any more evil or sin.

Even the fallen angels, mentioned in this Book of Enoch were given a definite time period, for their punishment for corrupting and destroying the original creation of God:- 10.000 years! (Enoch 18.16 "And He was wroth with them, and bound them til the time when their guilt should be consummated even for ten thousand years) There is eventually an end to all punishment!"

So, this story does eventually, have a happy ending!

REV.22:2 In the midst of the street of it, and on either side of the river, was there the tree of life, which bare twelve manner of fruits, and yielded her fruit every month: and the leaves of the tree were for the healing of the nations (those outside the Heavenly city who used to be wicked and evil, but in the future are altered and finally healed!)

The Concluding section of the Book

CHAPTER 91

1 And now my son Methuselah, call to me all thy brothers, and gather together to me all the sons of thy mother; for the word calls me, and the spirit is poured out upon me, that I may show you everything that shall befall you for ever.

Comment:1: Notice how Enoch is stating that in his Book of Enoch he is showing them the entire panorama of the future, from the Beginning of Creation unto Eternity... "everything that shall befall you for ever".

2 And thereupon Methuselah went and summoned to him all his brothers and assembled his relatives; and he spoke unto all the children of righteousness and said, "Hear ye sons of Enoch, all the words of your father, and hearken aright to the voice of my mouth; for I exhort you and say unto you, beloved: love uprightness and walk therein".

C.2 "Beloved" sounds like the term given for those who are very close to God, and means greatly loved.

MAT.3:17 &17.5 And suddenly a voice came from heaven, saying, "This is My Beloved Son, in whom I am well pleased."

John, who received the Book of Revelation directly from God, was also called John the "Beloved"

Also, Daniel, who also heard directly from God, in visions and dreams:

DAN.9:23 "At the beginning of your supplications the command went out, and I have come to tell you, for you are greatly beloved; therefore, consider the matter, and understand the vision:"

3 And draw not nigh to uprightness with a double heart, and associate not with those of a double heart, but walk in righteousness, my sons, and it shall guide you on good paths, and righteousness shall be your companion; for I know that violence must increase on the earth, and a great chastisement be executed on the earth, and all the unrighteousness come to an end; yea it shall be cut off from its roots and its whole structure be destroyed.

4 And unrighteousness shall again be consummated on the earth, and all the deeds of the unrighteousness and of violence and transgression shall prevail in a twofold degree. And when sin and unrighteousness and blasphemy and violence in all kinds and deeds increase, and apostasy and transgression and uncleanness increase, and great chastisement shall come from heaven upon all these, and the holy Lord will come forth with wrath and chastisement, to execute judgement on earth.

C.3 Here Enoch is directly telling them that Judgement is coming: 1) THE FLOOD, but that after that judgement of the Flood, that violence, evil, apostasy and transgression and uncleanness shall yet increase and become "twofold degree".

5 In those days, violence shall be cut off from its roots, and the roots of unrighteousness together with deceit and they shall be destroyed from under heaven

And all the idols of the heathen shall be abandoned, and the temples burned with fire, and they shall remove them from the whole earth, and they shall be cast into the judgement of fire, and perish in wrath and in grievous judgement for ever.

C.4 2) Another Judgement comes at the WRATH of GOD in the not too distant future, and after the TRIBULATION 3) "cut off from its roots and its whole structure be destroyed". & "unrighteousness come to an end" The final judgement at the Great White Throne Judgement after the Millennium.

6 And the righteous shall arise from their sleep, and wisdom shall arise and be given unto them; and after that the roots of unrighteousness shall be cut off, and the sinners shall be destroyed by the sword…shall be cut off them the blasphemers in every place, and those who planned violence and those who commit blasphemy shall perish by the sword.

DAN.12:2 And many of those who sleep in the dust of the earth shall awake, Some to everlasting life, Some to shame and everlasting contempt.

7 And after that there shall be another, the eighth week, that of righteousness, and as sword shall be given to it, that a righteous judgement may be executed to the oppressors, and sinners shall be delivered it to the hands of the righteous. And at its close, they shall acquire houses through their righteousness, and a house shall be built for the Great King in glory for evermore.

8 And all mankind shall look to their path of uprightness; and after that, in the ninth week, the righteous judgement shall be revealed to the whole world. All the works of the godless shall vanish from all the earth, and the world shall be written down for destruction.

9 And after this in the tenth week in the seventh part, there shall be the great eternal judgement, in the which He will execute vengeance amongst the angels. And the first heaven shall depart and pass away, and a new heaven shall appear, and all the powers of the heaven shall give sevenfold light.

C.5 It would appear that one week here*, is 700 years. It is stated that the 3rd Judgment happens in the tenth week in the seventh part. We all know that there are 7 days in a week. This is telling us that the Final Judgement of the Great White Throne Judgement of God will happen on the 7th day of the 10th week. Multiply 10 x 7 = 70. We know that there are 7000 years of World History leading up to the grand finale of the Great White Throne Judgement in the date 3000+AD. Nostradamus put the End at the date of 3700 AD, although most of us would tend to put the date around 3000+AD, depending on what calendar of time you use, which is another big subject! (See more details of this, in the Appendix*, at the back of this book.)

10 And after that there will be many weeks without number for ever. And all shall be in goodness and righteousness, and sin shall no more be mentioned for ever.

11 And now I tell you my sons, and show you the paths of righteousness and the paths of violence. Yea, I will show them to you again, that ye may know what will come to pass. And now hearken unto me, my sons, and walk in the paths of righteousness, and walk not in the paths of violence. For all who walk in the paths of unrighteousness shall perish forever.

CHAPTER 92

1 The book written by Enoch. Enoch indeed wrote this complete doctrine of wisdom, which is praised of all men and a judge of all the earth. For all my children who shall dwell on the earth. For future generations who shall observe uprightness and peace.

2 Let not your spirit be troubled on account of the times, for the Holy and Great One has appointed days for all things; and the righteous one shall arise from sleep, and shall shine, and walk in the paths of righteousness. All his path and conversation shall be in eternal goodness and grace.

Comment:1: "the righteous one" here seems to talking about **JESUS, the MESSIAH**.

LUK.24:51 And it came to pass, while he blessed them, he was parted from them, and carried up into heaven.

LUK.24:27 And beginning at Moses and all the prophets, he expounded unto them in all the scriptures the things concerning himself (Jesus-after His Resurrection).

MAR.16:9 Now when Jesus was risen early the first day of the week, he appeared first to Mary Magdalene, out of whom he had cast seven devils.

3 And He will be gracious to the righteous and give them eternal uprightness. And He will give him power so that he shall be endowed with goodness and righteousness. He shall walk in eternal light; and sin shall perish in darkness for ever and shall no more be seen from that day for evermore.

JOH.10:27 My sheep hear my voice, and I know them, and they follow me:

JOH.10:28 And I give unto them eternal life; and they shall never perish, neither shall any man pluck them out of my hand.

JOH.10:29 My Father, which gave them me, is greater than all; and no man is able to pluck them out of my Father's hand.

C.2 Jesus also talked in parables and also talked about sheep in His time and promised to give us all eternal life.

CHAPTER 93

1 And after that Enoch both gave and began to recount from the books, and Enoch said: Concerning the children of righteousness, and concerning the elect of the world, I will 1 speak thee things, yea, I Enoch will declare them unto you, my sons: According to that which appeared to me in the heavenly vision, and which I have known through the word of the holy angels, and have learnt from the heavenly tablets.

JUBILEES: 6.30 "And all the days of the commandment will be two and fifty weeks of days, and the entire year complete/ Thus it is engraved and ordained on the heavenly tablets"

2 And Enoch began to recount from the books and said: I was born the seventh in the first week, while judgement and righteousness still endured; and after me, there shall arise in the second week great wickedness, and deceit shall have sprung up; and in it shall be the first end. And in it a man shall be saved; and after it is ended unrighteousness shall grow up, and law shall be made for the sinners.

Comments:1: (See **Appendices X, XI, XII** in the back of this book for **time charts**)

Enoch is very accurately predicting the entire future of the world in 10 weeks.

Each week being around 700 years or a total of 10 x 7= 70 days. Each day = 100 years.

NB. A Jubilee = 50 years, which is exactly half of 100. This would mean that there are exactly 70 x 2=140 JUBILEES from the Beginning of the Creation until the FINAL JUDGEMENT and ETERNITY.

NUMEROLOGY: God seems to like not just the number 7, but also the number 10. (There were 10 Commandments. Some say that originally there were 10 planets?*)

We see these numbers all throughout the entire Bible.

Enoch was the 7th from Adam, born during the 7th Day of the 1st Week (See Appendix Time chart) There are 7000 actual years of World History=7 x10^3 =140 JUBILEES=7 X 2 X 10.

Incidental: There are 7 basic colours; 7 basic musical notes. 7 days in the week. In fact creation is full of 7s. (See Appendix for more details)

First week: The world was still alright when "judgement and righteousness still endured."

Second week: "Great wickedness" and "the first end" or 1st JUDGEMENT=THE FLOOD

A man shall be saved: That was NOAH. "After it is ended, unrighteousness shall grow up".

In other words, after the Great Flood of Noah, at the end of "Second week", then wickedness would return.

"Law shall be made for the sinners" God started giving His laws to Abraham, but not finalized until the time of Moses and the children of Israel.

3 And after that in the third week at its close, a man shall be elected as the plant of righteous judgement*[1]; and his posterity shall become the plant of righteousness*[2] for evermore. And after that in the fourth week, at its close, visions of the holy and righteous shall be seen, and a law for all generations and an enclosure shall be made for them.*[3]

Interpretations: *[1]ABRAHAM *[2]JESUS *[3] (MOSES)

4 And after that in the fifth week, at it close, the house of glory and dominion shall be built forever;*[1] and after that in the sixth week all who live in it shall be blinded,(time between the testaments 400 BCE until the time of CHRIST in 30 BCE) and the hearts of all of them shall godlessly forsake wisdom, and in it a man shall ascend *[2]; and at its close, the house of dominion shall be burnt with fire, and the whole race of the chosen shall be dispersed. (70 AD under the Romans)

C.2 Interpretation: *[1]King Solomon *[2]Jesus

5 And after that in the seventh week shall an apostate generation arise*[1], and many shall be its deeds, and all its deeds shall be apostate; and at its close shall be elected the elect righteous one the eternal plant of righteousness, to receive sevenfold instruction concerning all His creation.

C.3 Interpretation*1 (THE DARK AGES of False Religions)

6 For who is there of all the children of men that is able to hear the voice of the Holy One without being troubled? And who can think His thoughts? And who is there that can behold all the works of heaven? And how should there be one who could behold the heaven, and who is there that could understand the things of heaven and see a soul or a spirit and could tell thereof, or ascend and see all their ends and think them or do like them?

PSA.33:11 The counsel of the LORD stands for ever, the thoughts of his heart to all generations.

7 And who is there of all men that could know what is the breadth and length of the earth, and to whom has been shown the measure of all of them? Or is there anyone who could discern the length of the heaven and how great is its height, and upon what it is founded, and how great is the number of the stars, and where all the luminaries rest?

JOB.38:4 Where was thou when I laid the foundations of the earth? Declare, if thou hast understanding.

JOB.38:5 Who hath laid the measures thereof, if you know? Or who hath stretched the line upon it?

JOB.38:6 Whereupon are the foundations thereof fastened? Or who laid the corner stone thereof;

PSA.104:4 Who makes his angels spirits; his ministers a flaming fire:

ECC.3:21 Who knows the spirit of man that goes upward, and the spirit of the beast that goes downward to the earth?

CHAPTER 94

1 'And now I say unto you, my sons, love righteousness and walk therein; for the paths of righteousness are worthy of acceptance, but the paths of the unrighteousness shall suddenly be destroyed and vanish; and to certain men of a generation shall the paths of violence and of death be revealed, and they shall hold themselves afar from them, and shall not follow them'.

MAT.13:17 For verily I say unto you, 'That many prophets and righteous men have desired to see those things which ye see, and have not seen them; and to hear those things which ye hear, and have not heard them.'

PRO.16:29 A violent man entices his neighbour, and leads him into the way that is not good.

2 And now I say unto you the righteous: walk not in the paths of wickedness, nor in the paths of death, and draw not nigh to them, least ye be destroyed; but seek and choose for yourselves righteousness and an elect life, and walk in the paths of peace, and ye shall prosper.

3 And hold fast my words in the thoughts of your hearts; for I know that sinners will tempt men to evilly entreat wisdom, so that no place may be found for her, and no manner of temptation may diminish.

PSA.58:11 So that a man shall say, 'Verily there is a reward for the righteous: verily he is a God that judges in the earth.'

4 Woe to those who build unrighteousness and oppression and lay deceit as a foundation; for they shall be suddenly overthrown, and they shall have no peace. Woe to those who build their houses with sin, for from the foundations shall they be overthrown, and by the sword shall they fall. And those who acquire gold and silver in judgement shall suddenly perish.

OBA.1:4 Though thou exalt thyself as the eagle, and though thou set thy nest among the stars, thence will I bring thee down, says the LORD.

5 Woe to ye rich, for ye have trusted in your riches, and from your riches shall ye depart, because ye have not remembered the Most High in the days of your riches. Ye have committed blasphemy and unrighteousness, and have become ready for the day of slaughter, and the day of darkness and the day of the great judgement.

JAM.5:1 Go to now, ye rich men, weep and howl for your miseries that shall come upon you.

JAM.5:2 Your riches are corrupted, and your garments are moth-eaten.

JAM.5:3 Your gold and silver is cankered; and the rust of them shall be a witness against you, and shall eat your flesh as it were fire. Ye have heaped treasure together for the last days.

6 Thus, I speak and declare unto you: He who hath created you will overthrow you, and for your fall there shall be no compassion, and your Creator will rejoice at your destruction; and your righteous ones in those days shall be a reproach to the sinners and the godless.

PSA.54:5 He shall reward evil unto mine enemies: cut them off in thy truth.

CHAPTER 95

1 Oh that mine eyes were a cloud of waters that I might weep over you, and pour down my tears as a cloud of waters; that so I rest from my trouble of heart! Who has permitted you to practice reproaches and wickedness?

And so judgement shall overtake you, sinners.

LAM.3:47 Fear and a snare is come upon us, desolation and destruction.

LAM.3:48 Mine eye runs down with rivers of water for the destruction of the daughter of my people.

2 Fear not the sinners, ye righteous; for again will the Lord deliver them into your hands, that we may execute judgement upon them according to your desires.

Woe to you who fulminate anathemas which cannot be reversed; healing shall therefore be far from you because of your sins.

3 Woe to you who requite your neighbour with evil; for ye shall be requited according to your works. Woe to you lying witnesses, and to those who weigh out injustice, for suddenly shall ye perish. Woe to you, sinners for ye persecute the righteous; for ye shall be delivered up and persecuted because of injustice, and heavy shall its yoke be upon you.

CHAPTER 96

1 Be hopeful, ye righteous; for suddenly shall the sinners perish before you, and ye shall have lordship over them according to your desires.

2 And in the day of tribulation of the sinners, your children shall mount up as eagles, and higher than the vultures will be your nest, and ye shall ascend and enter the crevices of the earth, and the clefts of the rock for ever as conies before the unrighteous, and the sirens shall sigh because of you, and weep.

Comment:1: and the 'Sirens shall weep' **Enoch 96.2** "And the women also of the angels who went astray shall become sirens" **-Enoch 19.2**

Think how many stories there are from ancient mythology, as in Jason and the Argonauts about the dangers of Sirens. Beautiful Female spirits of the dead who possess different creatures in the physical realm, such as the mythological mermaids, with hypnotic melodious songs, to lure and seduce men to their destruction. Maybe there really was some truth to that idea.

C.2 Sirens 1) Micah 1:8 (Septuagint) Therefore, shall she lament and wail, she shall go barefooted, and being naked she shall make lamentation *as that of serpents*, and mourning as of the *daughters of sirens.*

Enoch 29:2 And the women also of the angels who went astray shall become sirens.' Enoch 29:2

The Book Of The Apocalypse Of Baruch 10:8 'I will call the Sirens from the sea'.

C.3 Sirens 2) The Oriental mystic prophet called Avak, stated that the original creation of God, was destroyed by Satan, when He rebelled, so that then, God proceeded to re-create order out of the confusion that Satan had made.

C.4 I am wondering, if there is any evidence, that God himself created *other good creatures* to *count-balance the evil versions* which were created by the fallen angels, who not only made love to human women, but later on, messed with the DNA of animals, birds and fish. It is a very interesting topic. We know that the Chinese believe that there is YING AND YANG, good and bad, and an opposite for everything. If you know of any examples of good hybrid creatures, then please let me know. I know of some of the mythological creatures, that supposedly could fly such as the Harpies, which were, supposed to be partly in a woman's form and that of a bird. They were thoroughly evil apparently.

It would be nice to find some good versions of the bad I suppose, a bit like C.S. Lewis' Chronicles of Narnia, which had all kinds of hybrids, such as the centaur, and Pegasus the flying horse, but in the case of Narnia those creatures were good. (See the **Appendix XXVI** concerning the good chimeras created by God Himself, such as the 4 beasts mentioned in Revelations chapter 4 & many other good examples)

C.5 From the Book of Enoch, unfortunately, we only see the bad fruit of the fallen angels making love with the women on earth and creating giants, and then later other fallen angels deliberately creating the hybrids, so that the spirits of the giants who had fallen in battle, and were now in the hidden state of the spirit world, could actually come back to earth in the form of centaurs etc. As you can see we only hear about the negative creatures that resulted from the fall of the angels.

All that to say that personally *if physical mermaids do exist* in the seas, and *I do think it very probable*, then they are *probably very dangerous and beguiling & like the serpent race.*

3 Wherefore fear not, ye that have suffered; for healing shall be your portion and a bright light shall enlighten you and the voice of rest ye shall hear from heaven.

4 Woe unto you, ye sinners, for your riches make you appear like the righteous, but your hearts convict you of being sinners, and this fact shall be a testimony against you far a memorial of your evil deeds. Woe to you who devour the finest wheat, and drink in large bowls, and tread underfoot the lowly with your might.

MAT.23:13 But woe unto you, scribes and Pharisees, hypocrites! for ye shut up the kingdom of heaven against men: for ye neither go in yourselves, neither suffer ye them that are entering to go in.

MAT.23:14 Woe unto you, scribes and Pharisees, hypocrites! for ye devour widows' houses, and for a pretence make long prayer: therefore, ye shall receive the greater damnation.

MAT.23:15 Woe unto you, scribes and Pharisees, hypocrites! for ye compass sea and land to make one proselyte, and when he is made, ye make him twofold more the child of hell than yourselves.

MAT.23:16 Woe unto you, ye blind guides, which say, 'Whosoever shall swear by the temple, it is nothing; but whosoever shall swear by the gold of the temple, he is a debtor!'

REV.3:17 Because thou say, I am rich, and increased with goods, and have need of nothing; and know not that thou art wretched, and miserable, and poor, and blind, and naked:

C.6 This sounds like those who pretend to be religious, but do so in order to gain power and riches, while totally ignoring the poor of the world. The worst kind of evil, is that which pretends to be righteous and good for the purpose of deceit and gain.

Many religions and charities today, are in this category, as they are a false front. Put there by the rich and wealthy!

5 Woe to you who drink water from every fountain, for suddenly shall ye

be consumed and wither away, because ye have forsaken the fountain of life. Woe to you who work unrighteousness and deceit and blasphemy; it shall be a memorial against you for evil. Woe to you, ye mighty, who with might oppress the righteous; for the day of your destruction is coming. In those days many and good days shall come to the righteous, in the day of your Judgement.

JAM.5:5 Ye have lived in pleasure on the earth, and been wanton; ye have nourished your hearts, as in a day of slaughter.

JAM.5:6 Ye have condemned and killed the just; and he doth not resist you.

C.7 The fountain of life is the WORD OF GOD. Your life will be empty and vain, if you don't have God's Word in your soul. It is important to drink of the true living waters of God's Word and not the deceitful words of man "whose breath is in his nostrils". Some people will say anything for money, power, popularity and fame.

Be selective in what you read as not all waters contain God's wisdom.

JAM.1:17 Every good gift and every perfect gift is from above, and cometh down from the Father of lights, with whom is no variableness, neither shadow of turning.

CHAPTER 97

1 Believe, ye righteous that the sinners will become a shame and perish in the day of unrighteousness. Be it known unto you (ye sinners), that the Most High is mindful of your destruction, and the angels of heaven rejoice over your destruction.

PSA.9:17 The wicked shall be turned into hell, and all the nations that forget God.

2 What will ye do, ye sinners, and whither will ye flee on that day of judgement, when ye hear the voice of the prayer of the righteous? Yea. Ye shall fare like unto them, against whom this word shall be a testimony; "Ye have been companions of sinners."

PSA.139:8 If I ascend up into heaven, thou art there: if I make my bed in hell, behold, thou art there.

JER.12:17 But if they will not obey, I will utterly pluck up and destroy that nation, says the LORD

3 And in those days the prayer of the righteous shall reach unto the Lord, and for you the days of your judgement shall come. And all the words of your unrighteousness shall be out before the Great One, and your faces shall be covered with shame and He will reject every work which is grounded in unrighteousness.

REV.6:10 And they cried with a loud voice, saying, 'How long, O Lord, holy and true, dost thou not judge and avenge our blood on them that dwell on the earth?'

MAT.12:36 But I say unto you, 'That every idle word that men shall speak, they shall give account thereof in the day of judgment'.

4 Woe to you, ye sinners, who live on the mid ocean and on the dry land, whose remembrance is evil against you. Woe to you who acquire silver and gold in unrighteousness and say: "We have become rich with riches and have possessions; and have acquired everything we have desired. And now let us do what we purposed: For we have gathered silver, and many are the husbandmen in our houses." And our granaries are brim full as with water. Yea and like water your likes shall flow away; for your riches shall not abide but speedily ascend from you; for ye have acquired it also in unrighteousness and ye soon be over to a great curse.

JAM.5:4 Behold, the hire of the labourers who have reaped down your fields, which is of you kept back by fraud, cries: and the cries of them which have reaped are entered into the ears of the Lord of Sabaoth.

JAM.5:5 Ye have lived in pleasure on the earth, and been wanton; ye have nourished your hearts, as in a day of slaughter.

JAM.5:6 Ye have condemned and killed the just; and he doth not resist you.

JER.22:13 Woe unto him that builds his house by unrighteousness, and his chambers by wrong; that uses his neighbour's service without wages, and giveth him not for his work;

LUK.12:19 And I will say to my soul, Soul, thou hast much goods laid up for many years; take thine ease, eat, drink, and be merry.

LUK.12:20 But God said unto him, 'Thou fool, this night thy soul shall be required of thee: then whose shall those things be, which thou hast provided?'

CHAPTER 98

1 And now I swear unto you, to the wise and to the foolish, for ye shall have manifold experiences on the earth. For ye men shall put on more adornments than a woman, and coloured garments more than a virgin; in royalty and in grandeur and in power, and in silver and in gold and in purple, and in splendour and in food they shall be poured out as water.

Comment:1: This sounds just like a description of the **GREAT WHORE OF REVELATION 17-18** which represents the GREAT MERCHANTS OF THE EARTH

REV.17:4 And the woman was arrayed in purple and scarlet colour, and decked with gold and precious stones and pearls, having a golden cup in her hand full of abominations and filthiness of her fornication:

DEU.22:5 The woman shall not wear that which pertains unto a man, neither shall a man put on a woman's garment: for all that do so are abomination unto the LORD thy God.

2 Therefore they shall be wanting in doctrine and wisdom, and shall perish thereby together with their possessions; and with all their glory and their splendour, and in shame shall be cast into the furnace of fire.

REV.18:19 And they (Rich Merchants) cast dust on their heads, and cried, weeping and wailing, saying, Alas, alas that great city, wherein were made rich all that had ships in the sea by reason of her costliness! for in one hour is she made desolate.

3 I have sworn unto you, ye sinners as a mountain has not become a slave, and a hill dies not become the handmaid of a woman, even so sin has not been sent upon the earth, but man of himself has created it, and under a great curse shall they fall who commit it; and barrenness has not been given to the woman, but on account of the deeds of her own hands she dies without children.

JAM.1:13 Let no man say when he is tempted, I am tempted of God: for God cannot be tempted with evil, neither tempts he any man:

JAM.1:14 But every man is tempted, when he is drawn away of his own lust, and enticed.

JAM.1:15 Then when lust hath conceived, it brings forth sin: and sin, when it is finished, brings forth death.

C.2 ABORTION: Abortion is a great crime against God, and an affront to His Holy Spirit, which has claimed the innocent lives of over 1,000,000,000 babies in the past 60 years or so. I have met women, who have suffered great loss, because of the decision to have an abortion.

In both cases, the women, that I am thinking about, could not have children, after they had had an abortion, which is now a great sorrow to them!

JER.2:34 'Also in thy skirts is found the blood of the souls of the poor innocents(BABIES): I have not found it by secret search, but upon all these.'

C.3 Millions of people say that Abortion is OK, but is it in the eyes of God?

JER.2:35 Yet you say, Because I am innocent, surely his anger shall turn from me. Behold, I will plead with thee, because you say, I have not sinned.

4 I have sworn unto you, ye sinners, by the Holy Great One, that all your evil deeds are revealed in the heavens, and that none of your deeds of oppression are covered and hidden. Do not think in your spirit nor say in your heart that ye do not know and that ye do not see that every sin is every day recorded in heaven in the presence of the Most High.

REV.20:12 And I saw the dead, small and great, stand before God; and the books were opened: and another book was opened, which is the book of life: and the dead were judged out of those things which were written in the books, according to their works.

C.4 Obviously every word we say and everything we do in life is recorded somewhere. We are told by scientists that our brain remembers everything that has ever happened to us, but that we don't consciously remember most events, but that somewhere in our subconscious mind every second of our life is recorded (One of the Books?)

5 From henceforth ye know that all your oppression wherewith ye oppress will be written down every day till the day of your judgement. Woe to you, ye fools, for through your folly shall ye perish; and ye transgress against the wise, and so good hap shall not be your portion.

PSA.14:1 The fool hath said in his heart, 'There is no God. They are corrupt, they have done abominable works, there is none that doeth good.'

PSA.5:5 The foolish shall not stand in thy sight: thou hates all workers of iniquity.

6 And now, know ye that ye are prepared for the day of destruction; wherefore do not hope to live, ye sinners, but ye are prepared for the day of great judgement, for the day of tribulation and great shame for your spirits.

7 Woe to you, ye obstinate of heart, who work wickedness and eat blood: From whence have ye good things to eat and to drink and to be filled? From all good things which the Lord the Most High has placed in abundance on the earth; therefore, ye shall no peace.

LEV.17:14 For it is the life of all flesh; the blood of it is for the life thereof: therefore, I said unto the children of Israel, Ye shall eat the blood of no manner of flesh: for the life of all flesh is the blood thereof: whosoever eats it shall be cut off.

DEU.12:16 Only ye shall not eat the blood; ye shall pour it upon the earth as water.

8 Woe to you who love the deeds of unrighteousness; wherefore do ye hope for good hap unto yourselves? Know that ye shall be delivered into hands of the righteous, and they shall cut off your necks and slay you, and have no mercy upon you.

PSA.1:5 Therefore the ungodly shall not stand in the judgment, nor sinners in the congregation of the righteous.

2PE.2:12 But these, as natural brute beasts, made to be taken and destroyed, speak evil of the things that they understand not; and shall utterly perish in their own corruption;

9 Woe to you who rejoice in the tribulation of the righteous; for no grave shall be dug for thee. Woe to you who set at nought the words of the righteous; for ye shall have no hope of life. Woe to you who write down lying and godless words; for they write down their lies that many may hear them and act godlessly towards their neighbour; therefore, they shall have no peace but die a sudden death.

PSA.10:2 The wicked in his pride doth persecute the poor: let them be taken in the devices that they have imagined.

PSA.5:9 For there is no faithfulness in their mouth; their inward part is very wickedness; their throat is an open sepulchre; they flatter with their tongue

ISA.48:22 There is no peace, says the LORD, unto the wicked.

CHAPTER 99

1 Woe to you who work godlessness, and glory in lying and extol them: ye shall perish and no happy life shall be yours. Woe to them who pervert the words of the righteous, and transgress the eternal law, and transform themselves into what they were not: they shall be trodden under foot upon the earth.

2PE.2:3 And through covetousness shall they with feigned words (lying) make merchandise of you: whose judgment now of a long time lingers not, (does not delay), and their damnation slumbers not.

Comment:1: "transform themselves into what they were not" That is a very ambiguous statement and could mean many things.

In modern times, wealthy men are seeking to transform themselves into gods, through the science of Transhumanism (X-MEN). However, it has all been done before in the times before the Great Flood of Noah.

In ancient times, some of the angels of God transformed into Devils and their offspring the Giants, when they died on the earth into demons, when they had entered the negative spirit world.

2 In those days make ready, ye righteous, to raise your prayers as a memorial, and place them as a testimony before the angels, that they may place the sin of the sinners for a memorial, and place them as a testimony before the angels, that they place the sin of the sinners for a memorial before the Most High.

C.2 Sounds like it is time to be very desperate in prayers night and day when the world has become so evil. I would go further and state that it has become dangerous not to pray fervently and frequently for our loves ones and their safety, as the world has indeed become so perverted, violent and dangerous and is heading in the same direction as in pre-flood times which will result in the 2nd destruction of mankind at the Wrath of God.

3 In those days the nations shall be stirred up, and the families of the nations shall arise on the day of destruction. And in those days the destitute shall go forth and carry off their children, and they shall abandon their children that are still sucklings, and not return for them, and shall have no pity on their beloved ones.

II Ezdras: "A man shall have no pity upon his neighbours, but shall make an assault upon their houses with the sword, and plunder their goods, because of hunger for bread, and because of great tribulation."

DAN.12:1 "And there shall be a time of trouble, such as never was since there was a nation even to that same time."

C.3 How can a mother abandon her suckling child? That simply is not human at all! It goes against every instinct of motherhood to protect her off-spring even at the threat to her own life, at least that is the norm!

Is it just possible that the kind of people it is talking about, have been programmed as in the long foretold "MARK of the BEAST" people, who have no conscience anymore, who are more like drones, or zombies and become increasingly motivated by fear and terror, to the point, that they abandon their own babies when the brain control system of the Mark of the Beast is finally broken.

REV.13:15 And he had power to give life unto the image of the beast, that the image of the beast should both speak, and cause that as many as would not worship the image of the beast should be killed.

REV.13:16 And he causes all, both small and great, rich and poor, free and bond, to receive a mark in their right hand, or in their foreheads:

MAT.24:21 For then shall be great tribulation, such as was not since the beginning of the world to this time, no, nor ever shall be.

MAT.24:22 And except those days should be shortened, there should no flesh be saved.

4 And again I swear to you, ye sinners, that sin is prepared of a day of unceasing bloodshed; and they who worship stones, and graven images of gold and silver and wood and stone and clay, and worship impure spirits and demons, and all kinds of idols not according to knowledge, shall get no manner of help from them.

REV.14:20 And the winepress (of the Wrath of God) was trodden without the city, and blood came out of the winepress, even unto the horse bridles, by the space of a thousand and six hundred furlongs. (A 200 mile long, river of human blood)

5 And they shall become godless by reason of the folly of their hearts, and their eyes shall be blinded through the fear of their hearts, and through the visions in their dreams. Through these they shall become godless and fearful; for they shall have wrought all their works in a lie, and shall have worshipped a stone, therefore in an instant they shall perish.

ISA.13:8 And they shall be afraid: pangs and sorrows shall take hold of them; they shall be in pain as a woman that travails: they shall be amazed one at another; their faces shall be as flames.

COL.2:8 Beware lest any man spoil you through philosophy and vain deceit, after the tradition of men, after the rudiments of the world, and not after Christ.

C.4 "Worshipped a stone" This is basically what the modern Evolutionists* believe, that everything came from a stone. (*See **Appendix XXIII** for more info)

1TI.6:20 Keep that which is committed to thy trust, avoiding profane and vain babblings, and oppositions of science falsely so called:

6 But in those days blessed are all they who accept the words of wisdom, and understand them, and observe the paths of the Most High, and walk in the path of His righteousness, and become not godless with the godless; for they shall be saved.

PRO.1:7 The fear of the LORD is the beginning of knowledge: but fools despise wisdom and instruction.

PSA.1:1 Blessed is the man that walks not in the counsel of the ungodly, nor stands in the way of sinners, nor sits in the seat of the scornful.

7 Woe to you who spread evil to your neighbours; for you shall be slain in Sheol (Hell or unseen state). Woe to you who make deceitful and false measures, and to them cause bitterness on the earth; for they shall thereby be utterly consumed. Woe to you who build your houses through the grievous toil of others, and all their building materials are the bricks and stones of sin; I tell you ye shall have no peace.

MAT.23:14 Woe unto you, scribes and Pharisees, hypocrites! for ye devour widows' houses, and for a pretence make long prayer: therefore, ye shall receive the greater damnation

8 Woe to them who reject the measure and eternal heritage of their fathers, and whose souls follow their idols; for they shall have no rest. Woe to them who work unrighteousness and help oppression, and slay their neighbours until the day of great judgement. For He shall cast down your glory, and bring affliction on your hearts, and shall arouse His fierce indignation, and destroy you all with the sword; and all the holy and righteous shall remember your sins.

C.5 Woe to them who abandon the godly standards of former generations, and who now live for expensive & extravagant possessions (idols), which give them no satisfaction or peace of mind. "slay their neighbours" This reminds me of a terrible tragedy which happened yesterday,14/06/17, in London, a real-life version of the movie "The Towering Inferno" The owners & managers of the building were warned of the dangers involved, but did nothing to ensure the on-going safety of the building, and as a result many casualties have happened. Just one example of "fatal neglect" of taking care of ones "neighbours". Jesus said to love thy neighbour as thyself. Not to slay him!

CHAPTER 100

ARMAGEDDON

1 And in those days in one place the fathers together with their sons shall be smitten, and brothers one with another shall fall in death till the streams flow with their blood; for a man shall not withhold his hand from slaying his sons and his sons' sons, and sinners shall not withhold his hand form his honoured brother; from dawn till sunset they shall slay one another.

EZE.38:21 And I will call for a sword against him throughout all my mountains, says the Lord GOD: every man's sword shall be against his brother.

2 And the horse shall walk up to the breast in the blood of sinners, and the chariots shall be submerged to its height. In those days the angels shall descend into the secret places and gather together into one place all those who brought down sin, and the Most High will arise on that day of judgement to execute great judgement amongst sinners.

REV.14:20 And the winepress was trodden without the city, and blood came out of the winepress, even unto the horse bridles, by the space of a thousand and six hundred furlongs.

Comment:1: Six hundred furlongs represents a 200 mile long river of human blood! Obviously, many millions of people are slaughtered at the Battle of Armageddon.

REV.16:16 And he gathered them together into a place called in the Hebrew tongue Armageddon.

3 And over all the righteous and holy He will appoint guardians from the amongst the holy angels to guard them as the apple of an eye. Until He makes an end of all wickedness and all sin, and though the righteous sleep a long sleep, they have nought to fear.

PSA.17:8 Keep me as the apple of the eye, hide me under the shadow of thy wings,

ZEC.2:8 "For he that touches you, touches the apple of His (God's) eye".

DAN.12:2 And many of them that sleep in the dust of the earth shall awake, some to everlasting life, and some to shame and everlasting contempt.

4 And then the children of the earth shall see the wise in security, and shall understand all the worlds of this book, and recognize that their riches shall not be able to save them in the overthrow of their sins.

5 Woe to you, Sinners on the day of strong anguish, ye who afflict the

righteous and burn them with fire; Ye shall be requited according to your works. Woe to you, ye obstinate in heart, who watch in order to devise wickedness: Therefore shall fear come upon you and there shall be none to help you.

II Ezdras: 15.53 "If ye had not always killed my chosen people, exulting and clapping your hands and talking about their death when you were drunk"

II Ezdras 16.70-73 "For in many places and in neighbouring cities there shall be a great insurrection against those who fear the Lord. They shall be like mad men sparing no one, but plundering and destroying those who continue to fear the Lord. For they shall destroy and plunder their goods, and drive them from their houses. Then the tested quality of my elect shall be manifest, as gold that is tested by fire"

6 Woe to you, ye sinners, on account of the words of your mouth, and on account of the deeds of your hands which your godlessness hath wrought, in blazing flames burning worse than fire shall ye burn. And now, know ye that from the angels He will inquire as to your deeds in heaven, from the sun and the moon and from the stars in reference to your sins because upon the earth ye execute judgement on the righteous.

7 And He will summon to testify against you every cloud and mist and dew and rain; for they shall all be withheld because of you from descending upon you, and they shall be mindful of your sins; and now give presents to the rain that it be not withheld from descending upon, nor yet the dew, when it has received gold and silver from you that it many descend.

8 When the hoar-frost and snow with their chilliness, and the snowstorms with all their plagues fall upon you, in those days ye shall not be able to stand before them.

C.2 Is our planet to be judged by an ICE-AGE?

CHAPTER 101

1 Observe the heaven, ye children of heaven, and every work of the Most High, and fear ye Him and work no evil in His presence. If He closes the windows of heaven, and withholds the rain and the dew from descending on the earth on your account, what will ye do then?

2 And if He sends His anger upon you because of your deeds, ye cannot petition Him; for ye spoke proud and insolent words against Him; for ye spoke proud and insolent words against His righteousness: therefore ye shall have no peace.

3 And see ye not the sailors of the ships, how their ships are tossed to and fro by the waves, and are shaken by the winds, and are in sore trouble? And therefore do they fear because all their goodly possessions go upon the sea with them, and they have evil forebodings of the heart that the sea will swallow them and they will perish therein.

4 Are not the entire sea and all its waters, and all its movements the work of the Most High, and has He not set limits to its doings, and confined it throughout by the sand? And at His reproof it is afraid and dries up, and all its fish die, and all that is in it; But ye sinners that are on the earth fear Him not.

5 Has He not made the heaven and the earth, and all that it therein? Who has given understanding and wisdom to everything that moves on the earth and in the sea. Do not the sailors of the ships fear the sea? Yet sinners fear not the Most High.

REV.9:20 And the rest of the men which were not killed by these plagues yet repented not of the works of their hands, that they should not worship devils, and idols of gold, and silver, and brass, and stone, and of wood: which neither can see, nor hear, nor walk:

REV.9:21 Neither repented they of their murders, nor of their sorceries, nor of their fornication, nor of their thefts.

CHAPTER 102

1 In those days when He hath brought a grievous fire upon you, wither will ye flee, and where will ye find deliverance? And when He launches forth His word against you, will you not be affrighted and fear, and all the earth shall be affrighted and tremble and be alarmed.

REV.19:21 And the remnant were slain with the sword of him that sat upon the horse, which *sword proceeded out of his mouth*: and all the fowls were filled with their flesh.

2TH.1:8 In flaming fire taking vengeance on them that know not God, and that obey not the gospel of our Lord Jesus Christ:

2TH.1:9 Who shall be punished with everlasting destruction from the presence of the Lord, and from the glory of his power;

2 And all the luminaries shall be affrighted with great fear, and all the earth shall be affrighted and tremble and be alarmed. And all the angels shall execute their commands, and shall seek to hide themselves from the presence of the Great Glory, and the children of earth shall tremble and quake; and ye sinners shall be cursed for ever, and ye shall have no peace.

REV.6:15 And the kings of the earth, and the great men, and the rich men, and the chief captains, and the mighty men, and every bondman, and every free man, hid themselves in the dens and in the rocks of the mountains;

REV.6:16 And said to the mountains and rocks, 'Fall on us, and hide us from the face of him that sits on the throne, and from the wrath of the Lamb'.

REV.6:17 For the great day of his wrath is come; and who shall be able to stand?

3 Fear ye not, ye souls of the righteous, and be hopeful ye that have died in righteousness; and grieve not if your soul into Sheol has descended in grief. And that in your life your body fared not according to your goodness, but wait for the day of judgement of the sinners and for the day of cursing and chastisement.

Comment:1: Sheol means the 'Invisible State of the Spirit World'

REV.14:13 And I heard a voice from heaven saying unto me, Write, '*Blessed are the dead which die in the Lord from henceforth*: Yea, says the Spirit, that they may rest from their labours; and their works do follow them'.

4 And yet when ye die the sinners speak over you: "As we die, die the righteous, and what benefit do they reap for their deeds? Behold, even as we, so do they die in grief and darkness, and what have they more than we, from henceforth we are equal. And what will they receive and what

will they see ever? Behold they too have died, and henceforth for ever they shall see no light."

PSA.9:17 The wicked shall be turned into hell, and all the nations that forget God.

C.2 The "Sinners" mentioned here, obviously neither believe in God or the afterlife, but only see things of the physical world and are totally blind to the existence of God's vast spirit world that is all around us and even in us.

PSA.14:1 The fool hath said in his heart, "There is no God". They are corrupt, they have done abominable works, there is none that doeth good.

1CO.15:58 Therefore, my beloved brethren, be ye steadfast, unmoveable, always abounding in the work of the Lord, forasmuch as ye know that your labour is not in vain in the Lord.

5 I tell you, ye sinners, ye are content to eat and drink, and rob and sin, and strip men naked, and acquire wealth and see good days. Have ye seen the righteous how their end falls out, that no manner of violence is found in them till their death; nevertheless they perished and because as though they has not been, and their spirits descended into Sheol in tribulation.

PSA.37:14 The wicked have drawn out the sword, and have bent their bow, to cast down the poor and needy, and to slay such as be of upright conversation.

PSA.37:15 Their sword shall enter into their own heart, and their bows shall be broken.

CHAPTER 103

1 Now therefore, I swear to you, the righteous, by the glory of the Great and Honoured and Mighty One in dominion, and by His greatness I swear unto you: I know a mystery and have read the heavenly tablets, and have seen the holy books, and have found written therein and inscribed regarding them: that all goodness and joy and glory are prepared for them, handwritten down for the spirits of those who have died in righteousness; and that manifold good shall be to you in recompense for your labours, and that your lot is abundantly beyond the lot of the living.

JOH.14:2 In my Father's house are many mansions: if it were not so, I would have told you. I go to prepare a place for you.

1CO.2:9 But as it is written, Eye hath not seen, nor ear heard, neither have entered into the heart of man, the things which God hath prepared for them that love him

1CO.15:58 Therefore, my beloved brethren, be ye steadfast, unmoveable, always abounding in the work of the Lord, forasmuch as ye know that your labour is not in vain in the Lord.

2 And the spirits of you who had died in righteousness shall live and rejoice. And their spirits shall not perish, nor their memorial from before the face of the Great One unto all generations of the world; wherefore no longer fear they contumely.

3 Woe to you, ye sinners, when ye have died, if ye die in the wealth of your sins, and those who are like you say regarding you: "Blessed are the sinners; they have seen all their days; and how they have died in prosperity and in wealth, and have not seen tribulation or murder in their life, and they have died in honour, and judgement has not been executed on them during their life."

II Ezdras 16.77 "Woe to those who are chocked by their sins and overwhelmed by their iniquities, as a field is choked with underbrush, and its path overwhelmed with thorns, so that no one can pass through."

78 "It is shut off and given up and consumed by fire."

JAM.5:5 Ye have lived in pleasure on the earth, and been wanton; ye have nourished your hearts, as in a day of slaughter.

4 Know ye, that their souls will be made to descend into Sheol, and they shall be wretched in their great tribulation; and into darkness and chains and a burning flame where there is grievous judgement shall your spirits

enter; and the great judgement shall be for all the generations of the world. Woe to you, for ye shall have no peace.

5 Say not in regard to the righteous and good who are in life: "In our troubled days we have toiled laboriously and experienced every trouble, and met with much evil and been consumed and have become few and our spirit small; and we have been destroyed and have not found any to help us even with a word: We have been tortured and destroyed and not hoped to see life from day to day.

6 We hoped to be the head and have become the tail. We have toiled laboriously and had no satisfaction in our toil; and we have become food of the sinners and the unrighteous, and they have laid their yoke heavily upon us. They have had dominion over us that hated us and smote us; and those that hated us we have bowed our necks, but they pitied us not."

Comment:1: "Become food" Enoch is probably referring to the cannibalistic giants who were as wild beasts who devoured mankind in his time.

"Laid their yoke heavily upon us" This sounds similar to the Children of Israel, when they were in Egypt under the task masters of the Egyptians.

EXO.1:13 And the Egyptians made the children of Israel to serve with rigour:

7 We desired to get away from them that we might escape and be at rest, but found no place whereunto we should flee and be safe from them; and are complained to the rulers in our tribulation, and cried against those who devoured us, but they did not hearken to our voice.

8 And they helped those who robbed us and devoured us and those who made us few; and they concealed their oppression, and they did not remove from us the yoke of those that devoured us and dispersed us and murdered us, and they concealed their murder, and remembered not that they had lifted up their hands against us.

C.2 Just before the Flood, would have been a terribly frightening time to live, as almost everyone was lawless! The existing flimsy governments did nothing to protect the people from the man-eating Giants, and were actually in league with them. It would seem that the Giants/Demi-gods were the absolute rulers, who had mankind leaders serving under them. They used the rest of mankind whenever they could get away with it as slaves, and when they got hungry they sometimes mindlessly devoured some of their slaves.* (In modern times the "Lord of the Rings" story comes to mind, concerning the Orcs and Trolls, who also devoured mankind.)

Jubilees 5.2 "And lawlessness increased on the earth, and behold and all flesh corrupted its way, alike men and cattle and beasts and birds and everything that walks on the earth. All of them corrupted their ways and their orders, and began to devour each other, and lawlessness increased on the earth and every imagination of the thoughts of all men was thus evil continually."

Jubilees 7.22 "And they begat sons the Naphalim, and they were all unalike, and they devoured one another; and the Giants slew the Naphil and the Naphil slew the Eljo, and the Eljo mankind, and one man another."

C.3 Here, ***distinct types and sizes of Giants are mentioned***. The larger ones destroying those ones, less large, than themselves. No wonder we find the remains of underground cities, where those before the Flood could hide from the cannibalistic monstrous sized Giants. Even in modern times, skeletons of Giants, as high as 45 feet high have been found upon numerous occasions, all over the world; but usually the evidence is taken away by the Smithsonian Institute, and either destroyed or hidden, as it would immediately disprove the theory of Evolution! Other giants of 35 feet high, & yet others of 25 feet high, and yet others of 15 feet high.

Goliath mentioned after the Flood, was a *midget giant*, in comparison, as a giant of only 9 feet 9 inches! (See **Appendix** for more about **giants**)

CHAPTER 104

1 I swear unto you, that in heaven the angels remember you for good before the glory of the Great One; and your names are written before the glory of the Great One. Be hopeful, for foretime ye were put to shame through ill and affliction; but now ye shall shine as the lights of heaven, ye shall shine and ye shall be seen, and the portals of heaven shall be opened to you.

LUK.10:20 .. but rather rejoice, because your names are written in heaven.

MAT.13:43 Then shall the righteous shine forth as the sun in the kingdom of their Father.

2CO.4:7 But we have this treasure (anointing of the Holy Spirit) in earthen vessels, that the excellency of the power may be of God, and not of us.

2CO.4:8-9 We are troubled on every side, yet not distressed; we are perplexed, but not in despair; persecuted, but not forsaken; cast down, but not destroyed;

REV.3:8 I know thy works: behold, I have set before thee an open door, and no man can shut it.

REV.4:1 After this I looked, and, behold, a door was opened in heaven.

2 And in your cry, cry for judgement, and it shall appear to you; for all your tribulation shall be visited on the rulers, and on all who helped those who plundered you. Be hopeful, and cast not away your hopes for ye shall have great joy as the angels of heaven.

REV.6:10 And they cried with a loud voice, saying, 'How long, O Lord, holy and true, dost thou not judge and avenge our blood on them that dwell on the earth?'

PSA.91:8 Only with thine eyes shalt thou behold and see the reward of the wicked.

PSA.37:40 And the LORD shall help them, and deliver them: he shall deliver them from the wicked, and save them, because they trust in him

HEB.10:35 Cast not away therefore your confidence (faith), which hath great recompense of reward.

NEH.8:10 Neither be ye sorry; for the joy of the LORD is your strength.

3 What shall ye be obliged to? Ye shall not have to hide on the day of great judgement and ye shall not be found as sinners, and the eternal judgement shall be far from you for all the generations of the world.

PSA.91:7 A thousand shall fall at thy side, and ten thousand at thy right hand; but it shall not come nigh thee.

PSA.91:1 He that dwelleth in the secret place of the most High shall abide under the shadow of the Almighty.

4 And now fear not, ye righteous, when ye see the sinners growing strong and prospering in their ways: and not companions with them, but keep afar from their violence; for ye shall become companions of the hosts of heaven.

PSA.37:35 I have seen the wicked in great power, and spreading himself like a green bay tree.

PSA.37:36 Yet he passed away, and, lo, he was not: yea, I sought him, but he could not be found.

EPH.5:11 And have no fellowship with the unfruitful works of darkness, but rather reprove.

PRO.16:29 A violent man entices his neighbour, and leads him into the way that is not good.

5 And, although ye sinners say: "All our sins shall not be searched out and be written down, nevertheless they shall write down all your sins every day; and now I show unto you that light and darkness, day and night, see all your sins."

MAT.12:36 But I say unto you, 'That every idle word that men shall speak, they shall give account thereof in the day of judgment.'

MAT.12:37 For by thy words thou shalt be justified, and by thy words thou shalt be condemned.

PSA.91:8 Only with thine eyes shalt thou behold and see the reward of the wicked.

Comment:1: If all men have to give an account before God of every idle word that they spoke in their life-time, then obviously someone is taking the time to write them all down. In fact according to medical science the human brain does not actually forget anything; it is all tucked up in the subconscious brain. So all God has to do is to re-play the sub-conscious brain of man like re-winding a tape-recorder:

REV.20:12 And I saw the dead, small and great, stand before God; and the books were opened: and another book was opened, which is the book of life: and the dead were judged out of those things which were written in the books, according to their works.

6 Be not godless in your hearts, and lie not and alter not the words of uprightness, nor charge with lying words of the Holy Great One, nor take account of your idols; for all your lying and all your godlessness issue not in righteousness but in great sin.

ACT.20:29 For I know this, that after my departing shall grievous wolves enter in among you, not sparing the flock.

ACT.20:30 Also of your own selves shall men arise, speaking perverse things, to draw away disciples after them

7 And now I know this mystery, that sinners will alter and pervert the words of righteousness in many ways, and will speak wicked words, and lie, and practice great deceits, and write books concerning their words; but when they write down truthfully all my words in their languages, and not change or (de)minish ought from my words, but write them down truthfully- all that I first testified concerning them.

ROM.1:18 For the wrath of God is revealed from heaven against all ungodliness and unrighteousness of men, who hold the truth in unrighteousness;

JUD.1:4 For there are certain men crept in unawares, who were before of old ordained to this condemnation, ungodly men, turning the grace of our God into lasciviousness, and denying the only Lord God, and our Lord Jesus Christ.

JUD.1:10 But these speak evil of those things which they know not: but what they know naturally, as brute beasts, in those things they corrupt themselves.

8 Then, I know another mystery, that books will be given to the righteous and wise to become a cause of joy and uprightness and much wisdom; and to them shall the books be given, and then shall all the righteous who have learnt therefrom all the paths of the uprightness be recompensed.

ECC.2:13 Then I saw that wisdom excels folly, as far as light excels darkness

ECC.12:12 And further, by these, my son, be admonished: of making many books there is no end; and much study (of man's books) is a weariness of the flesh.

ECC.12:13 Let us hear the conclusion of the whole matter: Fear God, and keep his commandments: for this is the whole duty of man.

ECC.12:14 For God shall bring every work into judgment, with every secret thing, whether it be good, or whether it be evil.

2TI.2:15 Study to shew thyself approved unto God, a workman that needs not to be ashamed, rightly dividing the word of truth.

CHAPTER 105

1 In those days the Lord bade them to summon and testify to the children of the earth concerning their wisdom; Show it unto them for ye are their guides, and a recompense over the whole earth. For I, and My Son, will be united with them for ever in the paths of uprightness in their lives; and ye shall have peace: rejoice, ye children of uprightness. Amen.

MAT.5:9 Blessed are the peacemakers: for they shall be called the children of God.

Comment: For I (God), and My Son (Jesus)

Fragment of the Book of Noah

CHAPTER 106

1 And after some days my son Methuselah took a wife for his son Lamech, and she became pregnant and bore him a son, and his body was white as snow and red as the blooming of a rose, and the hair of his head and his long locks were white as wool, and his eyes beautiful. And when he opened his eyes he lighted up the whole house like the sun, and the whole house was very bright.

EXO.34:29 And it came to pass, when Moses came down from mount Sinai with the two tables of testimony in Moses' hand, when he came down from the mount, that Moses knew not that the skin of his face shone while he talked with him.

REV.1:14 His head and his hairs were white like wool, as white as snow; and his eyes were as a flame of fire;

Comment:1: When the prophet and leader Moses went up into mount Sinai to receive the Ten Commandments, having spent so much time in the very presence of God, his face then shone brightly. Jesus himself was also described in the same sort of way. Noah was obviously a very special child, chosen from before birth, who already knew God very well and had been in His presence just before birth, and thus Noah's appearance at birth was very godlike, reflecting God's own presence, in the same way the moon reflects the sun.

2 And thereupon he arose in the hands of the midwife, opened his mouth, and conversed with the Lord of righteousness; and his father Lamech was afraid of him and fled, and came to his father Methuselah.

3 And he said unto him; "I have begotten a strange son, diverse from and unlike man, and resembling the sons of God of heaven; and his nature is different and he is not like us, and his eyes are as the rays of the sun, and his countenance is glorious.

4 And it seems to me that he is not sprung from me but from the angels, and I fear that in his days a wonder will be wrought on the earth. And now my father I am here to petition thee and implore thee that thou mayest go to Enoch, our father, and learn from him the truth for his dwelling-place is amongst the angels."

5 And when Methuselah heard the words of his son, he came to me to the ends of the earth; for he had heard that I was there, and he cried aloud, and I heard his voice and I came to him. And I said unto him; "Behold, here I am my son, wherefore has thou come to me?"

6 And he answered and said: "Because of a great anxiety have I come

to thee, and because of a disturbing vision have I approached. And now, my father, hear me; unto Lamech my son there that been born a son, the like of whom there is none, and his nature it not like man's nature, and the colour of his body is whiter than snow and redder than the bloom of a rose, and the hair of his head is whiter than wool, and his eyes are like the rays of the sun, and he opened his eyes and thereupon lighted up the whole house."

7 And he arose in the hands of the midwife, and opened his mouth and blessed the Lord of heaven; and his father Lamech became afraid and fled to me, and did not believe that he was sprung from him, but that he was in the likeness of the angels of heaven; and behold I have come to thee that thou mayest make known to me the truth.

8 And I, Enoch answered and said unto him: "The Lord will do a new thing in the earth, and this I have already seen in vision, and make known to thee that in the generation of my father Jared some of the angels of heaven transgressed the word of the Lord. And behold they commit sin and transgress the law, and have united themselves with women and commit sin with them, and have married some of them, and have begotten children by them.

9 Yea, there shall come a great destruction over the whole earth, and there shall be a deluge and great destruction for one year; and this son who has been born unto you shall be left on the earth, and his three children shall be saved with him: when all mankind that are on the earth shall die, he and his sons shall be saved."

C.2 Here Enoch is prophesying that the Great Flood will come and last for a year and that Noah & (his wife) and his 3 sons (and their wives) will be the only ones to survive. Noah entered the Ark in the 600th year of his life, and was in the ark for one year:

GEN.7:11 In the six hundredth year of Noah's life, in the second month, the seventeenth day of the month, the same day were all the fountains of the great deep broken up, and the windows of heaven were opened.

GEN.8:13 And it came to pass in the six hundredth and first year, in the first month, the first day of the month, the waters were dried up from off the earth: and Noah removed the covering of the ark, and looked, and, behold, the face of the ground was dry.

10 And they shall produce on the earth giants not according to the spirit, but according to the flesh, and there shall be a great punishment on the earth, and the earth shall be cleansed from all impurity.

11 And now make known to thy son Lamech that he who has been born is in truth his son, and call his name Noah; for he shall be left to you, and he and his sons shall be saved from the destruction, which shall come upon the earth on account of all the sin and all the unrighteousness, which shall be consummated on the earth in his days.

12 And after that there shall be still more unrighteousness than that which was first consummated on the earth; for I know the mysteries of the holy ones; for He, the Lord has showed me and informed me, and I have read them in heavenly tablets.

C.3 It is stating here that at the end of the world, the conditions on earth are going to be like those just before the great Flood of Noah, only much worse! That is a very scary thought! What is coming back to the surface of the earth? The giants and the chimeras and a host of other critters which scientists will unleash on the earth by their experiments at Cern, and other doors to hell dotted around the world?

C.4 Man is playing around with fire spiritually speaking, and is delving into the negative spirit world, and will inadvertently bring back the spirits of the evil dead, whether intentionally or deliberately. I suppose a bit like portrayed in Lord of the Rings. Those at Cern, think they are getting into higher dimensions of more intelligent creatures than man, but in fact they are getting into the lower dimensions of Hell, because of their unbelief in God. Man experiments around with other dimensions of what he interprets as just *other physical higher beings*, such as what he thinks of as just 'aliens', when in fact he is getting into demonology and the negative spirit world.

CHAPTER 107

1 And I saw written on them that generation upon generation shall transgress, till a generation of righteousness arises, and transgression is destroyed, and sin passes away from the earth, and all manner of good comes from it; and now my son, go and make known to thy son Lamech that his son, which has born is in truth his son, and that is no lie.

Comment: Enoch tells his son Methuselah, *hundreds of years* after he *himself had been translated,* that the son (Noah) born unto Lamech, (Methuselah's son), is indeed Lamech's. In other words, he is emphasizing that Noah, although born a child full of great light and wonders, is in fact Lamech's son and *not a son born of the angels*.

2 And when Methuselah had heard the words of his father Enoch, for he had shown him everything in secret, he returned and showed them to him and called the name of that son Noah; for he will comfort the earth after all the destruction.

CHAPTER 108

1 Another book which Enoch wrote for his son Methuselah, and for those who will come after him, and keep the law in the last days: Ye who have done good shall wait for those days till an end is made of those who work evil; and an end of the might of transgressors.

2TI.2:15 Study to shew thyself approved unto God, a workman that needs not to be ashamed, rightly dividing the word of truth.

2 And wait ye indeed till sin has passed away, for their names shall be blotted out of the *book of life* and out of the holy books, and their seed shall be destroyed for ever, and their spirits shall be slain, and they shall cry and make lamentation in a place that is a chaotic wilderness, and in the fire shall they burn, for there is no earth there.

JOH.5:29 And shall come forth; they that have done good, unto the resurrection of life; and they that have done evil, unto the resurrection of damnation.

PSA.69:28 Let them be blotted out of the *book of the living*, and not be written with the righteous.

REV.20:15 And whosoever was not found written in the *book of life* was cast into the lake of fire.

3 And I saw there something like an invisible cloud; for by reason of its depth, I could not look over, and I saw a flame of fire blazing brightly, and things like shining mountains circling and sweeping to and fro.

Comments:**1**: "Invisible Cloud" is visible to some extent to Enoch but not visible to the rest of those in Enoch's time. I would venture to say that this is talking about what today is called "The Veil that Separates". It is the separation between the spiritual world and the physical world. Notice that Enoch is not able to see all that is hidden by the invisible cloud.

"*Shining mountains circling and sweeping to and fro*". This sounds like large pyramidical UFOs and their motions. Some UFOs have the appearance of a fiery flame within them, and look like an incandescent pulsating fire, or even like a beating heart.

4 And I asked one of the holy angels who was with me and said unto him: "What is this shining thing? For it is not a heaven, but only the flame of a blazing fire, and the voice of weeping and crying, and lamentation and strong pain."

C.2 Talking about UFOs as, '*not a heaven, but only the flame of a blazing fire.*'

Here it sounds like Enoch is explaining that the specific UFOs seen here, have nothing to do with heaven or goodness, but these ones are in fact very evil

C.3 In this life, the fallen angels have apparently shown off to mankind, throughout the entire history of the world, upon thousands of different occasions, as to how powerful and seemingly invincible they are, or appear to be. Including showing off their craft such as UFOs. One day all their powers will account for nothing, as they, with their UFOs descend into the Lake of Fire; and both they and all their supernatural powers will be destroyed for ever.

ZEC.5:1 Then I turned, and lifted up mine eyes, and looked, and behold a *flying roll*

ZEC.5:3 Then said he unto me, 'This is the *curse* that goes forth over the face of the whole earth: for every one that steals shall be cut off as on this side according to it; and every one that swears shall be cut off as on that side according to it.'

C.4 These verses in Zechariah are amazing & sound a lot like the movie "Aliens & Cowboys". In other words, UFOs in the future, will become much more frequently seen, and become a terrible curse to mankind in the End of Days. That is why the fallen angels who pretend to be aliens unto mankind will end up getting very severe judgement, as being Satan's emissaries, they will have practically destroyed all of God's original creation, and also mankind for a 2nd time, during the coming GREAT TRIBULATION or the last 3 and a half years of the Anti-Christ's 7-year Covenant.

5 And he said unto me: "This place which you see; here are cast the spirits of sinners and blasphemers, and of those who work wickedness, and of those who pervert everything that the Lord hath spoken through the mouth of his prophets, even the things that shall be."

REV.22:18 For I testify unto every man that hears the words of the prophecy of this book, If any man shall add unto these things, God shall add unto him the plagues that are written in this book:

REV.22:19 And if any man shall take away from the words of the book of this prophecy, God shall take away his part out of the *book of life*, and out of the holy city, and from the things which are written in this book.

6 For some of them are written and inscribed above in the heaven, in order that the angels may read them and know that which shall befall the sinners, and the spirits of the humble, and of those who have afflicted their bodies, and been recompensed by God; and of those who have been put to shame by wicked men, who love God and loved neither gold nor silver, nor any of the good things which are in the world, but gave over their bodies to torture, who, since they came into being, longed not after earthly food, but regarded everything as a passing breath, and lived accordingly, and the Lord tried them much, and

their spirits were found pure so that they should bless His name.

PSA.31:18 Let the lying lips be put to silence; which speak grievous things proudly and contemptuously against the righteous

MAT.4:4 But he answered and said, 'It is written, Man shall not live by bread alone, but by every word that proceeds out of the mouth of God.'

2TI.2:12 If we suffer, we shall also reign with him: if we deny him, he also will deny us:

2TI.3:12 Yea, and all that will live godly in Christ Jesus shall suffer persecution.

1CO.9:27 But I keep under my body, and bring it into subjection: lest that by any means, when I have preached to others, I, myself, should be a castaway.

1PE.1:7 That the trial of your faith, being much more precious than of gold that perishes, though it be tried with fire, might be found unto praise and honour and glory at the appearing of Jesus Christ:

7 And all the blessings destined for them I have recounted in the books. And he that assigned them their recompense, because they have been found to be such as loved heaven more than their life in the world, and though they were trodden under foot of wicked men, and experienced abuse and reviling from them and were put to shame, yet they blessed Me.

1JN.2:15 Love not the world, neither the things that are in the world. If any man loves the world, the love of the Father is not in him.

1JN.2:16 For all that is in the world, the lust of the flesh, and the lust of the eyes, and the pride of life, is not of the Father, but is of the world.

1JN.2:17 And the world passes away, and the lust thereof: but he that doeth the will of God abides for ever.

8 And now I will summon the spirits of the good who belong to the generation of light, and I will transform those who were born in darkness, who in the flesh were not recompensed with such honour as their faithfulness deserved. And I will bring forth in shining light those who have loved My holy name, and I will seat each on the throne of his honour.

REV.20:4 And I saw thrones, and they sat upon them, and judgment was given unto them: and I saw the souls of them that were beheaded for the witness of Jesus, and for the word of God, and which had not worshipped the beast, neither his image, neither had received his mark upon their foreheads, or in their hands; and they lived and reigned with Christ a thousand years.

9 And they shall be resplendent* for times without number; for righteousness is the judgement of God; for to the faithful He will give faithfulness in the habitation of upright paths; and they shall see those who were, born in darkness, led into darkness, while the righteous shall be resplendent; and the sinners shall cry aloud and see them resplendent, and they indeed will go, where days and seasons are prescribed for them.

C.5 *Resplendent: splendid or dazzling in appearance.

DAN.12:2 And many of them that sleep in the dust of the earth shall awake, some to everlasting life, and some to shame and everlasting contempt.

DAN.12:3 And they that be wise shall *shine as the brightness of the firmament*; and they that turn many to righteousness *as the stars* for ever and ever.

THE RETURN OF THE MESSIAH

C.6 Here is a description of **Jesus** from the **OLD TESTAMENT:**

DAN.7:13 I saw in the night visions, and, behold, one like the Son of man came with the clouds of heaven, and came to the Ancient of days, and they brought him near before him.

DAN.7:14 And there was given him (The Son of man) dominion, and glory, and a kingdom, that all people, nations, and languages, should serve him: his dominion is an everlasting dominion, which shall not pass away, and his kingdom that which shall not be destroyed.

DAN.7:27 And the kingdom and dominion, and the greatness of the kingdom under the whole heaven, shall be given to the people of the saints of the most High, whose kingdom is an everlasting kingdom, and all dominions shall serve and obey him.

PSA.72:11 Yea, all kings shall fall down before him: all nations shall serve him.

PSA.72:19 And blessed be his glorious name for ever: and let the whole earth be filled with his glory; Amen, and Amen

PSA.96:10 Say among the heathen that the LORD reigns: the world also shall be established that it shall not be moved: he shall judge the people righteously.

PSA.96:11 Let the heavens rejoice, and let the earth be glad; let the sea roar, and the fullness thereof.

PSA.96:12 Let the field be joyful, and all that is therein: then shall all the trees of the wood rejoice.

PSA.96:13 Before the LORD: for he cometh, for he cometh to judge the earth: he shall judge the world with righteousness, and the people with his truth.

ISA.11:1 And there shall come forth a rod out of the stem of Jesse, and a Branch shall grow out of his roots:

ISA.11:2 And the spirit of the LORD shall rest upon him, the spirit of wisdom and understanding, the spirit of counsel and might, the spirit of knowledge and of the fear of the LORD;

ISA.11:3 And shall make him of quick understanding in the fear of the LORD: and he shall not judge after the sight of his eyes, neither reprove after the hearing of his ears:

ISA.11:4 But with righteousness shall he judge the poor, and reprove with equity for the meek of the earth: and he shall smite the earth: with the rod of his mouth, and with the breath of his lips shall he slay the wicked.

ISA.11:5 And righteousness shall be the girdle of his loins, and faithfulness the girdle of his reins.

DAN.2:44 And in the days of these kings shall the God of heaven set up a kingdom, which shall never be destroyed: and the kingdom shall not be left to other people, but it shall break in pieces and consume all these kingdoms, and it shall stand for ever.

DAN.7:9 I beheld till the thrones were cast down (The Anti-Christ and his demonic rulers), and the Ancient of days did sit, whose garment was white as snow, and the hair of his head like the pure wool: his throne was like the fiery flame, and his wheels as burning fire.

DAN.7:10 A fiery stream issued and came forth from before him: thousand thousands ministered unto him, and ten thousand times ten thousand stood before him: the judgment was set, and the books were opened.

C.7 Here is a description of **Jesus** from the **NEW TESTAMENT**:

MAT.24:27 For as the lightning cometh out of the east, and shines even unto the west; so shall also the coming of the Son of man be.

MAT.24:29 Immediately after the tribulation of those days shall the sun be darkened, and the moon shall not give her light, and the stars shall fall from heaven, and the powers of the heavens shall be shaken:

MAT.24:30 And then shall appear the sign of the Son of man in heaven: and then shall all the tribes of the earth mourn, and they shall see the Son of man coming in the clouds of heaven with power and great glory.

MAT.24:31 And he shall send his angels with a great sound of a trumpet, and they shall gather together his elect from the four winds, from one end of heaven to the other.

REV.1:13 And in the midst of the seven candlesticks one like unto the Son of man, clothed with a garment down to the foot, and girt about the paps with a golden girdle.

REV.1:14 His head and his hairs were white like wool, as white as snow; and his eyes were as a flame of fire;

REV.1:15 And his feet like unto fine brass, as if they burned in a furnace; and his voice as the sound of many waters.

REV.1:16 And he had in his right hand seven stars: and out of his mouth went a sharp two-edged sword: and his countenance was as the sun shines in his strength.

REV.19:11 And I saw heaven opened, and behold a white horse; and he that sat upon him was called Faithful and True, and in righteousness he doth judge and make war.

REV.19:12 His eyes were as a flame of fire, and on his head were many crowns; and he had a name written, that no man knew, but he himself.

REV.19:13 And he was clothed with a vesture dipped in blood: and his name is called The Word of God.

REV.19:14 And the armies which were in heaven followed him upon white horses, clothed in fine linen, white and clean.

REV.19:15 And out of his mouth goes a sharp sword, that with it he should smite the nations: and he shall rules them with a rod of iron: and he treads the winepress of the fierceness and wrath of Almighty God.

REV.19:16 And he hath on his vesture and on his thigh a name written, KING OF KINGS, AND LORD OF LORDS.

1TI.6:14 That thou keep this commandment without spot, unrebukable, until the appearing of our Lord Jesus Christ:

1TI.6:15 Which in his times he shall shew, who is the blessed and only Potentate, the KING OF KINGS, AND LORD OF LORDS;

SALVATION

Finally, I challenge you, that if you have not already prayed to receive Jesus into your heart, so that you can have eternal life, & be guaranteed an eternal place in Heaven, then please do so immediately, to keep you safe from what is soon coming upon the earth!

Jesus stated in **Revelations 3.20** "Behold, I stand at the door and knock, if any man hear my voice, and open the door, I will come in to him and live with him and him with me".

"He who believes on the Son of God has eternal life." **John 3.36**.

That means right now! Once saved, you are eternally saved, and here is a very simple prayer to help you to get saved:

"Dear Jesus, Please, come into my heart, forgive me all of my sins, give me eternal life, and fill me with your Holy Spirit. Please help me to love others and to read the Word of God in Jesus name, Amen."

Once you've prayed that little prayer sincerely, then you are guaranteed a wonderful future in Heaven for eternity with your creator, and loved ones. "For God is Love" **1 John 4.16**

Your Salvation does not depend on you going to church, and your good works. **Titus 3.5** states "Not by works of righteousness which we have done, but according to His mercy he *saved* us".

Your salvation only depends on receiving Christ as your saviour, not on church or religion!

"He that comes unto Me, **I will in no wise cast out" - Jesus**

Jesus explained that unless you become as a child, you won't even understand the KINGDOM OF HEAVEN. (**John 3.3**)

For a much more detailed explanation of **SALVATION AND ETERNAL LIFE** please refer to my website: http://www.outofthebottomlesspit.co.uk/418605189

APPENDIX

CONCLUSIONS

I Conundrums:1) How could Enoch write about Noah in chapter 12, when according to the Bible time chronology, Noah was not even born until about 70-90 years after Enoch had been "translated"?

2) How did Noah visit Enoch at the 'ends of the earth' in chapter 65 and also Methuselah visit Enoch also at the 'ends of the earth' in chapter 106?

Well, interestingly enough, there is a way to explain it all:

The fact is that Enoch never actually died, so that both Noah and Methuselah found a way to call on Enoch hundreds of years after his translation. But how?

Well, It is stated in the Book of Jubilees 4.23, that Enoch was taken by the angels into the Garden of Eden, when he was translated, where he wrote down on the heavenly tablets the history of the world from the beginning to the end. *If that all happened after his translation, then it would have been possible for him to write CH 12 about God sending the angel Uriel to Noah*, as quite some time had passed while Enoch was in the Heavenly Realm. Noah had already been born and grown up and been given his instructions from God concerning the coming Flood.

Ch 65 and 105, when both Noah and Methuselah met Enoch hundreds of years after his translation, gave ample opportunity for Enoch to pass on His books to either Methuselah or Noah. Noah subsequently took the Book of Enoch on the Ark, where it was kept and preserved after the flood. It was finally re-written and compiled again in around 200 BCE.

It also states in the Book of Jubilees, that Enoch was learning and writing for 6 Jubilees, which is 300 years, and was in the garden of Eden, during that time writing things down on tablets of stone.. According to Jewish tradition of the Ancient Sages, the Garden of Eden was inside the earth, and situated immediately below the cave where Abraham buried Sarah.(See my website under '**HOLLOW EARTH'**: http://www.outofthebottomlesspit.co.uk/421040248 Or chapter 3 of my book *Out of the Bottomless Pit*.)

Enoch's total life span on earth was 365 years. His son Methuselah, was born when Enoch was 65, so Enoch must have started his spiritual journeys sometime right after the birth of Methuselah. He was finally translated when he was 365 years old. By comparing the life of Enoch as told in the Book of Jasher and the Book of Jubilees with the Bible, one gets a clearer picture of the whole situation, and how it was even possible for Noah to talk with Enoch, after he had been translated.

II THE ENDS OF THE EARTH

Another conundrum is that both Noah and Methuselah stated that they visited

Enoch at "the ends of the earth" How did they get to the ends of the earth? If the earth is actually hollow, is it just possible that there used to be PORTALS from the outer surface to the inner surface of the earth. These portals would not have been visible to everyone, but only to a few select people on earth, including Noah and Methuselah, because they were *very desperate in prayer with God*, and very much needed to talk to Enoch. When both Methuselah and Noah mentioned travelling to see Enoch at the 'ends of the earth' after his translation, *they don't make it sound like it was impossible to find him*, or that they *had to travel very long distance and spend a long time locating Enoch. How could both of them on separate occasions have travelled a long distance in what seems like moments, according to their own description of the event?*

Enoch talks about portals in detail. I propose that all kinds of Portals used to exist, which were *dimensional gate-ways to other places* and for various purposes. I believe that there used to be portals linking the OUTER EARTH to the INNER EARTH. Also, other portals, linking this dimension with higher dimensions. There seems to be quite a bit of evidence of this. The famous Bermuda Triangles, seem to show that there are places on earth where portals move ships, planes and people to other dimensions and even other times, and sometimes back again. I have heard many stories of strange places on earth where some kind of invisible portals exist, and whole areas that are put as "off-limits" to the general population. (See my website under "THE BERMUDA TRIANGLE" www.outofthebottomlesspit.co.uk Or chapter 2 of my book *Out of the Bottomless Pit* Available at www.amazon.co.uk)

III THE 'TRANSLATION' OF ENOCH

The problem that we face today, is that normally most people are supposedly in most cases, too scared, to even contemplate communicating with the "Dead". In fact to most modern religions, it is simply taboo, based on Old Testament laws of Moses, where you could be "stoned to death" for communicating with the dead.

I believe that God in His great wisdom and foresight, realised that future communications with those who have passed on, might became problematic in the future for most human-beings, which is completely understandable.

So, God choose Enoch, to be a *type of intercessor between Himself and mankind*. The fact that *Enoch hadn't actually "died"*, would have given reassurance to both Methuselah and Noah, that it was actually perfectly OK, for them to communicate directly with Enoch even after his "translation to heaven", as he had not "died" but was translated to another higher plane, but still had a physical improved supernatural body, such as Jesus had after His Resurrection.

Powers and Ability to move fast, of those who have passed on to the positive spirit world:

The day is coming when nobody will move rapidly except us. (Those who have been SAVED through Jesus Christ) One of these days soon we will be trading in our old, worn-out, fleshly, earthy body for an entirely new Heavenly model! We'll be able to fly through the air and up through the clouds and all the way to the moon and the stars, and we'll fly with not just the speed of light, which is not fast enough to get around through such a big Universe! But our new spiritual bodies will move with the speed of thought! All you'll have to do is think yourself someplace and you'll be there! No time wasted, no cars, no stinky fumes, no flat tires, no accidents and you're there!

The flesh of the future, the supernatural, miraculous, resurrected, transformed, fleshly bodies of the future are going to be like the angels of God! We will look like we do now, only better! Just as Jesus did after His resurrection. He could eat and drink and they could feel Him and touch Him as well as see Him, and yet He was in a miraculous supernatural body, His new resurrected body (**Lk.24:36-43**). He said we were going to have bodies like His! (**1Jn.3:2; 1Cor.15:42-58**). He could appear or disappear, He could walk right through walls or locked doors, and He could fly with the speed of thought! Whissssst! - And you're there!

With the above thoughts in mind, I don't think it was so difficult for Enoch to communicate with both Methuselah and Noah from the positive spirit world or in his particular case the Garden of Eden, which is sort of in-between world half physical and half spiritual.

IV Background History of the Book of Enoch

What other evidences for Enoch's authenticity (as a sacred text) are there?

Why isn't it in the Bible today?

*[1] Since it's English translation in the 1800's from texts found in Ethiopia in 1768, The Book of Enoch (known today as 1st Enoch) has made quite a stir in academic circles. 1 Enoch has been authenticated as existing and in wide use before the church age (most scholars now date it at 200 BC). Multiple copies were discovered in 1948 in the Dead Sea Scrolls. This of course has caused many to wonder why it is not included in modern Bibles.

Enoch 1 relates the story of the fallen angels in great detail. It lists the names of 18 "prefect" angels - of 200 - who committed this sin. According to the text, these angels also taught mankind the "making of swords and knives, shields and breastplates (metallurgy); ... magical medicine, dividing of roots (medicinal and hallucinogenic use); incantations, astrology, the seeing of the stars, the course of the moon, as well as the deception of man."

By Noah's time, "The earth also was corrupt (wasting - KJV notation) before God, and the earth was filled with violence... all flesh had corrupted his way upon the earth." Gen 6:10-11. Afraid of the consequences, these angels appeal to Enoch to intercede with God on their behalf; God instead uses Enoch to deliver a message of judgment against them. Aside from the "taking of wives," God states that he would not forgive them for teaching mankind magical arts and warlike ways.

The increasing acceptance and popularization of this important book among theologians helps cast light on the extra-terrestrial hypothesis (ETH) in general. Enoch is an ancient writing, which states that angels & not true space aliens, as stated by many UFO cults, and popular modern authors Erich Von Daniken & Zachariah Sitchin visited ancient Earth and polluted mankind's DNA. While this case can easily be made solely from the canonized Bible. Enoch is yet another witness against these bad interpretations of Earth's pre-deluvian era (i.e., before the flood of Genesis 6). The fact that they also gave mankind technology which supposedly "advanced our race" (but which we actually used to destroy each other, and to incur God's judgment), lends itself to a more sinister understanding of today's UFO phenomenon

Genesis 6 / Book of Enoch	**Today / Any episode of the X-Files**
Supernatural Beings identified as angels	Supernatural Beings identified as ETs
Took as wives "any whom they chose"	Abduction Phenomenon
Hybrid Race of Nephilim	Missing Fetuses, Hybrids, Cloning
Introduced Destructive Technology: Weapons of Warfare / Psychotropic Drugs / Astrology & Sorcery	Hitler's Foo Fighters / Roswell Crash / "Back-engineering" of Stealth Bombers, etc / Occult Arts, New Age Doctrines
Worshipped as Gods (Annanuki) / Nephilim hybrids were "heroes of old, men of renown..." Gen 6:4 - the factual basis for Greco-Roman deities	Zechariah Sitchin / UFO Cults / Immunity for Abduction Crimes / Called "Spirit Guides, Ascended Masters" and/or "Space Brothers"
"And the Lord said, 'I will destroy man whom I have created from the face of the Earth' ... but Noah found grace in the eyes of the Lord." Genesis 6:7-8	"As it was in the days of Noah, so shall it be at the coming of the Son of Man..." Jesus Christ, Matthew 24:37

(Editor: See my 1st book, *Out of the Bottomless Pit* at www.amazon.co.uk , for much more information concerning the topic of Aliens, Alien Abductions and many Paranormal coverups.)

V What other evidences for Enoch's authenticity (as a sacred text) are there?

Why isn't it in the Bible today?

One reason given by churches:
Jesus said that angels can't have sex, proving this book's falsehood...

The idea that Jesus said that angels cannot have sex is a very common objection to The Book of Enoch, and the angelic understanding of Genesis

6 in general. However, it is also a very common misinterpretation of what he actually said. (Matt 22:30)

MAT.22:30 For in the resurrection they neither marry, nor are given in marriage, but are as the angels of God in heaven

This verse is not saying that people can't have sex in heaven. The opposite is true, where love and sex are a much more complete experience in the spirit world, according to those who have spoken from beyond, of which there are many examples written. (See the book 'Journey to Gragau' about a trip to hell and also about the nature of both angels and spirit helpers.)

Beyond that misunderstanding, there is no doubt today that The Book of Enoch was one of the most widely accepted and revered books of Jewish culture and doctrine in the century leading up to Jesus' birth.

It is usually noted first that New Testament author Jude directly quotes from 1 Enoch - "Behold he comes with ten thousand of his saints to execute judgment ..." (1 Enoch 2, Jude 14-15). Additionally, "the citations of Enoch by the Testaments of the Twelve Patriarchs... show that at the close of the second century B.C., and during the first century B.C., this book was regarded in certain circles as inspired" (1).

Aside from Jude, Peter and Paul's affirmations of the angelic/hybrid interpretation, recognition of 1 Enoch "... is given amply in the Epistle of Barnabus, and in the third century by Clement and Irenaeus" (1). The Catholic Church's Origen - known as "the father of theology" - affirmed both the Book of Enoch and the fact that angels could and did co-habitate with the daughters of men. He even warned against possible angelic and/or Nephilim infiltration of the church itself. Oddly, while thousands of his writings are still considered by them as "sacred"; this very issue got him labelled as a heretic when the faulty Sons of Seth "doctrine" was conceived! (2) Additionally, the Coptic Orthodox Churches of Egypt (est'd appx 50-100 A.D.) still include Enoch as canonized text in the Ethiopic Old Testament (2). This fact alone should carry great weight for Western Christians when honestly studying the "case" for Enoch. Given their 1900+ year history, the fact that they were never "ruled" by Rome's theology, and that they currently number over 10 million - this is a VERY significant portion of The Body of Christ that has historically esteemed 1 Enoch as inspired doctrine.

Some today (who do not seem to believe in the inspiration of scripture) claim that most major themes of the New Testament were in fact "borrowed" from 1 Enoch. "It appears that Christianity later adopted some of its ideas and philosophies from this book, including the Final Judgment, the concept of demons, the Resurrection, and the coming of a Messiah and Messianic Kingdom" (3). No doubt, these themes are major parts of 1 Enoch, and appear there as complete theologies a full 200 years before any other NT writings.

Christian author Stephen Quayle writes, "Several centuries before and after the appearance of Jesus in Jerusalem, this book had become well known to the Jewish community, having a profound impact upon Jewish thought.

The Book of Enoch gave the Jews their solar calendar, and also appears to have instilled the idea that the coming Messiah would be someone who had pre-existed as God (4)." Translator RH Charles also stated that "the influence of 1 Enoch on the New Testament has been greater than all of the other apocryphal and pseudepigraphical books put together" (3). The conclusions are somewhat inescapable given Enoch's dating and wide acceptance between 200 B.C. and 200 A.D. - either Christian authors, and especially the Nicene Council, did plagiarize their theology directly from Enoch, or the original version of Enoch was also inspired.

James H Charlesworth, director of Dead Sea Studies at Yale University, says in The Old Testament Pseudeipgrapha & The New Testament (Trinity Press International),

"I have no doubt that the Enoch groups deemed the Book of Enoch as fully inspired as any biblical book. I am also convinced that the group of Jews behind the Temple Scroll, which is surely pre-Qumranic, would have judged it to be quintessential Torah -- that is, equal to, and perhaps better than, Deuteronomy....Then we should perceive the Pseudepigrapha as they were apparently judged to be: God's revelation to humans (2 & 5)."

But perhaps the most telling argument for 1 Enoch's "inspiration" may well be that the Jewish understanding of the term "Son of Man" as a Messianic title comes - not truly from our Old Testament canon - but from the Book of Enoch! Ever wonder why Jesus refers to himself in the gospels as the "Son of Man" rather than the Son of God? (2) Of over 100 uses of the phrase "son of man" in the OT, it refers almost always to "normal" men (93 times specifically of Ezekiel, and certainly not as Messiah!), but is used only one time in the entire OT, in one of Daniel's heavenly visions, to refer to divinity. Despite the Old Testament's frequent lack of divine application of the phrase, 1 Enoch records several trips to heaven, using the title "Son of Man" unceasingly to refer to the pre-incarnate Christ. Of particular Messianic significance, Enoch describes the following scene (2):

The angels "glorify with all their power of praise; and He sustains them in all that act of thanksgiving while they laud, glorify and exalt the name of the Lord of Spirits forever and ever... Great was their joy. They blessed, glorified and exalted because the name of the Son of Man was revealed to them (1 Enoch 68:35-38)." Both His disciples, and especially the Sanhedrin knew what Jesus was claiming - 84 times in the gospels! - when referring to Himself as the "Son of Man." This claim was considered an obvious blasphemy to the Pharisees & Sadducees, but it is eternal life to all who confess that Jesus of Nazareth was, and is, the Son of Man, The Messiah, God in the flesh, The Holy One of Israel, God's Christ - the Lord of All to whom every knee shall bow (Philippians 2:8-10).

Using "normal rules" of scriptural interpretation, we are never to draw firm doctrine from only one passage of scripture. Right? Daniel's single use of "Son of Man" (in a "night vision" at that - Dan 7:13), would not be sufficient to claim that the phrase is indeed Messianic, especially given the other 107 times it is not used in that way. 1 Enoch is the missing "second witness" needed (according to all other rules of interpretation) to understand the phrase's double meaning as an enduring Messianic title. It has been argued ever since Enoch's first English translation, that by using this title so familiar to the Jews, Jesus was actually affirming the truth of this book, that the prophet was taken on many trips to heaven before his "final" translation, and that HE WAS THE ONE whom Enoch saw there - the pre-existent Son of Man, whom Enoch prophesied would judge the souls of all men.

Interestingly, Daniel is ALSO the only OT use of the term "watcher" to ever refer to angels (Daniel 4:13, 17, 23 KJV). Strong's Concordance defines a watcher as a "guardian angel" (Strong's 5894). "The distinguishing character of the Watcher (opposed to other angels in the canon) appears to be that it spends much time among men, overseeing what they are doing. It is also interesting to note that both times one of these angels appeared to Daniel, he took pains to note that it was "an holy one", suggesting that some Watchers are not aligned with God while others are (4). Found nowhere else in the OT canon but the book of Daniel, "watcher" is patently Enoch's term for these angels. Likewise, Daniel alone used Enoch's term "Son of Man" to refer to the pre-incarnate Christ, adding further intrigue to the case for 1 Enoch's inspiration, and an overall understanding of its doctrinal acceptance among both Old and New Testament writers.

What we lose out on today by not examining 1 Enoch - even if only for its historical significance - is that it is actually more splendid than ANY OTHER book in our canon in its exultation of Christ as King! It also gives clear, stern and oft-repeated warnings to the unsaved of swift destruction at the Coming of The Lord, but is also full of amazing promises of future glory for the elect! We are of course wise to stay clear of dangerous heresy, but... ask yourself if the below sounds like false doctrine? Keep in mind, this was written at least 200 years before Christ walked the earth, and perhaps before Noah's birth:

Then shall the kings, the princes, and all who possess the earth,
glorify Him who has dominion over all things, Him who was concealed;
for from eternity the Son of Man was concealed,
whom the Most High preserved in the presence of
His power and revealed to the elect.
He shall sow the congregation of the saints, and of the elect;
and all the elect shall stand before Him in that day.
All the kings, the princes, the exalted, and those who rule
over the earth shall fall down on their faces before Him,
and shall worship Him.
They shall fix their hopes on this Son of Man...
Then the sword of the Lord of Spirits shall be drunk from them (the lost);
but the saints and the elect shall be safe in that day; nor the face
of the sinners and the ungodly shall they thence-forth behold.
The Lord of Spirits shall remain over them;
And with this Son of Man shall they dwell, eat, lie down,
and rise up for ever and ever...
Enoch 61:10-13

So why is it not in the Bible?

Uncertain, as well as multiple authorship, and several slightly varying texts are among the main reasons cited for Enoch not "making it" into the generally recognized canon. In truth, the spiritual agenda(s) of the early Roman Church is most likely the ultimate reason however, and we will examine this agenda here as well. Let's begin with the first two though, before moving to the more incredulous, but quite valid "conspiracy theories".

"The Book of Enoch, like the book of Daniel, was originally written in Aramaic, and partly in Hebrew (1)." While there may have been Hebrew translations during the centuries B.C. (which early church leaders may or may not have had access to), today only the Ethiopic manuscripts exist, as well as some incomplete Greek and Latin translations, plus one Aramaic fragment from the Dead Sea Scrolls. By the time of Jesus' birth, "average" Jews were reading mainly the Greek Septuagint translation of their own Torah (completed 200 B.C.), as a result of their years of foreign captivity and then-current Roman occupation. To coin the vernacular, they had been assimilated. So unless an authentic Aramaic version appears miraculously today, there will never be any completely indisputable way to argue for a modern "canonization" of 1 Enoch, as the originals are lost, probably forever.

The honest problem facing the infant Roman Church of 390 A.D., when first assembling today's Bible, was that the existing copies of 1 Enoch varied, albeit in minor ways. "Unlike the (rest of the) Bible which was carefully copied and checked for errors by Jewish and Christian scribes throughout its history, The Book of Enoch is available in a number of ancient manuscripts that differ slightly from one another... and many errors have crept in... There is no way of knowing which versions are (exactly faithful to) the original and which are the errors. While this doesn't change its stories in any substantial manner, it does make it impossible to anchor beliefs or arguments on any given section... (4)."

Another less important but quite "legitimate" issue is that 1 Enoch is actually a collection of at least four different "books", possibly written by various authors over many centuries, and possibly not by the true Enoch of Genesis 5.

The Artisan Publishers' introduction to The Book of Enoch says "there can be no shadow of doubt" that there is a diversity of authorship and perhaps even time periods represented across the span of 1 Enoch, but that there is also "nonetheless, uniformity". They attribute this to the very possible idea that as God raised up prophets (after Malachi...?), they published under the safety of a revered pseudonym, to avoid persecution and possible death at the hands of the religious powers-that-were, who wanted no "fresh words" from God (1). This could well be the case, but would make the book(s) of Enoch no less inspired of God if true. However, only the NT Book of Hebrews (written centuries closer to the Bible's assembly, with multiple matching manuscripts) has been accepted as canon with such uncertain authorship - without even a good solid guess agreed upon, that is.

Since "the real" Enoch of Genesis 5 was transported to heaven - permanently

- it would be no stretch to imagine that it was also a normal experience during his lifetime. After all, the Bible says he walked with God for 300 years! (Genesis 5:22) The first 36 chapters (detailing the watchers' fall) are sometimes only reluctantly attributed to Enoch (given their pre-deluvian history), but there are varying theories regarding the rest of the book(s). For much of the 1800's, it was argued that the remaining chapters were actually the work of an early Christian scribe, but these claims were decisively put to rest with the discovery of the Dead Sea Scrolls, as were JT Milik's claims that chapters 37-71 were Christian. Charlesworth says "The consensus communis is unparalleled in almost any other area of research; no specialist now argues that I *Enoch 37-71 is (written by a first-century) Christian and (that it) postdates the first century... (2) and (5)." With this in mind, we must again face up to the very real dilemma of stating that either the entire New Testament was "drawn" in a natural, secular way from 1 Enoch - with no supernatural inspiration - or that 1 Enoch and The New Testament are both from God.

It is also considered that possibly a single author assembled older prophets' inspired works around 200 B.C. and simply added Enoch's name to them all, to ensure widespread acceptance - "Hardly a practice that inspires confidence in the text (4)." But in reality, it is no secret academically that certain canonized OT books, as well as Mark's gospel, may have been originally written by another - or even multiple - inspired author(s) and later were also assembled under the inspiration of God by a single author, who put either his own, or the original author's name, to the work. For example, most agree that Moses actually wrote Job's story from other existing texts (or that he knew him personally), before he even wrote Genesis. Most of the Major Prophets and historical books contain clear breaks in the time period, and were finally assembled many years later - as the author "was carried along by the Holy Spirit (1 Peter 2:21)." Christians need to get over the idea that "inspiration" means the writer went into some mystical trance, while God "possessed them" and wrote the Bible. Inspiration simply means they were obedient to God's leading, and wrote what He said OR supernaturally revealed to them, or even that he guided their research, helping them discern truth from error, for the purpose of writing "an orderly account (Luke 1:3)." Here, Luke states that his gospel was an extended research project!

In that vein, I.D.E. Thomas has recently suggested one other possibility perhaps not considered in academic circles before the 1986 publication of The Omega Conspiracy. "Thomas suggests that the compiler may have written his book from texts originally written by Enoch himself. In such a case it would make perfect sense for the compiler to attach Enoch's name to the book for which he had provided the material (4) and (6)."

Even with all of this said, there is still no "clean" explanation for Enoch's 1000-year disappearance from even popular literature though. Despite the above reasons for not canonizing the book, it is painfully apparent that the church did in fact suppress The Book of Enoch. Only in studying both the goals and motives - positive and negative - of the Roman Church do the truest reason for Enoch's "fall from grace" become apparent.

(But despite the arguments presented here, please note that I have no intention of bashing the early Roman Catholic Church. Always remember, they have done the world an incredible service by assembling and preserving God's Word for the 1600+ years yet to follow. To make a distinction, the greatest sins and travesties they often stand accused - and guilty of - were not the work or intent of the earliest Church fathers, but of the corrupt political system that grew up in the centuries after the Roman system's formation. "It was not until hundreds of years later (5th - 7th centuries), that the first vestiges of this church government rose where there was a Roman bishop as the head of the Church, making it an official Roman Church functioning similar to today's." (7))

To be honest, in reading Enoch there seems to be in the multitude of heavenly trips a physical distinction sometimes made between The Father and the Pre-Incarnate Son. The phrases "Lord of Spirits", "Ancient of Days," and "Son of Man" are used so often (perhaps interchangeably, perhaps not) that even a careful reading sometimes infers the (doctrinally acceptable - 1 Cor 15:24) separation of the eternal Godhead. On earth, "... all the fullness of the deity" was present in Jesus Christ, "the image of the invisible God." But 1 Enoch can at minimum cause confusion to the understanding of the Godhead - hard enough to grasp even today - in a way that other authors (Moses, Isaiah, Ezekiel, Paul and John) do not when speaking of their face-to-face encounters with God. (Did any gnostics still in the audience catch that phrase?) Even without the conflicting manuscripts or possible multiple authors coming into play (which careful examination of the rest of canon shows could have been worked out actually, if they so chose), I sincerely believe that if there was a legitimate, excusable motive for not including Enoch in the Bible, this was it.

This does not excuse why we had to wait 1000 years to re-discover this book however.

So finally, with the general integrity of the Holy Scriptures, and the legitimate reasons the early Roman Catholic Church may have rejected 1 Enoch covered respectfully (and in a way palatable for modern Christian academics), let's critically examine the real reasons behind the indisputable censure of 1 Enoch. There are many texts that - while not included as canon - have nonetheless retained their "position of honour" and even reverence among the (Western) historical Christian church. Among these are the Apocrypha (still included of course in modern Catholic Bibles - and, just FYI, even included in the original King James Bible), as well as The 12 Patriarchs, and writings too numerous to name by various "Church Fathers." All of these have remained in a relatively high-profile position throughout church history, more or less available for both scholars and laymen to draw from when studying the ancient origins of the Christian faith. Not so with Enoch.

Yes, ANY of the above are certainly "good enough" reasons to have disqualified Enoch from canonization. But only assuming you wanted to in the first place ...

With all of the evidence in, we have to own the fact that 1 Enoch was not merely "rejected for canonization." It was buried. Flat out suppressed. It was quite intentionally lost to history, with all copies destroyed or left to rot 10 stories deep under the Vatican. Enoch was not merely "left out of the Bible." It was dropped like a bad habit.

Enoch was suppressed and labelled as heresy specifically to *hide the truth of the fallen angels' past, present and future activity on earth*, according to Origen. [Adamantius **Origen,** was Greek (A.D. 184-254), was born in Alexandria, Egypt, and was one of the most famous "church fathers, & was also a prolific writer.]

The above articles: **APPENDIX V & VI which are 'Background History' of the Book of Enoch**, is printed from:- http://www.sherryshriner.com/church-coverup.htm

by permission of Sherry Shiner. *For more on this topic please visit Sherry's website.*

VI GIANTS: See Steve Quayle's website, concerning giants:-< www.stevequayle.com >

VII GENE DISINTEGRATION: ***Genetic Entropy*** presents compelling scientific evidence that the genomes of all living creatures are slowly **degenerating** - due to the accumulation of slightly harmful mutations. This is happening in spite of natural selection. The author of this book, Dr. John Sanford, is a Cornell University geneticist. Dr. Sanford has devoted more than 10 years of his life to the study of this specific problem. Arguably, he has examined this problem in greater depth than any other scientist. The evidences that he presents are diverse and compelling. He begins by examining how random mutation and natural selection actually operate, and shows that simple logic demands that genomes must degenerate. He then makes a historical examination of the relevant field (**population genetics**), and shows that the best scientists in that field have consistently acknowledged many of the fundamental problems he has uncovered (but they have failed to communicate these problems to the broader scientific community). He then shows, in collaboration with a team of other scientists, that state-of-the-art numerical simulation experiments consistently confirm the problem of genetic degeneration (even given very strong selection and optimal conditions). Lastly, in collaboration with other scientists, he shows that ***real biological populations clearly manifest genetic degeneration.***

Dr. Sanford's findings have enormous implications. His work largely ***invalidates classic neo-Darwinian theory.*** The mutation/selection process by itself is not capable of creating the new biological information that is required for creating new life forms. Dr. Sanford shows that not only is mutation/selection incapable of creating our genomes - it can't even preserve our genomes. As biochemist Dr. Michael Behe of Lehigh University writes in his review of

Genetic Entropy, "...not only does Darwinism not have answers for how information got into the genome, it doesn't even have answers for how it could remain there." Dr. Sanford has coined the term "genetic entropy" to describe this fatal flaw of neo-Darwinian theory. This fundamental problem has been something of a trade-secret within the field of population genetics, with the rest of the world largely being kept in the dark. Fortunately, this book finally discloses this very serious problem, using language that is for the most part accessible to all scholars and students having a basic understanding of biology. Get Dr Sanford's amazing insightful book on **'POPULATION GENETICS' AND 'GENE DE-GRADATION'**: https://answersingenesis.org/store/product/genetic-entropy-mystery-genome/?sku=10-3-114

VIII THE COSMIC BATTLE OF JESUS (*HUMILITY)* AGAINST SATAN (*PRIDE)*

Ever since time immemorial, this battle has been constantly waged. So where did it all start? It has been stated that before the physical creation, there existed a heavenly realm which was inhabited by spirit beings of all types. All originally were obedient to God. God realized however, in His infinite wisdom, that ultimately it would be better if everyone followed His orders, not because they felt forced to, or that they were so afraid not to obey God's every whim, but *by choice*.

The Bible tells us clearly, that God Himself, at the essence of His being is Love. We also know that Jesus is the opposite of Satan, and is the Spirit of Humility, and so also is His Holy Spirit Mother.

We are told by the scriptures, that God has simply always been, and that He is the Great 'I am that I am'. We have also learnt from scripture that Jesus is the Word of God, and it was Jesus along with the Holy Spirit of God, that were responsible for the physical creation. Apparently, they were hindered in the creation story by Satan himself at some time or other. Avak the Oriental Mystic prophet stated that Satan destroyed God's original Creation in the 'Great Heavenly Rebellion' of both himself and the fallen angels. So, then God recreated order out of the chaos that the Devil had made in his anger and rebellion.

WHY DID SATAN REBEL AGAINST GOD IN THE FIRST PLACE?

'Long, long ago, Lucifer stood at the right hand of God. He bore the light. He was not the light, but he held the light on high for all the inhabitants of the universe to see. He was the standard bearer, the mightiest of all archangels, and he exercised some of the power of Almighty God Himself in helping to rule the universe. Then pride took its grip. Though he held such a high and honoured position, Lucifer was no longer satisfied with bearing the light of God. He wanted to be God Himself.

WHAT TRIGGERED SATAN'S FALL?

Apparently, according to a very interesting prophecy that I had the privilege of reading, it all started when God came to present His 'Only Begotten Son Jesus' to all the Hosts of Heaven. Satan thought that he himself being the mightiest of all arch-angels, should be the next in line for this honour:

'Infested with pride, he refused to listen to God. He refused to listen to the other angelic forces and to the Heavenly inhabitants. He refused any, and all help to see the right. Because he refused to admit he was wrong and say he was sorry, because he chose to hold on to his pride, strong delusion set in. Refusing to humble himself before a powerful and awesome God, his own loving, patient, and understanding Father, Lucifer fell. He altered the course of his own destiny. He didn't *have* to fall; he *chose* to fall. He chose his own course, all because of his lust for power and his proud refusal to choose the humble way.

This is when insanity took tight hold on Lucifer. This is when of his own choosing he was transformed from Lucifer, the bearer of light, to Satan, the Devil, the father of lies. This is when the long trek began. From the moment of that decision, he set out on his hostile mission. From that time on, he set out to live at enmity with God, His creation, and His children.'

THE FALL OF THE FALLEN ANGELS

When Satan fell, he tried to persuade others of the angels to go with him. Those who accepted his lies became poisoned, drawn away by their own desires. Therefore, pride took hold and they were overcome. Hence, Satan and his band of dark angels began to roam the Earth. It wasn't long before they realized if they were to win others to their side, they would have to come up with a plan, a scheme of some sort, something that would convince others to join them rather than continue being loyal and dedicated to the loving and just ways of the Heavenly Father. Having declared his own independence from righteous rule, Satan went into business for himself. His goal was to win as many others over to his side as he could. His purpose was to spread his own insanity and delusion to others; to prove that you could live without God, that you could in fact *be* God.

This is how Satan's plan came into being. That is when he began laying the foundation for his counterfeit kingdom; that is when the plan of his great deception began. Sadly, the precepts of his plan thrive in the world today. They touch every corner of the world. His philosophy is booming throughout society at large.'

FALLING LOWER & LOWER

But step by step Satan is being forced down to the ground, lower and lower he is being driven down each day, and it's killing him. He is king over all the children of pride.* He loves to establish himself and his kingdom in high places, and among the rich and powerful of the Earth, where he can control the most people. Ultimately, he wants to control everything and everyone. He mistook God's assigning of significant duties and responsibilities to His creations as a sign of God's weakness and not His love and transcendent power and majesty. [*1] **JOB.41:34** He beholds all high things: he is a king over all the children of pride.

IX THE IMPORTANCE OF LOVE

'Well, firstly you have to understand the power and place that love has in our universe. Love, you must realize, is the most powerful force that there is. Love is the very essence of God[ii]. It is the foundation on which all things were built and continue to exist. Without love, all that is would not be. Love is the foundation of everything, and it is the only thing that keeps the world alive and going. Love actually has creative powers. Jesus came to show the world His Father's love. Satan rejects love, because real love is too invasive, too intrusive and revealing. It is too open when anyone has things to hide, and for that reason Satan hated and rejected Jesus. But even death could not quell Jesus' love. He rose a victor over the forces opposed to love. All His miracles were done in love, His disciples were won in love, and His commandment to them was to 'love one another.'[iii] So whatever is done in love, God's love, can never be wrong in the eyes of God. The Devil hates all that is love, and does what he can to twist and destroy the pure impulse of God that love produces.' (Source: From the book about Hell: 'Journey to Gragau' a very insightful book by A.W.Trenholm- Available at Amazon.com

THE DANGERS OF RELATIONSHIPS WITH FALLEN ANGELS MASQUERADING AS ANGELS OF LIGHT

We have read so far in this book 'Enoch *Insights*', about the fall of the angels and how they took unto them wives of all they chose.

I would like to elaborate on this topic, as many have suggested that **there has to be more to the Story of Adam and Eve and Satan as the serpent in the Garden of Eden**, than what is briefly mentioned in the Bible.

From the Book of Enoch, we also get the impression that ***only male angels fell***, but is that the whole picture?

I would like to point out the real danger of the angels as in regards to human women, in the beginning was their beauty! ***Not just the beauty of the human women, but the beauty of the angels themselves!***

The 'Watcher' angels were not supposed to materialize physically & to be seen by the women, at will.

EZE.27:3 And say unto Tyrus, 'O thou that art situate at the entry of the sea, which art a merchant of the people for many isles, Thus says the Lord GOD; 'O Tyrus, thou hast said, 'I am of perfect beauty'.

As you know that I have already written in this book, that I believe that Cain was fathered by Satan, the deceiver who deceived Eve, once she had already fallen; having eaten of the apple' from the 'tree of the Knowledge of Good and Evil' and was already living in disobedience.

In the time of Jared, the first 200 angels fell and came down on Mount Hermon. Why did so many millions of angels eventually also fall? The Bible tells us in Revelations 12, that one third of God's angels eventually fell. It is stated that they didn't all fall at once, but that many of them were seduced! By whom?

In **Enoch chapter 8.1-2** 'And Azazel taught men to make swords and knives, and shields, and breastplates, and made known to them the metals of the earth and the art of working with them, and bracelets, and ornaments, and the *use of antimony, and the beautifying of the eyelids, and all kinds of costly* *stones, and all colouring tinctures.'* And there arose much godlessness, and *they committed fornication*, and they were led astray, and *became corrupt in all their ways.*

Women were taught how to beautiful themselves, and to be experts at seducing both men and angels.

Initially, the first 200 fallen angels seduced the women on earth, later with the knowledge of how to be seductive, it would seem that the ***human women seduced millions of angels***. Why would they be tempted to do exactly that? Why would angels of God fall for them?

Why is it that most people don't get to see angels? It would seem that God has put a barrier in the spirit against too much fraternization between the spirit world and the physical world, because of the problems mentioned, that all started before the Great Flood.

I notice that **in Gothic art there are many pictures of female 'fallen angels'**. Is there actually any evidence for this? If the male original 'fallen angels' were irresistible to the beautiful women on earth, ***imagine how much more dangerously seductive women from the spirit world would be to men on earth?*** Not a good idea! It would be very distracting! For these reasons, I believe that God has made a barrier between the physical realm and the spiritual. It was probably very different before the Great Flood. That is not to say that sexual union doesn't still happen between 'fallen angels' and women on the earth, but it is not normally so visible as in the Pre-Flood times. In modern times, people talk about being abducted by 'Aliens and being sexually abused', but it is the same old thing as before the great Flood, just in a slightly different manner.

THE DANGERS OF VANITY, FOR WOMEN!

I think that it is a big temptation for women to want to be something higher than human, especially if their mate/partner is not the most spiritual of persons. Why is it that 80% of those who go into Gothic Art and even into witchcraft are all women? Is it because they desire the higher powers afforded by the fallen angels, without necessarily realizing what they are getting into? Why do women spend hours and hours dolling themselves up to look amazingly beautiful? Is it really to attract just their mate or boyfriend if they have one? *Or is there a much deeper reason?* Women say they do it because they want to be noticed. Understood! Everyone wants to be seen as nice and beautiful, if at all possible, but I think that there can also be a big danger here for women, if they over-do on this beautifying of themselves, just like the original women on the earth before the Great Flood. *Important not to attractive the wrong kind of people or worse yet evil entities.*

TIME-FRAME OF 7000 YEARS OF WORLD HISTORY (Approximate dates AC=After Creation)

CREATION AC 0 (±4000 BCE)

ENOCH	AC 600
NOAH	AC 1000
ABRAHAM	AC 2000
MOSES	AC 2500
DAVID	AC 3000
DANIEL	AC 3500
JESUS CHRIST	AC 4000
DARK AGES AC	5000
MODERN TIMES	AC 6000
2ND COMING OF CHRIST circa	AC 6000
MILLENNIUM	AC 6000-7000AC
GREAT WHITE THRONE JUDGEMENT	AC 7000
THE NEW HEAVEN & THE NEW EARTH	AC 7000 to ETERNITY

XI

AGE OF THE EARTH CHART

Bible Ref.	GENEALOGIES	EARTH'S	ACTUAL AGE	DATES
Gen 5.1,2	The creation of Adam		6 days	4160 BCE
Gen 5.3	Creation of Adam to birth of Seth	130 years	130 years	4030 BCE
Gen 5.6	Birth of Seth to the birth of Enos	105 years	235 years	3925 BCE
Gen 5.9	Birth of Enos to birth of Cainan	90 years	325 years	3835 BCE
Gen 5.12	Birth of Cainan to birth of Mahalaleel	70 years	395 years	3765 BCE
Gen 5.15	Birth of Mahalaleel to birth of Jared	65 years	460 years	3700 BCE
Gen 5.18	Birth of Jared to birth of Enoch	162 years	622 years	3538 BCE
Gen 5.21	Birth of Enoch to birth of Methuselah	65 years	687 years	3473 BCE
Gen 5. 25	Birth of Methuselah to b. of Lamech	187 years	874 years	3286 BCE
Gen 5.28-9	Birth of Lamech to birth of Noah	182 years	1056 years	3104 BCE
Gen 7.6	Birth of Noah to birth to the FLOOD	600 years	1656 years	2504 BCE
Gen 11.10	Flood to birth of Arphaxad	2 years	1658 years	2502 BCE
Gen 11.12	Birth of Arphaxad to birth of Salah	35 years	1693 years	2467 BCE
Gen 11.14	Birth of Salah to birth of Eber	30 years	1723 years	2437 BCE
Gen 11.16	Birth of Eber to birth of Peleg	34 years	1757 years	2403 BCE
Gen 11.18	Birth of Peleg to birth of Reu	30 years	1787 years	2372 BCE
Gen 11.20	Birth of Reu to birth of Serug	32 years	1819 years	2341 BCE
Gen 11.22	Birth of Serug to birth of Nahor	30 years	1849 years	2311 BCE
Gen 11.24	Birth of Nahor to birth of Terah	29 years	1878 years	2282 BCE
Gen 11.26	Birth of Terah to birth of Abram	70 years	1948 years	2212 BCE
Gen 21.5	Birth of Abram to birth of Isaac	100 years	2048 years	2112 BCE
Gen 25.26	Birth of Isaac to birth of Jacob	60 years	2108 years	2052 BCE
Gen 47.5-12	Birth of Jacob to entering into Egypt	130 years	2238 years	1922 BCE
Ex.12.40,41	Entering Egypt to Exodus	430 years	2668 years	1492 BCE
1 Kg.6.1	Exodus to Solomon's Temple	480 years	3148 years	1012 BCE
BC/AD	1012 BCE to year 0	1012 years	4160 years	0 AC/BCE
	Year 0 to TODAY	2017 years	2017 years	2017 AD

TOTAL YEARS from Creation to today 6177 years

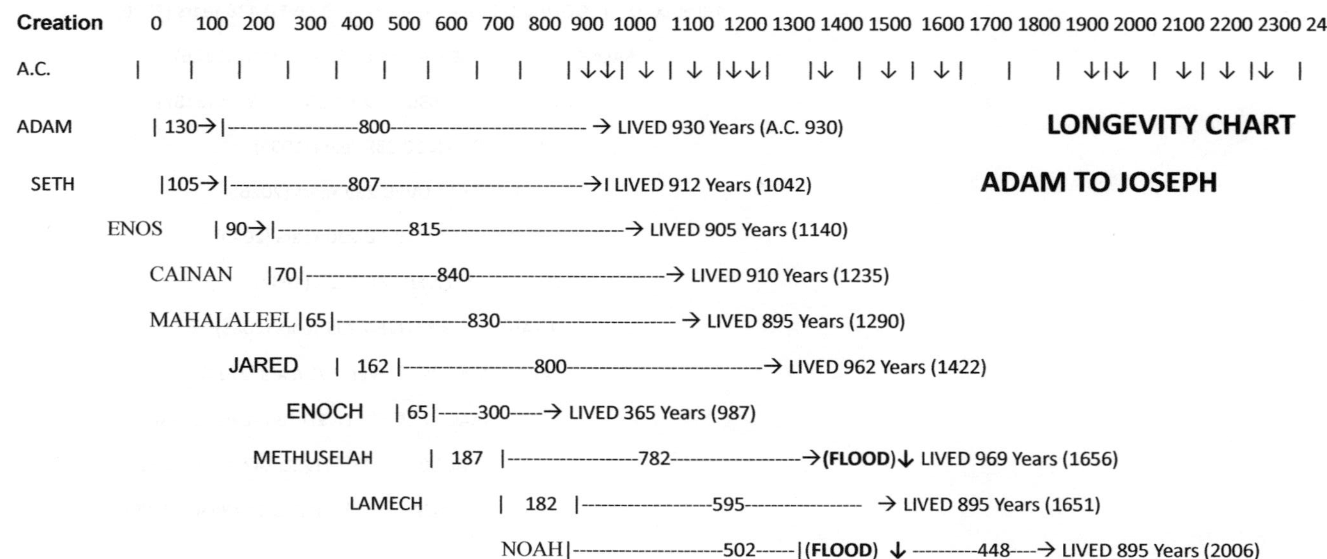
LONGEVITY CHART
ADAM TO JOSEPH
Years After |↓←(Around 4000 BCE)
Creation 0 100 200 300 400 500 600 700 800 900 1000 1100 1200 1300 1400 1500 1600 1700 1800 1900 2000 2100 2200 2300 2400
A.C.
ADAM | 130→|----800----→ LIVED 930 Years (A.C. 930)
SETH |105→|----807----→I LIVED 912 Years (1042)
ENOS | 90→|----815----→ LIVED 905 Years (1140)
CAINAN |70|----840----→ LIVED 910 Years (1235)
MAHALALEEL|65|----830----→ LIVED 895 Years (1290)
JARED | 162 |----800----→ LIVED 962 Years (1422)
ENOCH | 65|----300----→ LIVED 365 Years (987)
METHUSELAH | 187 |----782----→(FLOOD)↓ LIVED 969 Years (1656)
LAMECH | 182 |----595----→ LIVED 895 Years (1651)
NOAH|----502----|(FLOOD) ↓ ----448----→ LIVED 895 Years (2006)

XII

ARPHAXAD (**FLOOD**)↓35|-------------403-----→ LIVED 438 Years (2096)

SALAH|30|----------403------→ LIVED 433 Years (2126)

EBER|34|----------430----→ LIVED 464 Years (2187)

PELEG |30|209→ LIVED 239 Years (1996)

REU |32|207→ LIVED 239 Years (2026)

SERUG |30|200→ LIVED 230 Years (2049)

NAHOR |29|119→ LIVED 148 Years (1997)

TERAH |70|135→ LIVED 205 Years (2083)

ABRAHAM |100|75→ LIVED 175Years (2123)

ISAAC |60|120→ LIVED 180 Years (2228)

JACOB |91|56→ LIVED 147 Years (2255)

JOSEPH |110→ LIVED 110 Years (2309)

Years After |↓←(Around 4000 BCE)

Creation 2300 2400 2500 2600 2700 2800 2900 3000 3100 32003300 3400 3500 3600 3700 3800 3900 4000→ CONTINUING (NOT TO SCALE)
6000

A.C. | | | | | | | | | | | | | | | | | | | | ....

.

JOSEPH | 110 |→ LIVED 110 Years (2309)

KING DAVID LIVED | 70 |→ LIVED 70 Years (3000)

JESUS CHRIST |33 |→ LIVED 33 Years (4030

)

MODERN MAN→

70 Years(2017

OBS. Since the time of King David 3000 years ago, which was actually half of the World's History of approximately 6000 Years to date, the length of a man's life has generally stayed around ***70 Years on average***.

The exception to that, has been in different DARK AGES & THE INDUSTRIAL AGE, when millions of people's lives were cut short by plague and by pollution causing the disease called *consumption (T.B.)*, which also killed so many people during the coal mining age of the 19th century. In fact just 150 years ago, many people lived very short lives, such as 35 years, due to the heavy industrialization in the world.

XIII MYTHOLOGY & THE FALLEN ANGELS WHO *MASQUERADED AS GODS*

THE *SERPENT* DEITY RACE IS REAL? http://www.ancientpages.com/2017/10/24/mysterious-nagas-serpent-people-live-secret-underground-cities/

FLYING MACHINES IN ANCIENT INDIA: http://www.ancientpages.com/2014/05/27/vimanas-flying-machines-soaring-through-ancient-sky-of-india/

DRAGONS http://www.ancientpages.com/2016/11/02/dragons-dragon-kings-ancient-mythology/

XIV THE HOLLOW EARTH

CHAPTER 77 'PARADISE'

Is it just possible that 1) 'The Original Garden of Eden', was located inside the earth. 2) Then, *after the Flood,* mankind came to live on the outer surface of the earth?

There is evidence that not only are there cities inside the earth, but that also there are the remains of ancient cities, built long before the Great Flood.

In the book, '**Journey to Gragau**' by **Alan Trenholm***[1], Alan states that he went on a spirit trip down through the crust of the earth whilst riding a horse. He travelled widely inside the earth, and visited both Paradise and Hell.

Whist riding the horse down into Hell, through the many strata of the earth's crust, just before entering the Inner Earth, he states that he felt a clammy hand reach out and grab his leg, which was presumably one of the inmates of Hell itself.

His spirit guide explained to Alan that the "clammy hand" that he felt, was belonging to one of the "rock people". When Alan asked his very first question; "*Who are the rock people*?' The explanation given is what *gives it all away* concerning *when man moved from the INNER EARTH to the OUTER EARTH!* She explained that the "rock people" were spirits of the people from before the Flood, who were buried in the rubble of their former cities, and in imprisonment in the strata of the earth, because they didn't honour God. Instead they honoured themselves, and their cities, often built with the price of human blood and sacrifice. The incident mentioned about a being that grabbed Alan's leg, happened *just before he entered the inner surface of the earth*, howbeit, in the *lower dimension* of Hell. The important point here that it shows that "being" was *buried in the rubble of cities on the inside of the earth and not the outside.*

From this we can indeed deduce that as the first cities of man were built on the inner surface of the physical earth, that it is more than likely that *mankind first came onto the outer surface of the earth where we live today after the Flood at Noah's time.* This is just one example concerning cities inside the earth, and the rubble of ancient cities.

[See the dramatic, amazing and insightful book, *[1] "Journey to Gragau" by Alan Trenholm. Alan's "spirit trip" down to Hell, which he claims was 100% real: **'Journey to Gragau'** - www.amazon.com]

This could also explain why much of the Book of Enoch, & the topography of the earth as described by Enoch sounds like, that when he was actually describing the earth, most of the time like he was actually talking about the INNER EARTH, because that is where he lived before the Great Flood.

Remember that Enoch has talked about dinosaurs and dragons, and large creatures and both sea and land monsters. He also talks a length about the land of a 'thousand mountains', often volcanic in nature, and something that simply does not exist today; at least not on the outer surface of the planet, as we now know it today. He has also described trees as being exceedingly high and unlike the trees in our modern world. He also went to the ends of the earth and saw the Northern Polar Entrance.

Enoch stated that the seas only occupied one seventh of the earth's surface. Sounds like a very different world being described by Enoch. Today the outer surface of the earth, where we live is 80% seas. What a contrast that is!

I believe that Enoch also visited the *uninhabited outer surface of the earth where we live today*. We know from Enoch's book, that he also visited both the higher dimensions of Heaven itself, as well as the lower dimensions of both Hell and the Lake of fire.

To learn a lot more about these fascinating topics, I highly recommend the above-mentioned book by Alan Trenholm, about Hell, the Lake of fire, demons and fallen angels, as it gives an *amazing amount of insightful information about the lower worlds and the future of our planet.*

CONDITIONS BEFORE & AFTER THE FLOOD

Let's compare conditions on the earth before the Flood and after the Flood

Before the Flood	After the Flood
People lived up to almost 1000 years	Noah 350 more years after Flood and total age of 950 years
	Shem 500 years after the Flood total 600 years
	Son of Shem ARPHAXAD 438 years
	90 YEARS LATER ARPHAXAD'S great-grandson Peleg lived only 209 years
	Another 90 YEARS LATER Peleg's great grandson Nahor only lived to be 148 years
	(Noah was still alive when Nahor 8 generations after Noah, had already died!)
	Isaac 180 years
	Jacob 147 years
	Joseph 110 years
	(There were 13 generations from Noah to Joseph and a total of 640 years)
	Less than 800 years later in 2000 BCE, King David stated that a man's life was 70 years

Comments: Something was very different about the surface of the earth and the heavens above the earth, after the FLOOD. God had cursed man at the time of the FLOOD, and stated that a man's life would be 120 years only.

Why did men live to be almost 1000 years old before the Flood and less and less after the flood and their ages dwindled down from 950 to only 70 years in only 1600 years.

I propose that *before the flood mankind lived inside a very protected earth*. After the Flood mankind now lived on the outer surface of the earth, that was no longer protected as greatly as before the Flood. *The earth lost its protective shield of water about the earth*. We started to feel the influence of cosmic rays, which reduced the length of people's lives.

CONCLUSIONS: I believe that not only is the earth Hollow, but also the moon, and the sun and the stars, as hollow objects are much easier to cause to spin. Solid objects are not. Because of centrifugal forces, when one puts clothes in a washing machine, all the clothes that occupied the centre of the machine, once put in the centrifuge, all material is flung to the sides of the machine. The same is true of the earth and all other astral bodies.

My theory is that the entire universe down to the earth, within earth, & Hell &Tartarus below that, consists of globes and circular orbits.

1) The Earth is the centre of the universe

2) The Earth is hollow

3) All astral bodies are hollow

4) The sun and the moon rotate around the earth and not the earth around the sun.

5) The universe is not oval or ovuloid but is actually global in shape, with the earth at the very centre of it.

6) Before the Flood, the Earth was protected by a layer of water around 5-15 metres thick, 100 miles above the earth's surface all away around the earth. (Apparently 100 miles up in the atmosphere, is where both gravitational and centrifugal forces which are in opposite direction to each other, cancel each other out.) This caused the earth to act like a green-house and was the reason why the vegetation grew to be so big.

7) The protection above the earth, also acted like a "pressurized hyperbaric oxygen chamber", and thus large creatures like dinosaurs, which today scientists can't understand how they could have been breathing with such small lungs. Well there's your answer: the earth had a much higher oxygen content than today and it was also pressurized, thus making it much easier to breath for the dinosaur.

BIBLE VERSES ABOUT THE HOLLOW EARTH

PHI.2:10 That at the name of Jesus every knee should bow, of things in heaven, and things in earth, and things under the earth

EPH.4:9 (Now that he ascended, what is it but that he also descended first into the lower parts of the earth?

EXO.20:4 Thou shalt not make unto thee any graven image, or any likeness of anything that is in heaven above, or that is in the earth beneath, or that is in the water under the earth.

GEN.1:6 And God said, 'Let there be a firmament in the midst of the waters, and let it **divide** the **waters** from the **waters.'**

ISA.40:22 It is he that sits upon the circle of the earth, and the inhabitants thereof are as grasshoppers; that stretches out the heavens as a curtain, and spreads them out as a tent to dwell in:

AMO.9:2 Though they dig into hell, thence shall mine hand take them; though they climb up to heaven, thence will I bring them down:

PHI.2:10 That at the name of Jesus every knee should bow, of things in heaven, and things in earth, and things under the earth;

EZE.31:16 I made the nations to shake at the sound of his fall, when I cast him down to hell with them that descend into the pit: and all the trees of Eden, the choice and best of Lebanon, all that drink water, shall be comforted in the nether parts of the earth.

> (See 2nd Book '**EZRA** ***insights***' by the same author for a lot more about the **Hollow Earth** or the '**Womb of the Earth'** as God Himself calls the inside of our planet in **II EZDRAS**.)

XV INNER EARTH

MY OWN THEORY ABOUT THE ORIGINAL CREATION

My own idea, (which needs yet to be proven), is that not only was there a layer of water above the atmosphere, as other scientists have speculated, but that also above the INNER EARTH, around 50-100 miles above the surface of the INNER EARTH there was also an INNER canopy of water for the same reason, which made the inner earth also like a greenhouse.

The outer waters above the earth acted like a changeable lens, and the inner earth waters acted like a perfect internal mirror. There were portals in the earth or better said dimensional gates, which allowed light to get through the surface of the earth in selected places around the world in perfect order. At least 12 portals that we know of. Unfortunately, since the Flood, those portals no longer work the way they used to in Pre-Flood times, and in modern times they have become dangerous areas known as the 12 Bermuda triangles around the world, where ships and planes and even high altitude satellites get caught in the dimensional voids or areas between dimensions, which we call Bermuda triangles. ***See Chapter 2 From my first book, *Out of the Bottomless Pit* about the Bermuda Triangles. Five in the northern hemisphere and 5 in the southern Hemisphere. The two so-called Poles of the Earth, would have also conceivably been light sources to the INNER EARTH as they are today in modern times. A total of 12 PORTALS.

I propose that God's original creation was far more fantastic and beautiful than He is given credit for.

What if Adam and Eve were indeed placed in the Garden of Eden inside the earth. They might have been able to see the inner sun, but what about all the beautiful Cosmos of stars, not to the mention the Sun and the Moon, which normally one could only see from the outer surface of the earth?

God would certainly have created the earth in such a way, that His first children Adam and Eve could clearly have see His magnificent creation of the Sun, the Moon and the stars!

Obviously if that 1st assumption is correct, then God must have arranged the planet in such a way that Adam and Eve could still easily see the beautiful stars and the sun and Moon and planets, but how was that even possible?

The Bible tells us that God is the Father of Lights, and I put it to you that the earth was in the beginning both like a projector with moveable lenses, and a mirror and original light sources.

What was seen of the universe by Adam and Eve on the INNER EARTH in the Garden of Eden was a perfect internal REFLECTION.

The waters above the earth acted as a giant moveable lens, letting in the light. The inner waters above the inner earth acted as a perfect mirror.

There are invisible portals (today known as Bermuda Triangles) which sometimes, act as dimensional gate-ways, which before the flood allowed the light to travel through the very surface of the earth. Today 10 of the Bermuda Triangles (Gate-ways) are at around 30 degrees Latitude, in 5 points equidistant in the Northern Hemisphere, and 5 points equidistant in the southern Hemisphere. Strangely enough in modern times these Bermuda Triangles are mostly listed as to the immediate right of a land mass. I propose that as Enoch mentioned in his book, that there used to be a lot less water in the seas of our planet. Originally, all the "light portals" or "Bermuda Triangles" today, would have, for convenience been on the land area, and not in the sea.

The light then focused on the waters above the inner earth surface, which was like a perfect mirror, which reflected all the light of the cosmos and the sun and moon and stars back down onto the surface of the inner earth.

When it comes to LIGHT, water itself has amazing qualities and has been known to sometimes act as a lens, and sometimes act as a mirror, and at other times as a magnifying glass. Whether acting as a lens or a mirror would depend on different factors, but primarily on the temperature of the waters.

Amazingly enough I have just found some evidence to support my theory of the INNER WATERS & OUTER WATERS. The inner waters acting more like a perfect mirror in order to reflect the light perfectly onto the surface of inner earth. The light would have come through the portals (Bermuda Triangles).

Today I was reading a very famous book called, 'Flying Saucers From The Earth's Interior (1960) by Raymond W Bernard. He was talking about many different explorers & scientists who have descended through the North Pole

(Northern Aperture), and have tried different experiments to show that the earth is in fact Hollow. One of the amazing things that the scientists and explorers mention is that in going through the hole at the north and on their way onto the under surface of inner earth, at some point the *sky acts very odd* and appears as *a mirror in the sky*, which he stated that no one, at that time, understood the cause of this phenomenon. Although scientists suspected ice-crystals. Well when I read this, I was completely blown away, as one would say, because my theory above, is that there used to be a layer of water above the outer surface of the earth, which acted more like a lens and sometimes like a magnifying glass, and another layer of water above the INNER EARTH, which because of the uniform temperature, somehow acted more like a perfect internal mirror, allowing for total internal reflection.

The fact that scientific observers have found one area of the sky where this mirror effect is still evident, and formed by water in the form of ice-crystals is very encouraging. Apparently, this connecting northern aperture which directly connects our outer world with the inner world, is the only remaining location on the entire planet, where the mirror waters in the sky are yet still working!

The Inner Earth today has a uniform temperature of around 73 degrees F by all reports. I also think that God being the amazing and incredible creator that He is, that He created the outer-earth waters above the earth, as a giant changeable lens.

When night time came, the stars and in fact the whole universe would have been seen as being much closer to the earth

At night time, somehow the waters above the earth, acted as a giant magnifying glass.

If the above theory is correct, then at different times of the year, Adam and Eve could have clearly seen the 12 Astrological Star arrangements in the sky from Aries to Taurus, as though they were all very close-up.

It must have been absolutely both spectacular and astoundingly beautiful, and breath-taking.

The curse of the Bermuda Triangles wouldn't even exist today, if man hadn't been so rebellious, destructive, violent and perverse, in the first place, which resulted in the judgement of the Flood, and also unfortunately, caused the destruction of the giant projector of the earth, mentioned above.

All we apparently have left of that original light projector, is the defective "Light Portals" (Bermuda Triangles)

XVI (*See Enoch Chapter 82.5)

Prisca Sapientia (Ancient Wisdom)

The ancient "sacred year" consisted of 360 days, the numbering of which was a common practice among the ancients, according to the historian Immanuel Velikovshy:

When the year changed According to Error Flynn's Book, 'Temple at the centre of Time' there used to be 360 Days in the year. This fact is borne out by the Egyptians, Babylonians, Assyrians, Persians, the Chinese. The Chinese later added 5 more days to make 365, but why?

From 360 to 365, the Chinese added five and one-quarter days to their year. Plutarch wrote that in the time of Romulus, the Roman year was made up of 360 days only, and various Latin authors say the ancient month was thirty days in length.

Ancient absolute constants in mathematics, were revealed unto Moses by God Himself

Here is some amazing information about ABSOLUTE CONSTANTS in MATHS:

1x2=2

1x2x3=6

1x2x3x4=24

1x2x3x4x5=120

1x2x3x4x5x6=720

1x2x3x4x5x6x7=5,040= (7 x 360) x 2 or (14 x 360)

These feats are accomplished through simple arithmetic using the base number 2,540 and variations of 7 and 360.

The moon's diameter is determined by subtracting the number of degrees in a circle, 360, from 2520, equalling 2160 miles

The average distance between the surface of the earth and the moon is found by multiplying 77.77 times pi seven times

77.77x= 234,888 statute miles

The point being that many calculations concerning the distance, the weight, the diameter, the circumference of the planets and moon, sun and stars, can be made using the constants of 7, & 360 in particular. How is that even possible? Co-incidence? I don't think so! It looks like that it is God's Absolute Maths of Creation. David Flynn has done an excellent job in the discovering the ancient wisdom or Prisca Sapientia:-

(See Errol Flynn's book, 'At the centre of Time' Available on Amazon.com)

XVII

BOOK OF ENOCH chapter 91:

7000 YEARS OF WORLD HISTORY

"IN THE TENTH WEEK, IN THE SEVENTH PART"

One week here = 700 years

One day=100 years

Years After Creation	0	1st WEEK 700	2nd WEEK 1400	3rd WEEK 2100	4th WEEK 2800	5th WEEK 3500	6th WEEK 4200	7th WEEK 4900	8th WEEK 5600	9th WEEK 6300	10th WEEK 7000
Date	4000 BCE	3300 BCE	2600 BCE	1900 BCE	1200 BCE	500 BCE	200 AD	900 AD	1600 AD	2300 AD	3000 AD

DATE		NOTABLE EVENT
1st WEEK: YEAR	0	CREATION
1st WEEK: YEAR	700	ENOCH (born in 622; 7th part of the first WEEK. Enoch was also the 7th from Adam.)
2nd WEEK: YEAR	1400	NOAH
3rd WEEK: YEAR	2100	ABRAHAM
4th WEEK: YEAR	2800	KING DAVID
5th WEEK: YEAR	3500	CAPTIVITY IN BABYLON
6th WEEK: YEAR	4200	THE EARLY CHURCH ESTABLISHED & RECOGNIZED BY ROME
7th WEEK: YEAR	4900	THE CRUSADES IN THE HOLY LAND
8th WEEK: YEAR	5600	THE KING JAMES BIBLE (1601AD)
9th WEEK: YEAR	2300	MILLENNIUM
10th WEEK: YEAR	3000	GREAT WHITE THRONE JUDGEMENT & NEW HEAVEN AND NEW EARTH

DATE **NOTABLE EVENT** **QUOTE FROM ENOCH** **COMMENTS**

1st WEEK: YEAR 0 CREATION

700, ENOCH (born in 622; 7th part of the first WEEK. Enoch was also the 7th from Adam.)

(Enoch 93.2) "I was born the seventh in the first week, while judgement and righteousness still endured"

2nd WEEK: YEAR 1400 NOAH "second week great wickedness" "first end. And in it a man shall be saved"

3rd WEEK: YEAR 2100 ABRAHAM "third week" "plant of righteous judgement" "his posterity" "the plant of righteousness" (JESUS) MOSES (2500) "visions of the holy and righteous shall be seen, and a law for all generations"

4th WEEK: YEAR 2800 KING DAVID "fourth week" "fifth week, at it close*, the house of glory and dominion shall be built forever;(KING SOLOMON) (3100)

5th WEEK: YEAR 3500 CAPTIVITY IN BABYLON "in the sixth week" "shall be blinded",(time between the testaments 400 BCE until the time of CHRIST in 30 BCE.) "a man shall ascend" (Jesus) "At its close, the house of dominion shall be burnt with fire, and the whole race of the chosen shall be dispersed." (70 AD under the Romans)

6th WEEK: YEAR 4200 THE EARLY CHURCH ESTABLISHED & RECOGNIZED BY ROME "seventh week" "apostate generation arise" (THE DARK AGES of False Religions)

7th WEEK: YEAR 4900 THE CRUSADES IN THE HOLY LAND

8th WEEK: YEAR	5600	THE KING JAMES BIBLE (1601AD) eighth week, sword shall be given to it, that a righteous judgement may be executed to the oppressors, and sinners shall be delivered it to the hands of the righteous. And at its close, they shall acquire houses through their righteousness, and a house shall be built for the Great King in glory for evermore.
	"at its close shall be elected the elect righteous one the eternal plant of righteousness, to receive sevenfold instruction concerning all His creation." (The KING JAMES BIBLE?) "ninth week", the righteous judgement shall be revealed to the whole world. All the works of the godless shall vanish from all the earth, and the world shall be written down for destruction.	
	(2024?) or later?	2ND COMING OF CHRIST & THE WRATH OF GOD
9th WEEK: YEAR	2300	MILLENNIUM
10th WEEK: YEAR	3000	GREAT WHITE THRONE JUDGEMENT & NEW HEAVEN AND NEW EARTH "tenth week in the seventh part, there shall be the great eternal judgement, in the which He will execute vengeance amongst the angels. And the first heaven shall depart and pass away, and a new heaven shall appear, and all the powers of the heaven shall give sevenfold light." (Enoch 92.9)

XVIII

THE FEMALE HOLY SPIRIT

MAT.12:31 Wherefore I say unto you, 'All manner of sin and blasphemy shall be forgiven unto men: but the blasphemy against the Holy Ghost shall not be forgiven unto men.'

MAR.3:29-30 But he that shall blaspheme against the Holy Ghost hath never forgiveness, but is in danger of eternal damnation; because they said, He hath an unclean spirit.

LUK.12:10 And whosoever shall speak a word against the Son of man, it shall be forgiven him: but unto him that blasphemes against the Holy Ghost it shall not be forgiven.

Comment: Why did Jesus make a distinction between Himself and the Holy Spirit here? If God and Jesus and the Holy Spirit were all masculine, which is how they are portrayed by most modern churches, then perhaps Jesus would not have made this distinction!

Let me put in simple terms to understand. A man who has a beautiful wife, whom he both loves and adores, and also has a strong son. If perchance another man comes and gives a blow to his son, it is conceivable that the father will make light of it, and forgive the man. However, if the man hits his wife, I guarantee that he would neither forgive him or let him go unpunished. I do think that these above Bible verses prove one thing: The Holy Spirit has got to both feminine and God's wife. Nothing but wrath to those who would hurt and offend her!

THE FEMININE HOLY SPIRIT for more info:-

http://www.peopleofthekeys.com/news/docs/library/Dream+Queen

1) http://www.pistissophia.org/The_Holy_Spirit/the_holy_spirit.html
2) http://www.hts.org.za/index.php/HTS/article/view/3225/html

3) http://www.menorah.org/trinity1.html
4) https://www.saxo.com/dk/the-holy-spirit-the-feminine-nature-of-god-how-the-feminine-component-of-jehovah-god-was-erased-from-early-christian-and-jewish-belie_taylor-patricia-taylorpatricia-taylor_haeftet_9781440174841

XIX: Book of the Luminaries Ch 72-75.

GEO-CENTRIC UNIVERSE: http://www.outofthebottomlesspit.co.uk/418830180

The following LINK, if you scroll down a little, talks about the 'Book of Enoch' chapters 72-75: Implying that Enoch is stating that the earth revolves around the sun:

BIBLICAL CREATION: http://www.outofthebottomlesspit.co.uk/421607713

XX: TOPIC LIST ON MY WEBSITE

HOLLOW EARTH:	http://www.outofthebottomlesspit.co.uk/421040248
TRIPS TO HELL:	http://www.outofthebottomlesspit.co.uk/421128236
FALLEN ANGELS:	http://www.outofthebottomlesspit.co.uk/419028514
GIANTS:	http://www.outofthebottomlesspit.co.uk/411784132
MORE ON GIANTS:	http://www.outofthebottomlesspit.co.uk/411783108
ELONGATED SKULLS:	http://www.outofthebottomlesspit.co.uk/413325017
LIES OF EVOLUTION:	http://www.outofthebottomlesspit.co.uk/420555449
CHIMERAS:	http://www.outofthebottomlesspit.co.uk/420942516
ANCIENT TECHNOLOGY:	http://www.outofthebottomlesspit.co.uk/421401449
ANCIENT TECHNOLOGY II:	http://www.outofthebottomlesspit.co.uk/413536147
DRAGONS & DINOSAURS:	http://www.outofthebottomlesspit.co.uk/413522871
HEAVEN:	http://www.outofthebottomlesspit.co.uk/412320663
UFOs:	http://www.outofthebottomlesspit.co.uk/412116965
MORE ON UFOs:	http://www.outofthebottomlesspit.co.uk/418799994
VOLCANOES:	http://www.outofthebottomlesspit.co.uk/412290629
EARTHQUAKES:	http://www.outofthebottomlesspit.co.uk/413523034
GEO-ENGINEERING:	http://www.outofthebottomlesspit.co.uk/421385649
CHEMTRAILS:	http://www.outofthebottomlesspit.co.uk/412291091
ALIEN DISCLOSURE:	http://www.outofthebottomlesspit.co.uk/421678370
TRANSHUMANISM:	http://www.outofthebottomlesspit.co.uk/412370179
TRANSHUMANISM II:	http://www.outofthebottomlesspit.co.uk/413033606
ICE-AGE I:	http://www.outofthebottomlesspit.co.uk/412667930
ICE-AGE II:	http://www.outofthebottomlesspit.co.uk/420939961
CLIMATE CHANGE LIES 1:	http://www.outofthebottomlesspit.co.uk/412303615
CLIMATE CHANGE LIES 2:	http://www.outofthebottomlesspit.co.uk/413299970
CLIMATE CHANGE LIES 3:	http://www.outofthebottomlesspit.co.uk/421618708
STRANGE HYBIDS:	http://www.outofthebottomlesspit.co.uk/421556550
SALVATION:	http://www.outofthebottomlesspit.co.uk/418605189
ABOUT THE AUTHOR:	http://www.outofthebottomlesspit.co.uk/413469553

XXI The Cherubim, Seraphim, and Ophannim http://waterbloodspir-it.com/CAL.html

XXII ASTRONOMICAL FAKERY: http://www.peopleofthekeys.com/news/docs/library/Astronomical+Fakery%21

XXIII THERE ARE ABSOLUTES: http://www.peopleofthekeys.com/news/docs/library/There+Are+Absolutes

XXIV

BEHEMOTH

JOB.40:15 Behold now behemoth, which I made with thee; he eats grass as an ox.

JOB.40:16 Lo now, his strength is in his loins, and his force is in the navel of his belly.

JOB.40:17 He moves his tail like a cedar: the sinews of his stones are wrapped together.

JOB.40:18 His bones are as strong pieces of brass; his bones are like bars of iron.

JOB.40:19 He is the chief of the ways of God: he that made him can make his sword to approach unto him.

JOB.40:20 Surely the mountains bring him forth food, where all the beasts of the field play.

JOB.40:21 He lies under the shady trees, in the covert of the reed, and fens.

LEVIATHAN

JOB.41:1 Canst thou draw out Leviathan with an hook? or his tongue with a cord which thou lets down?

JOB.41:5 Wilt thou play with him as with a bird? or wilt thou bind him for thy maidens?

JOB.41:6 Shall the companions make a banquet of him? shall they part him among the merchants?

JOB.41:7 Canst thou fill his skin with barbed irons? or his head with fish spears?

JOB.41:10 None is so fierce that dare stir him up: who then is able to stand before me?

JOB.41:14 Who can open the doors of his face? his teeth are terrible round about.

JOB.41:15 His scales are his pride, shut up together as with a close seal.

JOB.41:20 Out of his nostrils goes smoke, as out of a seething pot or caldron.

JOB.41:21 His breath kindles coals, and a flame goes out of his mouth.

JOB.41:23 The flakes of his flesh are joined together: they are firm in themselves; they cannot be moved.

JOB.41:26 The sword of him that lays at him cannot hold: the spear, the dart, nor the habergeon.

JOB.41:27 He esteems iron as straw, and brass as rotten wood.

JOB.41:28 The arrow cannot make him flee: sling-stones are turned with him into stubble.

JOB.41:29 Darts are counted as stubble: he laughs at the shaking of a spear.

JOB.41:30 Sharp stones are under him: he spreads sharp pointed things upon the mire.

JOB.41:31 He makes the deep to boil like a pot: he makes the sea like a pot of ointment.

JOB.41:32 He makes a path to shine after him; one would think the deep to be hoary.

JOB.41:33 Upon earth there is not his like, who is made without fear.

JOB.41:34 He beholds all high things: he is a king over all the children of pride.

LEVIATHAN sounds like a physical manifestation of SATAN

REV.12:7 And there was war in heaven: Michael and his angels fought against the *dragon*; and the *dragon fought* and *his angels,*

REV.12:8 And prevailed not; neither was their place found any more in heaven.

REV.12:9 And the *great dragon* was *cast out,* that *old serpent*, called the *Devil,* and *Satan,* which *deceives the whole world:* he was *cast out into the earth*, and his *angels were cast out with him.*

XXV

CHIMERAS

ARE THEY ALL BAD?

"Thou shalt not make to thyself an idol, nor likeness of anything, whatever things are in the heaven above, and whatever are in the earth beneath, and whatever are in the waters under the earth."

(Exodus 20:4)

Waters Under The Earth

After a discussion with a good friend, who also has a very active website, together we came up with the following article concerning MERMAIDS:

Concerning a video purporting to prove that mermaids do in fact exist and confirmed by a high ranking US Navel officer who revealed the US Navy had kept one alive in captivity for two to three years.

The Navy supposedly did DNA testing on the "mermaid" and found that their DNA was almost identical to humans.

I would state that if mermaids really do in fact exist, they would most likely be dangerous and harmful and do wonder if any good hybrids exist?

It should be noted that every major culture in the world has references to "mermaids".

MORE ON MERMAIDS

"Therefore shall she lament and wail, she shall go barefooted, and being naked she shall make lamentation as that of serpents, and mourning as of the daughters of sirens." Micah 1:8 (Septuagint)

"And the women also of the angels who went astray shall become sirens." Enoch 29:2

"And the sirens shall sigh because of you-and weep." Enoch 96:2

2 Baruch: THE BOOK OF THE APOCALYPSE OF BARUCH THE SON OF NERIAH

"I will call the Sirens from the sea." 10:8

2 Baruch is a Jewish pseudepigraphical text thought to have been written in the late 1st century AD or early 2nd century AD, after the destruction of the Temple in AD 70. It is attributed to the biblical Baruch and so is associated with the Old Testament, but not regarded as scripture by Jews or by most Christian groups.

Regarding Hybrids

Since Satan can only imitate what God has done perhaps he was attempting to imitate the following verses in Ezekiel and Revelation and also make a deliberate attempt to provoke God at the same time.

"And their judges and rulers went to the daughters of men and took their wives by force from their

"And their judges and rulers went to the daughters of men and took their wives by force from their husbands according to their choice, and the sons of men in those days took from the cattle of the earth, the beasts of the field and the fowls of the air, and taught the mixture of animals of one species with the other, in order therewith to provoke the Lord; and God saw the whole earth and it was corrupt, for all flesh had corrupted its ways upon earth, all men and all animals." Jashur 4:18

Ezekiel Chapter 1:5-12

"And in the midst as it were the likeness of four living creatures. And this was their appearance; the likeness of a man was upon them. And each one had four faces, and each one had four wings. And their legs were straight; and their feet were winged, and there were sparks, like gleaming brass, and their wings were light. And the hand of a man was under their wings on their four sides. And the faces of them four turned not when they went; they went every-one straight forward. And the likeness of their faces was the face of a man, and the face of a lion on the right of the four; and the face of a calf on the left of the four; and the face of an eagle to the four. And the four had their wings spread out above; each one had two joined to one another, and two covered their bodies. And each one went straight forward: wherever the spirit was going they went, and turned not back."

Ezekiel Chapter 10:8-22

"And I saw the cherubs having the likeness of men's hands under their wings. And I saw, and behold, four wheels stood by the cherubs, one wheel by each cherub: and the appearance of the wheels was as the appearance of a carbuncle stone. And as for their appearance, there was one likeness to the four, as if there should be a wheel in the midst of a wheel. When they went, they went on their four sides; they turned not when they went, for whichever way the first head looked, they went; and they turned not as they went. And their backs, and their hands, and their wings, and the wheels, were full of eyes round about the four wheels. And these wheels were called Gelgel in my hearing. And the cherubs were the same living creature which I saw by the river of Chobar.

This is the living creature which I saw under the God of Israel by the river of Chobar; and I knew that they were cherubs. Each one had four faces, and each one had eight wings; and under their wings was the likeness of men's hands. And as for the likeness of their faces, these are the same faces which I saw under the glory of the God of Israel by the river of Chobar: and they went each straight forward."

Revelation 4:6-9

"And before the throne [there was] a sea of glass like unto crystal: and in the midst of the throne, and round about the throne, [were] four beasts full of eyes before and behind. And the first beast [was] like a lion, and the second beast like a calf, and the third beast had a face as a man, and the fourth beast [was] like a flying eagle. And the four beasts had each of them six wings about [him;] and [they were] full of eyes within: and they rest not day and night, saying, Holy, holy, holy, Lord God Almighty, which was, and is, and is to come. And when those beasts give glory and honour and thanks to him that sat on the throne, who liveth for ever and ever."

Revelation 5:13-14

"And every creature which is in heaven, and on the earth, and under the earth, and such as are in the sea, and all that are in them, heard I saying, Blessing, and honour, and glory, and power, [be] unto him that sitteth upon the throne, and unto the Lamb for ever and ever. And the four beasts said, Amen. And the four [and] twenty elders fell down and worshipped him that liveth for ever and ever."

Good hybrids?

Jashur 36:31-35

"And afterward about one hundred and twenty great and terrible animals came out from the wilderness at the other side of the sea, and they all came to the place where the asses were, and they placed themselves there.

And those animals, from their middle downward, were in the shape of the children of men, and from their middle upward, some had the likeness of bears, and some the likeness of the keephas, with tails behind them from between their shoulders reaching down to the earth, like the tails of the ducheephath, and these animals came and mounted and rode upon these asses, and led them away, and they went away unto this day.

And one of these animals approached Anah and smote him with his tail, and then fled from that place. And when he saw this work he was exceedingly afraid of his life, and he fled and escaped to the city. And he related to his sons and brothers all that had happened to him, and many men went to seek the asses but could not find them, and Anah and his brothers went no more to that place from that day following, for they were greatly afraid of their lives."

Jashur 61:15-16

"And Zepho went and he saw and behold there was a large cave at the bottom of the mountain, and there was a great stone there at the entrance of the cave, and Zepho split the stone and he came into the cave and he looked and behold, a large animal was devouring the ox; from the middle upward it resembled a man, and from the middle downward it resembled an animal, and Zepho rose up against the animal and slew it with his swords.

And the inhabitants of Chittim heard of this thing, and they rejoiced exceedingly, and they said, What shall we do unto this man who has slain this animal that devoured our cattle?"

It would seem a case could be made surmise the possibility that mermaids-sirens do exist. [See the following LINKS for much more information about Mermaids]

MERMAIDS- A REAL SKULL: https://youtu.be/sp33OgYJrJE?t=3331

(Comment from Editor:10/11/17: it is an excellent video, if one can forget the LIE OF EVOLUTION in the film)

MORE ON MERMAIDS- https://youtu.be/4-CAGrGssG8?t=232

CHIMERAS: http://www.outofthebottomlesspit.co.uk/420942516

Lightning Source UK Ltd.
Milton Keynes UK
UKHW02f0041070518
322190UK00005B/38/P

9 781782 225805